BIBLE
ALMANAC

BY ANNA TRIMIEW

CONSULTANT:
GARY BURGE, PH.D.

PUBLICATIONS INTERNATIONAL, LTD.

Anna Trimiew is a freelance writer and a former school teacher who holds a master's degree from Gordon-Conwell Theological Seminary. Her previously published work includes *Who's Who in the Bible, Bringing the New Testament to Life,* and other religious literature, including Bible study materials.

Gary Burge is a professor in the department of Biblical, Theological, Archaeological & Religious Studies at Wheaton College. He holds a Ph.D. in New Testament from King's College, The University of Aberdeen in Aberdeen, Scotland and a Master of Divinity degree from Fuller Theological Seminary. He is a member of the Biblical Archaeological Society.

Louis Weber, C.E.O.
Publications International, Ltd.
7373 North Cicero Avenue
Lincolnwood, Illinois 60646

Permission is never granted for commercial purposes.

Manufactured in U.S.A.

8 7 6 5 4 3 2 1

ISBN: 0-7853-2664-2

Picture credits:

Front cover: **Superstock:** Sistine Chapel, Rome.

Art Resource: 16; Werner Braun: 157; Paul Leslie Garber: 179; David Harris: 131; Richard Nowitz: 8; Zev Radovan: 93, 132, 209; Jane Taylor courtesy of Sonia Halliday: 197, 211; Bruce & Kenneth Zuckerman: 90.

Diagrams and map illustrations by Myron Netterlund.

CONTENTS

INTRODUCTION

he Bible is a compelling book, filled with drama, action, emotion, and inspiration. Readers everywhere are guided, encouraged, and fascinated by its message and by the sheer variety of information within its pages. The Bible is the world's all-time best-seller, and its truths have been passed on from generation to generation.

Although people are attracted to the timeless stories and the universal questions that the Bible answers, its setting is unfamiliar to most of us. Even a quick look through the pages of the Bible makes it clear that we are plunged into a world that is very different from our own. Its clothes, customs, and family patterns are unlike ours, and we are unaccustomed to the ancient world of work and worship.

It is also important to remember that the Bible was not originally written in our language. (The Old Testament was written mostly in Hebrew, and the New Testament in Greek.) As we read through the Scriptures, we see the original writings through the wisdom and eyes of translators. In addition, we discover that the Bible is not one book, but a collection of 66 different books (plus the Deuterocanonical writings) written by several different authors—kings, priests, and fishermen among them—spanning nearly 2,000 years of history.

All these things make the Bible hard to figure out, and questions invariably arise: Why was the Bible written? Who were the writers? Who were the people we are reading about? What did they do? Where did they live? When did these events take place?

Bible Almanac was written to answer questions like these. Its purpose is to help readers understand what the Bible is all about. This book is designed to bring the biblical world to life in a readable, up-to-date, and accurate way. In this "guided tour" through the pages of the Scriptures, the reader is introduced to each Bible book, to historical events, and to the language of the Bible. People and customs are drawn into focus; religion, beliefs, and ideas are opened up to a clearer view.

The angel appearing to Joshua

As the story of the Bible is brought to life, the people of this ancient world become familiar, rooted in real places with their lives spread plainly before us. We realize that these biblical characters loved and hated, succeeded and failed, celebrated and cried—just like people everywhere. In a refreshing way, the kings, queens, priests, farmers, and carpenters of the Bible become part of our own world.

Within these pages, you'll find a storehouse of information, with answers to many of your questions about the Bible. Discover a cornucopia of fascinating—and sometimes humorous—scriptural facts. Deepen your knowledge and understanding of the world's best-selling book, and enjoy its richness.

THE STORY OF THE BIBLE

ANY OF US ARE FAMILIAR with the sight of a big, black Bible on a bookshelf. When we take it down and open its pages, we discover that the Bible is, in fact, not just one book. It is made up of an entire collection of books containing many different writings: law, history, poetry, prophecy—even sermons, hymns, and personal letters. A deeper look reveals that the Bible is composed of two main sections: the Old Testament and the New Testament. But how did the books of the Bible come to be written? Who were the writers? When did they write these books? This chapter will help provide some insight on the history behind this amazing body of work.

The compelling story of Moses and the Ten Commandments (as told in the Book of Exodus) is just one of the many wonders described in the Bible.

The Old Testament

The first 39 books of the Bible are known as the Old Testament. They were first written down in Hebrew and Aramaic, the ancient languages of the Jews. We do not have any of the original manuscripts today. When the Old Testament authors finished their scrolls, they did not have copy machines or mechanical presses to make copies of their writings. The work of copying belonged to Jewish scribes, who would

laboriously make handwritten copies of the original writings. When the documents became worn out, the scribes made new copies from the old copies. Unfortunately, many of these scrolls have not survived over time. They deteriorated in the climate of the Bible lands. As a result, today there are few surviving copies of these early holy books, first written down about 1400 B.C.

Before 1947, the oldest known manuscripts of the Hebrew Old Testament dated from the ninth and tenth centuries A.D. These were copies of the first five books of the Bible. In 1947, however, there was an amazing discovery. Arab shepherds found a priceless treasure in the caves near the Dead Sea. They discovered the Dead Sea Scrolls. These second-century B.C. copies of all the books of the Old Testament (except Esther) were from the library of a Jewish religious group at Qumran (near the Dead Sea in Israel) who lived about the time of Jesus. This remarkable find revealed that the Old Testament text had changed very little over a thousand years. In fact, the Qumran manuscripts were so similar to the ninth-century documents, it showed that the scribes had done an outstanding job of accurately passing on the sacred writings. By this we know that the Old Testament as we now have it is probably very similar to the way it was originally written.

How the Old Testament Was Put Together

Jewish tradition holds that the scribe Ezra (whose story is told in the Book of Ezra) compiled the books of the Old Testament. Lacking evidence, however, we do not know for certain how the books actually came together in the collection we now have. We do know that by the time of Jesus, the Hebrew sacred writings usually comprised the 39 books we accept as the Old Testament. And Jesus himself makes it clear which books he and his apostles accepted as their "Bible."

The Jews arranged their sacred books into three major divisions: the Law, the Prophets, and the Writings. When Jesus spoke to his disciples about the Old Testament, he referred to these same groupings. Besides, most of the books of our Old Testament are quoted somewhere in the New Testament. It seems, then, that Jesus and his followers were familiar with the same Old Testament we have today.

Besides the 39 Old Testament books, the Jews had other holy texts. These books and chapters are known as the *Apocrypha*, and may be found in some Bibles. In the Greek version, these writings were given the same respect as other Old Testament books. However, in the Hebrew Bible, they were not considered to have the same authority as the other books of the Bible. Most Roman Catholic Bibles today will include the Apocrypha.

Other Ancient Versions of the Old Testament

One of the most important translations of the Old Testament is the Greek version known as the *Septuagint*. Jews who spoke Greek and many Christians of the first centuries

Manuscript Making

In ancient days, the art of making books was very different from printing and publishing as we know it. Back then, scribes used a quill pen and ink to write on parchment or vellum scrolls (made from animal skins) to make individual copies of the Bible. In Egypt, a writing surface was made from papyrus reeds. Scrolls were usually attached to two wooden handles and could be as long as 40 feet! When scrolls became tattered or old, copies were made and the old ones were buried in special ceremonies.

Although we do not have original scrolls of any Bible book today, we believe that we have reliable copies of the earliest texts. Scribes took painstaking care to copy out the sacred writings by hand generation after generation. Copyists usually worked together, writing at the dictation of the chief scribe. Seldom did they make mistakes, and when errors were found the copy was corrected. These expensive handwritten manuscripts were generally owned and used by churches or groups. Few individuals could afford to purchase such costly writings.

At first, the New Testament books were written in the traditional manner—on papyrus or parchment scrolls. However, by the late first century A.D. a new way of making copies of the Scriptures developed. Sheets of papyrus or vellum were folded and sewn together at the spine to make a book, known as a *codex*. This book form was a great improvement over the long, awkward scroll, and copyists could write on both sides of each page.

Many important papyrus manuscripts of the New Testament exist today. Over the past 250 years, scholars have worked hard to ensure that our New Testament today is as close as possible to the original words of the authors.

A.D. used the Septuagint. It has been suggested that this text was put together during the reign of Pharaoh Ptolemy Philadelphus (285–246 B.C.). As Christianity spread to people of other cultures and languages, the Old Testament was translated into Latin and many other languages.

The Text of the New Testament

The writers of the New Testament finished their work in the first century A.D. Today we have many fragments of the New Testament text from as early as the second century A.D. Originally written down in Greek, there are perhaps 15,000 complete manuscripts and fragments available today to help scholars put together the final 27 books of the Bible. In addition, scholars have available several early translations of the New Testament in Latin, Syriac, Coptic, and other languages. There are also New Testament quotations in the writings of the early church fathers. With all this information, scholars have had to be cautious in selecting and preserving the most accurate texts of the original writings.

By the fifth century A.D., the text of the New Testament was standardized from a common text found in many Greek manuscripts. The first printed edition of the standard Greek text came in 1516, prepared and published by the Dutch scholar Erasmus. Up to this point, there had been no thought to examine the accuracy of this text. During the next two centuries, however, some Bibles noted certain alterations from the standardized version, including the text of Stephanus used in translating the King James Version in England (1611), and the edition of Elzevir (1633), which became the model for New Testament translations in Europe. They had discovered older texts that were quite different from the fifth-century standard text.

As scholars continued their work of translation, they became more involved in the history and accuracy of texts. It became clear that certain texts were more reliable than others. Manuscripts were then grouped together according to their similarities. We now know that certain families of older texts (such as the Alexandrian and the Western texts) are closer to the original writings than the standard fifth-century text.

How the New Testament Books Were Collected

When the first Christians met together to worship, they probably read from the Old Testament, following the Jewish synagogue tradition. Since the focus of their worship was Jesus Christ, they likely added to their meetings an account of some part of his life and ministry. At first, the reports might have been first-hand accounts from people who knew Jesus. But as the church grew in numbers (and eyewitnesses began to die), it became important to write these stories down. This was how Matthew, Mark, Luke, and John came into being. These four Gospels became an important part in the worship and life of the early church.

As the Christian movement expanded, the apostles wrote letters to the young churches and various key individuals, providing guidance on Christian life and beliefs. These letters were considered useful to the church as a whole, and so they were preserved. This also occurred with the Book of Acts, which was accepted because it continued Luke's Gospel account and provided the only full record of the beginnings of Christianity.

By A.D. 200, the church was officially using the four Gospels as their authority for the life and teaching of Jesus. By this time also, Paul's letters were accepted as equally important. Then, during the third and fourth centuries, the remaining books of the New Testament were approved.

This process was formally established when church leaders compiled a list of books similar to our New Testament at the Council of Laodicea (A.D. 363) and the Council of Carthage (A.D. 397).

Now we have the entire Bible in our hands, Old and New Testaments, all 66 books. Many scholars and critics believe that the world's best-seller (often referred to as the "Holy Writ" or the "Word of God") is an accurate record of the authors' words, handed down without significant loss from generation to generation throughout the centuries.

Ten Quick Bible Facts

- The first books of the Bible were written nearly 3,500 years ago.

- Approximately 40 different people wrote the books of the Bible.

- Some Bible authors dictated their words to a scribe or secretary who wrote them down.

- The first five books of the Bible were written about 1400 B.C., and the last books were written about A.D. 96–100

- The grouping of books in the Hebrew Bible is different from the ordering of the books in the Christian Bible.

- The Hebrews hid or buried old copies of their Bible.

- Scribes were so careful in copying that they counted all the words and letters in the original and in the copy to check for errors.

- The Dead Sea Scrolls were found in old jars in caves by the Dead Sea.

- The New Testament was written within the span of 50 years.

- The New Testament books came together because of the needs of the early church.

Translating the Scriptures

After the New Testament was written and Christianity began spreading, the work of translation started. The Bible appeared in Latin, Armenian, Gothic, Coptic, and other languages. People wanted to read the Bible in their own tongue. These translations were not produced on scrolls but in codex form. This was a step forward in Bible making and the growing work of translation. Today, the Bible has been translated in more than 1,700 languages.

Ancient Versions of the Bible

Common Version: Jerome is the first Bible translator known to us. His Latin translation, the Vulgate (or Common Version) was the standard Bible of the Roman Catholic Church for centuries. A respected scholar, Jerome wrote his famous translation around A.D. 400.

Syriac Bible: Although Syriac, a dialect of Aramaic (the language of Jesus), is no longer spoken, this fourth-century translation (known as the Peshitta) is still used in Syria, Iran, India, and elsewhere.

Coptic Bible: A Coptic version was needed as Christianity spread south to Egypt and beyond. Translation began in the third century, and the Coptic Bible is still used today.

Gothic version: When Christianity swept through the Roman Empire after Emperor Constantine's conversion (A.D. 312), new Bible translations were needed. The Germanic Goths received almost the whole Bible in their language, Gothic, from the missionary translator Ulfilas.

Armenian Bible: Translated by St. Mesrop in the fifth century, this Bible is still the standard version used today in the ancient Armenian Church scattered throughout the world.

Old Slavonic Bible: St. Cyril invented the Cyrillic alphabet, and before long the entire Bible was translated in Old Slavonic. This version is the official Bible of the Russian Orthodox Church.

Middle Ages—English Translations

When the Roman Empire broke up, Christianity spread to northern and eastern Europe, and the need for new Bible translations increased. Early English translations were made from the Latin Bible, which was first read and taught in England by monks. It is believed that the first English translation was done by a seventh-century monk named Caedmon. Another English churchman, named Bede, translated the Gospels into English. King Alfred the Great (who reigned A.D. 871–901), another translator, gave his people parts of Exodus, Psalms, and Acts in their own language. He even included parts of the Ten Commandments in the laws of the land! In the 1300s, William of Shoreham and Richard Rolle translated the Psalms into English.

John Wycliffe

This well-known Oxford theologian (c. 1329–1384) was the first to translate the entire Bible from Latin into English. He believed that the Bible should be in the hands of every reader, not the exclusive property of churches and church leaders. Wycliffe and his team of translators followed the Latin text closely—even in its awkward order of words! By 1395 John Purvey revised Wycliffe's work into more understandable English.

Some copies of the Bible had notes that expressed the controversial theological views of Wycliffe and his followers. The pope reproved Wycliffe, and banned his English versions from the popular market. But the popularity of the English Bible endured. Hundreds of copies continued to circulate even up to the time of printing—more than 100 years later.

Printing, Gutenberg, and the Reformation

At Mainz in Germany, Johann Gutenberg pioneered the process of printing from movable type. The Bible, printed in Latin in 1456, was the first major work to emerge from his press. Ten years later, it was printed in German at Strasbourg. Following this, an Italian Bible and a French New Testament rolled off the press. Next, the first Dutch Scriptures appeared in 1477. Then in 1478, the entire Bible was produced in Catalan for Spain. All these printed versions were based on existing manuscripts and translated from the Latin.

Erasmus

In 1516, the renowned Dutch scholar Erasmus was the first to publish the Greek New Testament.

Martin Luther

While the young monk Martin Luther was studying his Latin Bible in Germany, he was struck by Paul's teaching in the Book of Romans. Luther's life was transformed by his new understanding of God and salvation, and he became a Bible scholar in earnest. He decided to translate the Bible into plain, everyday German. Luther was determined that everyone should be able to read the Bible. The translation was completed in 1532, and has remained the most famous German Bible since then.

William Tyndale

William Tyndale, a Cambridge scholar and follower of Erasmus, went to Germany to complete his work of translating the New Testament into English. His first printed version appeared at Worms, Germany, in 1526. Copies soon arrived in England and were eagerly studied. However, the

Bishop of London rejected this work and had the translation burnt in large quantities. Undaunted, Tyndale went on to produce a better version, and by 1566, his second revision had been printed 40 times!

Myles Coverdale

In 1535, Myles Coverdale published the entire Bible in English. It was printed overseas but quickly found its way into England. At the request of the clergy, the Coverdale Bible (with a dedication to King Henry VIII included in its pages) was authorized by the king for circulation among the people.

Coverdale's work was based on the scholarship of Tyndale, Luther, and the Latin versions of the Bible. His translation of the Psalms is still printed in *The Book of Common Prayer*. Coverdale is known for including chapter summaries (similar to the Authorized or King James Version), and for separating the Apocrypha from the Old Testament books in his version.

The Great Bible

This translation appeared in 1539 and contained a preface by the Archbishop of Canterbury, Thomas Cranmer, encouraging everyone to read the Bible. The Great Bible was intended for use by churches, and all controversial notes were dropped from its pages.

Before King Henry VIII's death in 1547, large numbers of Tyndale's and Coverdale's translations were destroyed, but the Great Bible remained in many churches (even though services were once more conducted in Latin).

The Geneva Bible

In 1560, English scholars working in Geneva, Switzerland, came out with a Bible revision dedicated to Queen Elizabeth I. The Geneva Bible, as it was called, tried to remain faithful to the style and phrasing of the Hebrew language. It included the Apocrypha, with a note about the importance of these books.

The Geneva Bible became popular both in Britain and Switzerland, and was printed 70 times during Elizabeth's reign! It also became the official Bible of the churches in Scotland.

It has sometimes been called the *Breeches Bible*, because in its translation of Genesis 3:7, it notes that Adam and Eve made "breeches" (rather than "loincloths") for themselves.

The Bishops' Bible

The Great Bible, revised by Bishop Parker and others in 1568, became known as the Bishops' Bible. The aim was to improve the text, remove offensive language, and avoid controversial notes and interpretations.

The King James or Authorized Version of 1611

When James I became king of England in 1603, he agreed to a new Bible revision. He helped organize the work, which was then handed to six groups of scholars. The revision was based on the Bishops' Bible, but the original Bible languages were used. Margin notes explained Hebrew and Greek words, linked parallel passages, and new chapter summaries were included.

When it was published, there was a dedication to King James and a long preface explaining how the work of revision and translation was done. This popular version (which, in the beginning, included the Apocrypha) enjoyed great status and authority for 350 years. People enjoyed the flow and dignity of its language. Since the early edition of the King James Version, the spelling has been updated, margin references expanded, and chapter summaries shortened.

The Douai Bible

A year before the King James Version, the first Roman Catholic Bible—the Douai Version—was published in

France. Gregory Martin and others who worked on this project tried to translate the Vulgate word for word. They ended up with a version that was difficult to understand. Bishop Challoner, unhappy with their results, called for two revisions of the Old Testament—and five of the New Testament!

Dutch, French, and Other European Languages

Besides English and German, the Reformation gave rise to Bible translations in many other languages. The first complete Dutch Bible was produced in 1525. During the following century, other versions were published, including the standard Protestant Bible—the States-General version of 1637. This is still used today along with other modern versions.

The French have produced many Bibles, the most popular among Protestants being The Segond Version of 1880 and the Synodale of 1910.

The story of Bible translation in other western European countries is similar. However, in eastern Europe old versions were used for centuries. In Russia, the entire Bible was not translated into Russian until 1876. Today there is much Bible translation being done throughout Europe.

Major Modern English Versions

In the centuries following the first publication of the Authorized Version, there were several revisions and new translations. Some of them were based on better manuscripts than the "Received Text" from which the Authorized Version was originally made.

English Revised Version

In 1870, the Church of England decided to make a revision of the King James Version. Talented teams of scholars were appointed and told to make as few changes in the text as possible. When the Revised Version New Testament emerged in 1881, it aroused great interest and speculation in England and America. In the revision, many well-known words and verses had been left out because they were lacking any real manuscript authority. The entire Bible was issued in 1885, but because it was oriented toward British spelling and figures of speech, it lost support in the United States.

Revised Standard Version

An agency of the World Council of Churches began working on a revision of the American Standard Version in 1929. Based on the latest scholarly Greek texts, the New Testament section of the RSV was published in 1946, and the Old Testament came out in 1952. It was considered a more reliable and readable translation than most others up to this point, but it was criticized because of the new wording of some key passages.

New English Bible

Dr. C. H. Dodd was the director of a new translation, suggested by the Church of Scotland in 1946. The New Testament was first published in 1961; the Old Testament appeared in 1970. This official interchurch translation in Britain was the first major version to move away from the Tyndale and Authorized Version tradition.

All the latest biblical research was considered in putting together the New English Bible. The Dead Sea Scrolls gave light to Old Testament texts, and newly discovered manuscripts revealed the meanings of some difficult words.

Living Bible

This highly popular Bible was written by Kenneth Taylor, who established his own publishing company (Tyndale House) in order to produce a paraphrase of the entire Bible written in everyday language. The New Testament was published in 1956, and the entire Bible came out in 1971.

Good News Bible

This version was produced by the American Bible Society between 1966 and 1976. Its aim was to have a reliable and accurate translation using the language of everyday speech. Based on a careful study of linguistics, it has provided a pattern for translations in many languages all over the world.

Jerusalem Bible

In 1966, the Jerusalem Bible was published by Roman Catholic translators. Based on the original languages, this modern, lively version is widely used by both Catholics and Protestants. The Jerusalem Bible (first translated into French) includes the introduction and notes from the French translation. The New Jerusalem Bible was published in 1986.

New International Version

This translation was produced in 1973 (New Testament) and 1978 (Old Testament) by a team of Protestant evangelical scholars mainly from the United States. They used the best research to produce an updated, formal Bible in the tradition of earlier English versions.

New King James Version

The New Testament of the NKJV was published in 1979 by Thomas Nelson Publishers. Based on the 1894 edition of the Textus Receptus, it both preserved the integrity of the text and eliminated archaic, difficult-to-read expressions. In 1982, the complete New King James Version was published by Thomas Nelson, and it became quite popular.

Translation, Version, Revision— What's the Difference?

What type of Bible do you read? Is it a recent translation? An updated version? A revision of an older version? If this all seems a bit confusing, perhaps some definitions of these terms will help:

Translation: There are two different types of translations. In one instance, the translator tries to render the exact words of the original language into the receptor language—for example, English. Using another approach, the translator takes the words or terms of the original language and tries to find the closest natural meaning in the receptor language. In this second method, the translation should have the same impact on the modern reader as the original had upon its audience.

Version: A translation from the original texts that is prepared by a committee of scholars.

Revision: A revised edition of an existing translation.

New Revised Standard Version

Responding to the need for a readable, accurate Bible—with gender-inclusive language—this new work was developed from the most ancient biblical texts available. Pioneered by Bruce M. Metzger and a stellar translation committee, the NRSV was published in 1989.

Jewish Translations

The Holy Scriptures According to the Masoretic Text, A New Translation (put out in 1917), aimed to combine the heart of Jewish culture with the best of biblical scholarship. In 1955, the Jewish Publication Society appointed a committee to make a new Jewish translation of the Bible, the *Tanakh*. The New Jewish Version was published in 1962 (and revised in 1973).

Statistics of Modern Bible Translation

Today, more than 5,440 languages are known to be spoken throughout the world. The work of Bible translation involves about 1,745 of these languages. However, of these, the entire Bible (or the New Testament) has been translated in under 600 languages:

Europe and the Middle East	46 languages
Asia-Pacific	285 languages
Africa	249 languages
Americas and the Caribbean	6 languages

There are also another 1,159 translations and revisions presently in progress:

Europe and the Middle East	12 languages
Asia-Pacific	465 languages
Africa	402 languages
Americas and the Caribbean	280 languages

The Work of Bible Translators

After the Middle Ages, the first translations of the Bible were made by Roman Catholics. By 1613, Jesuit missionaries had published the New Testament in Japanese. A Protestant version in Malay was then put together by workers of the Dutch East India Company. And the first entire Bible was translated in a complex American Indian language by John Eliot in 1633.

William Carey's work in India was a big step forward in this important task. Along with some colleagues and helpers, Carey spent 40 years working on translations of the Scriptures in 37 different languages or dialects, including Burmese and Chinese.

The History of Bible Translation

B.C.	300	—	Greek
	200		
	100		
A.D.	100	—	Latin, Syriac
	200	—	Coptic
	300	—	Gothic, Georgian, Ethiopic
	400	—	Armenian
	500	—	Nubian
	600	—	Chinese
	700	—	Arabic, Anglo-Saxon
	800	—	German, Slavonic, Frankish
	900		
	1000		
	1100	—	French
	1200	—	Icelandic, Dutch, Spanish, Italian, Polish
	1300	—	English, Danish, Czech, Persian
	1400		
	1500	—	Swedish
	1600	—	Finnish
	1700	—	Portuguese, Tamil
	1800	—	Norwegian, Russian, Swahili, Hindi, Urdu, Bengali, Japanese
	1900	—	Hausa, Afrikaans, and more than 1,000 other languages

In 1804, the British and Foreign Bible Society was founded. They put out the Hindustani New Testament in 1812 and the first modern African translation in 1816. Several other societies emerged decades ago and continued the work of Bible translation. These groups helped establish projects, they gave money where it was needed, and they had translations printed and distributed. In the case of the Netherlands Society, they trained their own linguists and sent them out as translators.

As the modern missionary movement grew, so did the work of translation. And although nationals were involved, the primary translators were usually missionaries. Thus, during the first half of the twentieth century, Bible translation moved along at a rapid pace.

Today, the largest missionary society in the world is the Wycliffe Bible Translators, founded in 1934. Their translators are first thoroughly trained in linguistics before beginning even the simplest task in figuring out a text. After months—or years—of difficult translating work, the reward is to see the joy the translation brings to someone who is able to read the Scriptures in their local language for the first time!

Another large group, the United Bible Societies, organizes more than 60 national societies all over the world. Both Protestants and Catholics are part of this work, which covers some of the major languages of the world—including Hindi, Chinese, and Arabic.

Today's translator is often a national—rather than a missionary—working to improve an existing translation developed by a foreigner. Translators often work together, sharing ideas, noting criticisms of the text, and drafting revisions. Bible society officers keep in close touch with translating projects throughout the world.

Besides Wycliffe Bible Translators and the United Bible Societies, there are several other translators at work today. However, there are still hundreds of language groups without an existing translation for their use. Clearly, there is plenty of work to be done. And Bible society scholars estimate that as languages keep changing, a revision—if not a new translation—will be needed every 30 years for each language.

Ten Quick Titles—Bibles for Children

Children's Bibles are a popular item on the publishing market right now. Some of these Bibles are really adult translations with art for children. Other so-called Children's Bibles are, in fact, just Bible storybooks with nice pictures. However, a few publishers have taken existing Bible translations and simplified them for children. Here is a list of Bibles designed especially for children and young people:

1. The Bible for Children
2. Simplified Living Bible
3. Children's New Testament
4. Precious Moments Children's Bible
5. International Children's Bible
6. The Everyday Bible
7. The New Testament in Modern English
8. A Book about Jesus (contains passages from the four Gospels)
9. Good News Travels Fast: Acts of the Apostles
10. A Few Who Dared (portions of the Old Testament)

Opening up the Bible

Why do millions of people the world over read the Bible on a regular basis? What appeal does this ancient book have for the average person today?

There are a number of reasons why people are fascinated by the Bible, and drawn to its stories and teachings. First, the Bible is all about God and his dealings with humanity. The lives of biblical characters and their experiences with God reflect our personal stories, too. The spiritual journeys of those who have gone before give us insight and direction for our own lives.

Also, as we look at the history of humanity, it becomes evident that the Bible has played a central role in many cultures: shaping laws, politics, and religion—influencing human rights and the fabric of social life. This influence continues today in many parts of the world.

The Books of the Bible

The Bible is a unique book that has a distinct theme and special appeal. The Old Testament stresses that there is only one true God, and he alone must be worshiped. In the New Testament, Jesus repeats the same assertions and goes a step further: He claims to be God's only son, and declares that only he can point the way to the father. Jesus invites anyone to come to him. And as we look at each book of the Bible, we discover that compelling message woven throughout the people, places, and events of the Old and New Testaments.

Genesis

Message: Genesis is about beginnings: the creation of the world, a new beginning after the great flood, and the beginning of the Jewish nation.

Key passages and events: The creation and corruption of the world (chapters 1–3); Cain kills his brother Abel (4); Noah and the flood (6–9); the Tower of Babel (11); the story of Abraham (12–25); the destruction of Sodom and Gomorrah (19); Jacob's story (27–35); Joseph's story (37–50)

Setting: An area of the Middle East known as the "fertile crescent"

Time of events: About 2000–1650 B.C.

Author: Attributed to Moses

Exodus

Message: Under Moses' leadership, God rescues his people from slavery in Egypt and begins to show them how to live a new life.

Key passages and events: Moses in the reeds (chapters 1–2); the ten plagues (7–12); the Passover (12–15); crossing the Red Sea (14); the Ten Commandments and the Law (20–24); the tent of worship (tabernacle) (26)

Setting: The Nile Delta in Egypt and the Sinai peninsula

Time of events: About 1325–1225 B.C.

Author: Attributed to Moses

Leviticus

Message: An account of how to offer sacrifices and carry out ceremonial law, Leviticus concerns itself with the duties of the priests and Levites. It also describes the religious festivals that marked the year for the Israelites.

Key passages and events: Laws about offerings and sacrifices (chapters 1–7); Aaron and his sons ordained as priests (8–9); ritual health laws (11–15); the Day of Atonement (16); worship and the festivals (17–27)

Setting: The Sinai peninsula

Time of events: Between 1325–1225 B.C.

Author: Attributed to Moses

Numbers

Message: The story of the clans of Israel living as nomads in the Sinai peninsula after their departure from Mount Sinai.

Key passages and events: Life in the desert (chapters 1–14); Korah's rebellion (14); water from the rock (20); the bronze snake (21); Balak and Balaam (24); the new land, Canaan (34)

Setting: Mount Sinai and the Sinai peninsula

Time of events: Between 1325–1225 B.C.

Author: Attributed to Moses

Deuteronomy

Message: The second record of God's laws, this book stresses obedience to God. As Israel is about to enter the Promised Land, Moses gives the people his final oration.

Key passages and events: Moses' reflections (chapters 1–4); obedience and God's laws (5–26); instructions for the new land (27–28); the covenant renewed (29); Joshua, the new leader (31); Moses' blessing (32–33); Moses' death (34)

Setting: The plain east of the River Jordan
Time of events: Approximately 1230 B.C.
Author: Attributed to Moses

Joshua

Message: The story of the Israelite invasion of Canaan (known as Israel, the Promised Land), led by Joshua.

Key passages and events: Joshua commissioned as leader (chapter 1); Rahab and the spies (2); crossing the Jordan (3); the fall of Jericho (5–6); the conquest of Canaan (9–12); the land divided among the tribes (13–19); Joshua's farewell message and death (23–24)

Setting: The plain east of the River Jordan; Canaan
Time of events: About 1230–1200 B.C.
Author: Unknown

Judges

Message: In spite of Israel's disobedience, God provides national heroes to rescue his people during the time between Israel's taking of Canaan and the first kings.

Key passages and events: Deborah and Barak defeat the Canaanites (chapters 4–5); Gideon's fleece and the Midianites (6–7); Jephthah, his daughter, and the battle with the Ammonites (10–12); Samson's story (13–16)

Setting: Canaan, the land of Israel
Time of events: About 1200–1070 B.C.
Author: Uncertain

Ruth

Message: The story of Ruth is one of love, loyalty, and God's care for everyone who is faithful to him, whatever their nationality.

Key passages and events: Ruth's husband dies (chapter 1); Ruth goes to Moab with her mother-in-law, Naomi (1–2); Ruth and Boaz (3); Ruth marries Boaz and has a son (4)

Setting: Bethlehem and Moab

Time of events: 1375–1050 B.C.

Author: Unknown

1 and 2 Samuel

Message: The history of Israel from the last of the judges, Eli and Samuel, and the first two kings, Saul and David.

Key passages and events: *1 Samuel:* Samuel's birth, call, and leadership (chapters 1–7); Saul becomes Israel's first king (8–15); God chooses David as Israel's future king (16); David kills Goliath (17); David and Jonathan (20); David outlawed (18–30); the deaths of Saul and Jonathan (31); *2 Samuel:* David mourns (1); David is crowned king (2–4); David conquers Jerusalem (5); David brings the Covenant to Jerusalem (6); David's adultery with Bathsheba and murder of Uriah (11–12); David's family troubles (13–20); David's song and final words (22–23)

Setting: Canaan, the land of Israel

Time of events: About 1200–1070 B.C.

Author: Unknown

1 and 2 Kings

Message: The story of Israel's history from David's death, through the kingdom division following Solomon's death, to the fall of Jerusalem and destruction of the temple by the Babylonians.

Key passages and events: *1 Kings:* Solomon asks for wisdom (chapters 3–4); the building and dedication of the temple (5–8); the Queen of Sheba's visit (10); Solomon's failure and death (11); the kingdom is divided (12); Elijah's and Baal's contest (17–19); King Ahab and Naboth's vineyard (21); *2 Kings:* Elijah is taken to heaven (2); Elisha and his miracles (2–6); the curing of Namaan (5); Queen Athaliah and the boy king, Joash (11); Israel's capture by Assyria (17); King Hezekiah and the Assyrian threat (18); King Josiah's discovery (22–23); Jerusalem falls to Babylon (25)

Setting: The two kingdoms of Israel and Judah

Time of events: About 970–586 B.C.

Author: Uncertain

1 and 2 Chronicles

Message: Chronicles tries to convince the Jews (now back home in Jerusalem after their exile in Babylon) that, in spite of their troubled history, they are still God's people. These books cover the same events as those in 2 Samuel and Kings.

Key passages and events: *1 Chronicles:* Family trees from Adam to the first kings (chapters 1–9); death of King Saul (10); the story of King David (11–21); David's preparations for building the temple and worship (22–29); *2 Chronicles:* King Solomon's story (1–9); the kings of Judah (10–36); last days and the fall of Jerusalem (36)

Setting: Israel and Judah

Time of events: About 1000–586 B.C.

Author: Uncertain (possibly Ezra)

Ezra

Message: The story of two groups of Jews who return to their homeland from exile in Babylon. They reconstruct the temple and, under the leadership of Ezra the priest, begin to observe the Law.

Key passages and events: The first group returns to Jerusalem (chapters 1–2); in spite of opposition, the temple is rebuilt (3–6); the second group returns with Ezra (7–10)

  Setting: Jerusalem

  Time of events: About 538–428 B.C.

  Author: Uncertain (possibly Ezra)

Nehemiah

Message: Nehemiah, a Jewish exile and great leader, directs another group of exiles back to Jerusalem. He becomes governor of Judea and initiates the rebuilding of the city walls. His reforms overlap Ezra's work.

Key passages and events: Nehemiah returns to Jerusalem and the walls are rebuilt (chapters 1–7); a list of the returned exiles (7); Ezra reads the Law and the people repent (8–10); the dedication of the new walls (12); Nehemiah's reforms (12–13)

  Setting: Jerusalem

  Time of events: About 458–432 B.C.

  Author: Nehemiah

Esther

Message: The beautiful Jewish girl, Esther, becomes queen to the Persian Emperor, Ahasuerus (Xerxes). With the help of her guardian, Mordecai, she thwarts a plot to have all Jews in the Emperor's kingdom killed.

Key passages and events: The emperor's wife, Vashti, is rejected (chapter 1); Esther is crowned queen (2); Haman's plot (3–4); the courage of Esther (5); the deliverance of the Jews (6–10)

  Setting: Susa (Persia)

Time of events: About 460 B.C.
Author: Unknown

Job

Message: This dramatic poem deals with the problem of human suffering. It tells the story of Job, a good man, who loses everything yet still has deep faith in God.

Key passages and events: Job's disasters (chapters 1–2); the friends of Job (3–37); God reveals his greatness to Job (38–42); the deliverance of Job (42)

Setting: Unknown
Time of events: Unknown
Author: Unknown

Psalms

Message: A compilation of 150 hymns, prayers, and poems expressing the range of human emotions. The common thread throughout this collection is deep faith and love for God.

Key themes and passages: Instruction (Psalms 1, 19, 39); praise (8, 29, 93, 100); thanksgiving (30, 65, 103, 107, 116); repentance (6, 32, 38, 51, 130); trust (3, 27, 31, 46, 56, 62, 86); distress (4, 13, 55, 64, 88); hope (42, 63, 80, 84, 137); history (78, 105)

Time of events: Collections of Psalms were made throughout Israel's history

Author: Different writers (many titles are linked to King David)

Proverbs

Message: A collection of wise sayings. The main theme is to find and follow godly wisdom and apply it to everyday living.

Key themes: Wisdom and folly; the righteous and the wicked; how to speak wisely; wealth and poverty; hopes and fears; joys and sorrows; anger; hard work and laziness

Time of events: Wisdom literature flourished throughout Israel's Kingdom period

Author: Solomon and other wisdom teachers

Ecclesiastes

Message: Life is short, and there is nothing that lasts. The author trusts in God, but believes that we can never know what God's intentions are. Clearly, for this writer, the life of faith is difficult.

Key words: "For everything there is a season, and a time for every matter under heaven" (Ecc 3:1)

Time of events: Uncertain

Author: Solomon or a later Jewish sage

Song of Solomon

Message: A collection of six beautiful songs expressing the wonder of unselfish love between a young husband and his wife.

Key themes and passages: Courtship (chapters 1–3); the wedding (3–5); growth in marriage (5–8); the nature and power of love (8)

Setting: The countryside in springtime

Time of events: About 971–931 B.C.

Author: Uncertain (possibly Solomon)

Isaiah

Message: Isaiah the prophet is called by God to warn of judgment on all who turn away from him. The prophet's message is that Israel must depend on God alone. Along with Isaiah's prophecies, the book is full of promises about the coming Messiah and future restoration.

Key themes and passages: Isaiah's vision and call (chapter 6); God with us (7); the future king (9); the peaceful kingdom (11); the road of holiness (35); Isaiah and the Assyrian siege (36–37); comfort and the mighty God (40); the Lord's servant (42); a light to the nations (49); the suf-

fering servant (52–53); God's invitation (55); future glory
(60); deliverance (61)

    Setting: Jerusalem
    Time of events: About 790–722 B.C.
    Author: Isaiah

Jeremiah

    Message: Jeremiah hated to bring bad news, but all of his
prophecies came true. He spoke of coming judgment on
Israel because of sin and idolatry. Jeremiah's prophecies
belong to the reigns of Judah's last five kings.

    Key themes and passages: God calls Jeremiah (chapter
1); God's word to his wayward people (2–6); captivity and
destruction predicted (13–17, 25); the potter's house (18–19);
the promise of restoration (30–33); the king destroys Jeremiah's scroll (36); Jeremiah in captivity (37–38); fall of
Jerusalem (39, 52); messages to other nations (46–51)

    Setting: Judah
    Time of events: About 627–586 B.C.
    Author: Jeremiah

Lamentations

    Message: These five poems express the sorrow of the
Jews at the destruction of Jerusalem by the Babylonians.
Mostly written in an acrostic form (based on the letters of
the Hebrew alphabet), these laments express fear that God
has abandoned his people. However, the writer puts his
faith in God's unfailing mercy.

    Key passage: Hope (La 3:21–27)
    Setting: Jerusalem
    Time of events: Probably 586 B.C.
    Author: Uncertain (attributed to Jeremiah)

Ezekiel

    Message: Much of Ezekiel's message is about sin and
judgment. The prophet/priest proclaimed that God in his

glory and holiness could not tolerate impurity and idolatry. He predicted the fall of Jerusalem, but spoke of the hope of repentance, restoration, and renewed worship.

Key themes and passages: Ezekiel's vision (chapter 1); his call (2–3); Ezekiel dramatizes the siege of Jerusalem (4–5); God's glory leaves the temple (8–10); death of Ezekiel's wife (24); the valley of the dry bones (37); vision of a new temple (40–48)

Setting: Babylon

Time of events: About 593–571 B.C.

Author: Ezekiel

Daniel

Message: Exiled in Babylon from boyhood, Daniel's story is one of uncompromising courage and faith in the midst of persecution. The Book of Daniel also includes visions of the future and a prayer.

Key themes and passages: Daniel in Babylon (chapters 1–6); the fiery furnace (3); Belshazzar's feast (5); Daniel escapes the lions (6); visions of four empires (7–8); Daniel's prayer (9); visions of future conflict (10–11); the time of the end (12)

Setting: Babylonia

Time of events: About 605–536 B.C.

Author: Daniel

Hosea

Message: Compassionate Hosea speaks out against Israel's corrupt civic and religious life. His own experience with family problems makes the prophet sensitive to Israel's unfaithfulness. He warns Israel of destruction and implores the people to return to God and enjoy his blessing.

Key themes and passages: Hosea's sorrow for his wife (chapter 1); unfaithful Israel (2); Hosea's wife returns (3); God loves his people but must judge their sin (4–13); promised restoration if Israel repents (14)

THE STORY OF THE BIBLE

Setting: Northern kingdom of Israel
Time of events: About 790–715 B.C.
Author: Hosea

Joel

Message: The image of locusts is used as a sign of the coming judgment day of the Lord. The prophet Joel calls for national repentance. He also looks forward to a time of rich blessing when God's Spirit will be poured out on everyone.

Key themes and passages: A plague of locusts (chapter 1); call to repentance (2); the gift of the Spirit (3); judgement against the nations (3)

Setting: Judah
Time of events: Uncertain
Author: Attributed to Joel

Amos

Message: The prophet's message is one of social justice. He speaks out against the unfairness, greed, and hypocrisy of Israel and other nations.

Key themes and passages: Prophecies against other nations (chapters 1–2); prophecies against Israel (2–6); five visions (7–9); a promise of restoration (9)

Setting: Northern kingdom of Israel
Time of events: About 790–722 B.C.
Author: Amos

Obadiah

Message: In this short prophecy against the Edomites—a nation that had taken advantage of Jerusalem—Obadiah warns that God will destroy Edom. In the future, Obadiah declares, Israel will not only get back their land, but they will also get the land of the Edomites.

Setting: Jerusalem
Time of events: Uncertain
Author: Obadiah

Jonah

Message: Jonah dislikes the idea that God's mercy extends beyond Israel—particularly to that nation's enemies. In this riveting story, God sets out to transform Jonah's thinking.

Key themes and passages: Jonah's disobedience—the storm and the great fish (chapters 1–2); Jonah's obedience—the action and words of the Lord (3–4)

Setting: The Great Sea and Assyria

Time of events: 793–753 B.C.

Author: Jonah

Micah

Message: The prophet is appalled by the false sacrifices and empty worship of Israel. His central concerns are for social justice and true religion. His hope is in God's future peace and blessing.

Key themes and passages: Judgment will come (chapters 1–2); God's reign of peace (4); a king from Bethlehem (5); what God requires (6)

Setting: Israel and Judah

Time of events: 750–722 B.C.

Author: Micah

Nahum

Message: This book is an oracle against Nineveh, capital of the cruel and powerful Assyrians. Nahum's message does include a call to repentance.

Key themes and passages: The certainty and description of God's judgment against Nineveh (chapters 1–2); the reasons for God's judgment (3)

Setting: Judah

Time of events: Around 612 B.C.

Author: Nahum

Habakkuk

Message: The prophet faces the difficult question: How can God allow the wicked to prosper? Why is it that evil Babylonia overpowers weak, less evil nations? The prophet concludes that true faith will not be disappointed because God, who is in control, can be trusted.

Key themes and passages: Habakkuk's distress (chapter 1); a dirge from God: the "woes" of Habakkuk (2); Habakkuk's prayer and God's majestic presence (3)

Setting: Judah

Time of events: 612–597 B.C.

Author: Habakkuk

Zephaniah

Message: The prophet predicts only doom for disobedient Jerusalem. But he believes that a remnant of the nation will survive and enjoy a great future.

Key themes and passages: The day of judgment (chapters 1–2); doom for the nations and hope for the remnant (2–3)

Setting: Judah

Time of events: 640–609 B.C.

Author: Zephaniah

Haggai

Message: The prophet Haggai urges God's people who have returned from exile, to finish the job of rebuilding the temple. They had abandoned the project, and instead, built fine homes for themselves. The people respond to Haggai's challenge, and the work of rebuilding continues.

Key themes and passages: A command to rebuild the temple (chapter 1); God's blessing on the obedient (2); a word for Zerubbabel, the governor (2)

Setting: Jerusalem
Time of events: 520 B.C.
Author: Haggai

Zechariah

Message: The prophet declares that a new age is beginning. Zechariah speaks not only about the blessing and hope of Jerusalem, but of the whole world. Zechariah also speaks of the coming of a Messiah, a king of love and justice who will be sent by God.

Key themes and passages: A new age is starting (chapters 1–8); eight symbolic visions (1–6); a message of rejoicing (8); the nations surrounding Israel (9); the blessings of the Messiah (9); the redemption of Israel (12–13); the return of the King (14)

Setting: Jerusalem
Time of events: 520–515 B.C.
Author: Zechariah

Malachi

Message: The prophet challenges Israel to keep God's commandments and encourages the people to rely on God for future blessing.

Key themes and passages: God's love for Israel (chapter 1); broken promises and judgment (2); paying tithes (3); God's promise of mercy (3–4)

Setting: Jerusalem
Time of events: About 430 B.C.
Author: Malachi

The Apocrypha

Christians agree that the 39 books of the Hebrew Scriptures are the core of the Old Testament. Questions arise over the status of the books called *Apocrypha* (meaning "hidden") by Protestants and called *Deutero-canonical* by Roman Catholics. The apocryphal books (written about 200 B.C.) were found and accepted by the early Christians when they took over the Greek Old Testament (Septuagint) as their Bible. Today, all Catholic Bibles contain the Deuterocanonical books. Some Protestant Bibles contain the Apocrypha. Many do not. And significant numbers of Christians believe that the apocryphal books are not part of the Scriptures, and therefore not authoritative.

The Apocrypha includes many types of literature, including wisdom, history, and visionary writing. There are even stories with startling supernatural details. In the book of Tobit, the liver and heart of a fish—with the help of a guardian angel—can drive away demons and cure blindness!

APOCRYPHAL OR DEUTEROCANONICAL BOOKS

Tobit
1 Maccabees
Judith
2 Maccabees
Additions to Esther
3 Maccabees
Wisdom
4 Maccabees
Sirach (Ecclesiasticus)
Prayer of Manasseh

Baruch
Psalm 151
1 Esdras
2 Esdras
Letter of Jeremiah
Prayer of Azariah and
    the Song of the
    Three Jews
Susanna
Bel and the Dragon

The Time Between the Testaments

Ezra, Nehemiah, and Esther give us the last glimpse of the Jews in the Old Testament. After Malachi, and until the start of New Testament times, the biblical prophets were silent. What do we know about this period?

- Alexander the Great from Greece conquered Palestine and the surrounding lands. He introduced Greek language and customs to Palestine (333–332 B.C.).

- When Alexander died, his empire went to four generals. Palestine was first conquered by the Egyptian kingdom, and then in turn, by the kingdoms founded in Syria and Mesopotamia.

- Antiochus (one of the Syrian conquerors) tried to force the Jews to adopt Greek beliefs and ways of worship. In his zeal to destroy Jewish faith in God, he set up a statue of the Greek God Zeus in the temple at Jerusalem and even sacrificed a pig in the temple.

- The Jews revolted against Antiochus. The Maccabee family who led the revolt became the new rulers. However, Jewish independence did not last long.

- Palestine was then conquered by the expanding Roman empire. Jewish priests were killed, and the Jews were once again dominated by the rule of outsiders.

- Augustus Caesar became emperor of the Roman Empire in 27 B.C. By the time Jesus came, the Jews were under the rule of the Romans (who continued to encourage the Greek way of life).

Matthew

Message: This Gospel links the Old Testament and the New. It portrays Jesus as the Messiah, the one foretold by the prophets. Matthew emphasizes the concerns of Jewish Christians.

Great events: Jesus' birth (chapter 1); Jesus' baptism (3); the temptation of Jesus (4); the transfiguration (17); Jesus' entry into Jerusalem (21); trials and crucifixion (26–27); Jesus' resurrection (28)

Famous passages: Sermon on the Mount (5–7); the Lord's Prayer (6); the Great Commission (28)

Time of writing: A.D. 60–80

Setting: Galilee and Jerusalem

Author: The Apostle Matthew

Mark

Message: Jesus is depicted as a man of action. He is the "Son of man" (of Daniel's vision) who wants his identity kept hidden.

Great events: John the Baptist prepares the way (chapter 1); Jesus' baptism (1); choosing 12 followers (3); feeding the 5,000 (6); the last supper (14); Jesus' arrest, trial, and death (14–15); the resurrection (16)

Famous passages: Jesus and the children (9–10); casting out the money changers (11)

Time of writing: A.D. 60–70

Setting: Galilee and Jerusalem

Author: John Mark, colleague of Peter

Luke

Message: Jesus came first to the Jews, his chosen people; now salvation comes to everyone. However, salvation is for the needy, those without hope. Luke portrays Jesus as the Savior, a man of prayer, full of the Holy Spirit.

Great events: The angel's message and the birth of Jesus (chapters 1–2); Jesus' baptism and temptation (3–4); the transfiguration (9); Jesus' entry into Jerusalem (20); the last supper (22); trial and crucifixion (22–23); Jesus' resurrection (24)

Famous passages: The angel's message to Mary (1); Mary's song (1); the shepherds and the angels (2); the parable of the great feast (14); the parable of the prodigal son (14); a blind beggar (18); Jesus and Zacchaeus (19)

Time of writing: Between A.D. 60–80
Setting: Galilee and Jerusalem
Author: Luke, colleague of Paul

John

Message: Jesus is the "Word of God" who desires to draw people to faith. John tells the story of Jesus' life in the framework of seven signs and seven sayings, and he presents Jesus as light, life, and love.

Great events: Jesus at the wedding (chapter 3); the woman at the well (4); the raising of Lazarus (11); Jesus' anointing (12); the triumphal entry (12); the last supper (13); Jesus' arrest, trial, and death (18–19); the empty tomb (20); Jesus appears to Thomas (20)

Famous passages: The Word (1); God's great love (3); the light of the world (8); Jesus washes the disciples' feet (13); Jesus, the way, the truth, and the life (14); the coming Holy Spirit (16)

Time of writing: Between A.D. 60–90
Setting: Galilee and Jerusalem
Author: The Apostle John

Acts of the Apostles

Message: Acts recounts the history of the early church from its small beginnings to its great expansion throughout the Roman Empire.

Great events: The ascension (chapter 1); the gift of the Holy Spirit (2); Saul's conversion (9); the voyage to Rome (27–28)

Famous passages: Peter's sermon (2); the jailer at Philippi (16); Paul before Agrippa (26)

Time of writing: About A.D. 60–80

Setting: The Roman Empire
Author: Luke, colleague of Paul

Romans

Message: In his letter to the Romans, Paul shows how a person's life is changed by believing the good news.
Key passage: Justification by faith (chapter 5)
Time of writing: About A.D. 55–60
Author: The Apostle Paul

1 Corinthians

Message: In his first letter to the Corinthians, Paul deals with social, moral, and spiritual issues confronting the young church.
Key passage: Love is greatest (chapter 13)
Time of writing: Between A.D. 55–60
Author: The Apostle Paul

2 Corinthians

Message: Paul, in his second letter, sets out the essentials of being in Christian service.
Key passage: True spiritual service (chapters 2–4)
Time of writing: Between A.D. 55–60
Author: The Apostle Paul

Galatians

Message: Paul wants his readers to know that a person does not need to keep the Law of Moses to be saved. Faith in Christ alone brings salvation.
Key passage: Living by faith (chapter 2)
Time of writing: Between A.D. 45–55
Author: The Apostle Paul

Ephesians

Message: Paul explains how vital the unity of all things in Christ is—in the church, between Jews and Gentiles, in marriage, and at the workplace.

Key passage: Practical Christian living (chapters 4–5)
Time of writing: About A.D. 60
Author: The Apostle Paul

Philippians

Message: Paul expresses love and joy for the Christians at Philippi. He is grateful for the gift they sent him, and commends a coworker to them.

Key passage: Greeting, thanksgiving, and prayer (chapter 1)
Time of writing: Between A.D. 55–60
Author: The Apostle Paul

Colossians

Message: Paul tells the Christians at Colossae that in order to be reconciled to God, all they need is Jesus Christ.

Key passage: The supremacy of Christ (chapters 1–2)
Time of writing: Between A.D. 55–60
Author: The Apostle Paul

1 Thessalonians

Message: Paul is encouraged by the faith of the Thessalonian Christians, and he wants to inspire them further. He advises them not to speculate on Christ's return but to live exemplary lives until the day of his coming.

Key passage: Be ready for Christ's return (chapters 4–5)
Time of writing: Between A.D. 45–50
Author: The Apostle Paul

2 Thessalonians

Message: Paul writes to clear up misunderstandings about Christ's second coming. The apostle stresses that what the believers should be most concerned with is the quality of their daily Christian lives.

Key passage: Practical Christian living (chapter 4)
Time of writing: Between A.D. 45–50
Author: The Apostle Paul

1 Timothy

Message: Paul writes to advise and encourage the young church leader, Timothy. Besides pastoral instruction, Paul tells Timothy how to deal with practical and spiritual problems in the congregation.

Key passage: Leadership in the church (chapter 3)
Time of writing: Between A.D. 60–65
Author: The Apostle Paul

2 Timothy

Message: Paul uses his own life as an example to encourage Timothy to persevere in the faith.

Key passage: Hardships ahead (chapter 3)
Time of writing: Between A.D. 60–65
Author: The Apostle Paul

Titus

Message: Paul instructs the leader of the church of Crete in what to teach, how to guide the believers, and in practical matters of church life.

Key passage: What to teach and how (chapter 2)
Time of writing: Between A.D. 60–65
Author: The Apostle Paul

Philemon

Message: Paul asks Philemon to treat Onesimus not as a runaway slave, but as a beloved Christian brother.

Key passage: True brotherhood (vss. 13–16)
Time of writing: Between A.D. 60–65
Author: The Apostle Paul

Hebrews

Message: This letter ties together the Old and New Testaments. Directed to Jewish Christians, the writer points out that Jesus has completed all that the Old Testament began.

He argues powerfully against a return to Judaism and its institutions—the life of faith in Christ is what counts.

    Key passage: Heroes of the faith (chapter 11)
    Time of writing: Before A.D. 70
    Author: Unknown

James

    Message: True Christianity is faith and action, word and deed.

    Key passage: Hearing and doing, faith and actions (chapters 1–2)
    Time of writing: Between A.D. 50–70
    Author: James, brother of Jesus

1 Peter

    Message: Peter writes to encourage Christians as they face coming persecution. He brings joy and hope, because he believes that faith is purified in struggle, and that persecution makes the union of Christians stronger.

    Key passage: Suffering for doing right (chapters 3–4)
    Time of writing: Between A.D. 60–65
    Author: The Apostle Peter

2 Peter

    Message: Watch out for corrupt teaching, the writer warns his Christian readers; concentrate on true knowledge of God, and live as though awaiting the return of Christ.

    Key passage: Knowledge of God and the truth (chapter 1)
    Time of writing: Uncertain
    Author: The Apostle Peter

1 John

    Message: This letter is written to Christians to confirm their faith.

    Key passage: Walking in the light (chapter 1)

Time of writing: Between A.D. 50–70
Author: The Apostle John

2 John

Message: The major concerns of this short letter are truth and love in the body of Christ.
Key passage: Walking in love (vss. 5–6)
Time of writing: Between A.D. 50–70
Author: The Apostle John

3 John

Message: Written to Gaius, a church leader, commending him; this letter also warns against ambitious Diotrephes.
Key passage: Commendation for hospitality (vss. 5–8)
Time of writing: Between A.D. 50–70
Author: The Apostle John

Jude

Message: Beware of false teachers.
Key passage: Guidelines for avoiding apostasy (vss. 17–23)
Time of writing: Between A.D. 60–80
Author: Jude

Revelation

Message: The final victory of Jesus Christ over all forces that oppose God. Revelation's message is conveyed through a pattern of visions, and the book ends with a description of heaven, with God and his redeemed people as one—all evil and pain overcome forever.
Key passage: The victorious Christ (chapters 19–20)
Time of writing: Between A.D. 80–100
Author: The Apostle John

EVENTS IN THE BIBLE

THIS REMARKABLE VOLUME that we call "The Bible" is, among other things, a history book. And to gain more than a casual understanding of the Bible, we need to get a clear picture of the historical events recorded in it. The Bible starts with the dawn of life, then takes us on an amazing journey through Old Testament history, the life of Christ, the ministry of the apostles, and the growth of the new church. From beginning to end, the story of the Bible depicts the creative, active hand of God at work in the world he made. This section highlights some of the important—and interesting—moments from Scripture.

The book of Genesis describes Adam and Eve's original sin, which caused a curse on all humanity.

Major Milestones in the Bible

The following is a roughly chronological list of significant biblical events. They have been divided into periods that start in the Old Testament and finish in the New Testament.

Events From Creation to Abraham

- God created all things, including the first human beings.

- The man and woman were put in charge of the earth and God gave them rules to live by.

- Adam and Eve disobeyed God's instructions. Sin entered the world.

- Adam and Eve had children. One of their sons, Cain, murdered his brother Abel.

- God gave Adam and Eve a third son, Seth. God promised to send the world a Redeemer; he would come from Seth's family.

- Rampant wrongdoing spread throughout the world.

- God sent a great flood to punish sinful humanity. He preserved Noah, his family, and some animals in an ark (a large wooden ship).

- After the flood, God put a rainbow in the sky to remind everyone that he would never again destroy all humanity by water.

- Proud city-dwellers in Babel tried to build a tower to heaven. God put a stop to their arrogance by scattering the people and breaking them up into different language groups.

The Patriarchs of Israel*

Abraham	2166 B.C.–1991 B.C
Isaac	2066 B.C.–1886 B.C.
Jacob	2006 B.C.–1859 B.C.
Joseph	1915 B.C.–1446 B.C.

*Dates are approximate

Events From Abraham to Moses

- Around 2000 B.C. God told Abraham to leave his homeland, Ur, and go to a new land.

- God promised Abraham a son through whom all nations on earth would be blessed.

- Abraham and his wife Sarah took matters into their own hands and secured an heir (Ishmael) through Hagar, Sarah's servant girl.

- Thirteen years after Ishmael's birth, the promised heir, Isaac, was born to Abraham and Sarah in their old age.

- Abraham's faith was tested when God told him to sacrifice Isaac. The boy's life was spared, and Abraham's trust in God and obedience to him grew.

- Isaac's second son, Jacob, lived about 1850 B.C. God chose Jacob to inherit the promises he had given to Isaac.

- Jacob stole the birthright (the right to succeed to Isaac's promises and blessings) from Esau, his brother. Because of this, Jacob left home to escape Esau's fury.

- After years of hard work and difficulties, Jacob had a family and became wealthy. He and his family returned to his father's home in Palestine. Jacob made peace with Esau.

The Wives and Sons of Jacob (Israel)

LEAH	RACHEL	BILHAH	ZILPAH
Reuben	Joseph	Dan	Gad
Simeon	Benjamin	Naphtali	Asher
Levi	Judah	Issachar	Zebulun

Each of these sons was the father of a large family (known as a "tribe" or "clan" in the Bible). Later on, Joseph's two sons, Ephraim and Manasseh, took their father's place as "children of Israel." About 400 years after Jacob (called Israel) died, the Israelites were brought out of Egypt to the land God had promised Abraham. In the new land, each clan was given its own area in which to live.

- Jacob's sons, jealous of their younger brother Joseph, sold him into slavery to an Egyptian caravan.

- Joseph rose from slavery in Egypt to become second in command under the pharaoh.

- Joseph rescued his family from starving when a famine drove them to Egypt in search of food. He forgave his brothers, and Joseph's family settled in a rich part of Egypt.

Events From Moses to Saul

- Jacob's descendants had many children. The pharaohs, afraid of an uprising, enslaved the Jews in Egypt.

- All Israelite boy babies were ordered killed.

- The pharaoh's daughter found an Israelite baby in a waterproof basket in the river. She named him Moses and took him (along with his mother as nursemaid) to the Egyptian court to be brought up and educated.

- Moses lived from about 1526 to 1406 B.C.

- When he was about 40 years old, Moses killed an Egyptian for beating an Israelite. Afraid for his life, Moses disappeared into the Midian Desert.

- God spoke to Moses from a burning bush. He told Moses to go back to Egypt and lead the Israelites into Palestine, the land he had promised to Abraham.

- God sent Aaron, Moses' brother, along with him to speak for Moses.

- After Egypt experienced plagues, destruction, and death at the hand of God, the pharaoh agreed to let the Israelites leave.

- Moses led the people out of Egypt, through the parted waters of the Red Sea, and on to Mount Sinai.

- At Mount Sinai, God gave Moses the laws (including the Ten Commandments) and social plans that would mold the Israelites into a holy nation.

- The Israelites complained, disobeyed God, and turned away from him. Because of their lack of trust, God condemned them to wander in the wilderness for 40 years.

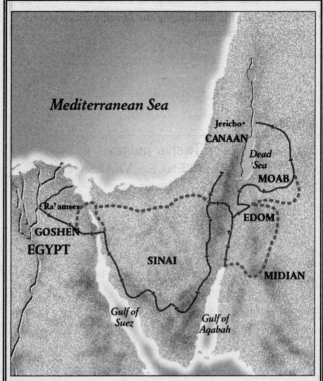

The Exodus

- Moses spoke to the people for the last time on the plains of Moab. After his farewell address, God led him to the top of Mount Nebo to see the land the Israelites would enter. There Moses died.

- Joshua, one of the spies who had first looked at Canaan, the land promised to the Israelites, led the people in conquering and settling the new land.

- In all, Joshua and his troops conquered 31 kings in the new territory.

- Joshua divided the land among the Israelite tribes according to God's directions.

- After Joshua's death, the great leaders of this period were charismatic figures known as "judges." The most memorable of these leaders were: Othniel, Deborah (the only woman judge), Gideon, Jephthah, Samson, Eli, and Samuel.

The Twelve Judges

NAME	REFERENCE	YEARS OF RULE (approximate)
Othniel	Jdg 3:7–11	1367–1327 B.C.
Ehud	Jdg 3:12–30	1304–1224 B.C.
Shamgar	Jdg 3:31	Uncertain
Deborah	Jdg 4–5	1224–1184 B.C.
Gideon	Jdg 6–8	1177–1137 B.C.
Tola	Jdg 10:1, 2	1134–1089 B.C.
Jair	Jdg 10:3, 5	1134–1089 B.C.
Jephthah	Jdg 10:6–12:7	1089–1083 B.C.
Ibzan, Elon, Abdon	Jdg 12:8–15	1083–1058 B.C.
Samson	Jdg 13–16	c. 1069 B.C.

- When Samuel was just a boy, God spoke to him about his future role as Israel's prophet and judge.

- Samuel, Israel's first great prophet and last of the judges, anointed Saul to be the first king over Israel.

- Saul turned against David, the young, fearless shepherd who killed the giant Goliath. David served as Saul's court musician.

- God then chose David as the next king of Israel.

- After Saul's death, King David brought the ark of the covenant (the wooden box that held the stone tablets on which were written the Ten Commandments) to Jerusalem, the capital city.

- David was a man of significant political and religious strength. The nation of Israel was more unified and stronger under David than it had ever been.

- David sinned against God: Among other things, he seduced Bathsheba, then had her husband killed; he took a census of the men of Israel because he lacked trust in God for military victory.

- Both David and the nation of Israel suffered because of David's sin.

- David's son, Solomon, was Israel's next king.

- In spite of Solomon's legendary wisdom, he often acted unwisely: His lavish lifestyle burdened the common people with high taxes; he made compromising trade agreements; he put together a harem of foreign brides who encouraged him to worship pagan gods and introduce pagan worship rituals in Jerusalem.

- God still planned to raise a Redeemer from Abraham's family, through the House of David.

- When Solomon died, his sons and generals fought for the throne.

- Rehoboam took the southern half of the country and called it Judah. He claimed to be the chosen king.

- Jeroboam set up his government in the northern half of the country and kept the name of Israel. Jeroboam claimed to be the chosen king.

- Both kingdoms became pagan, fell to foreign powers, and God's people were carried away into exile.

- Elijah the prophet warned King Ahab that God would punish the people for their wickedness.

- Elijah, in a contest with the prophets of the pagan god Baal, asked God to end the drought. God sent a cloudburst, and the pagan prophets were killed.

- Elijah condemned King Ahab and his wife Jezebel for their sins.

- Elijah was carried away to heaven in a chariot. His mantle fell on Elisha, his successor.

- Elisha parted the waters of the Jordan River, brought rain in times of drought, increased food supplies, performed other miracles, pronounced judgment on kings, and destroyed enemies with supernatural powers.

- Elisha performed more miracles than any other prophet in the Old Testament.

- Isaiah, Jeremiah, Amos, Hosea, Micah, Ezekiel, and other prophets followed Elisha and warned Israel and Judah that God would punish their wickedness.

- While God's people were in exile, Isaiah and Ezekiel had words of consolation for them from God.

Events From the Exile to the Return

- The Jews were taken into exile several times.

- "The Exile" refers to the 70-year Babylonian captivity of Judah.

- During the Exile, God used Ezekiel and Daniel to bring comfort and hope to the people.

- The Jews returned from the Exile to Palestine in two stages: One group was led by Sheshbazzar and Zerubbabel. The second was led by Ezra and Nehemiah.

- The Jews rebuilt the temple in Jerusalem. Zechariah and Haggai encouraged the people in their work.

- Toward the end of this time, Malachi reproached the Jews for slipping back into sinful patterns.

Events Between the Testaments

- Four hundred years elapsed between the writing of Malachi and the time of Jesus.

- Restored Israel came under the rule of Greek princes and generals, part of Alexander the Great's massive empire.

- The Seleucid King Antiochus III conquered Palestine in 198 B.C. However, the Roman legions defeated his army in 190 B.C.

- The Maccabee family began a civil war against the Seleucid governors and captured Jerusalem in 164 B.C.

- John Hyrcanus I of the Maccabee family established his own dynasty known as the Hasmoneans.

- The Hasmoneans ruled until 63 B.C., when Rome conquered Palestine. The Romans later installed the Herodian family as the new puppet government in Palestine.

Events During the Life of Christ

- Jesus was born in Bethlehem. Angels announced his birth and declared Jesus the long-promised Davidic king.

- Mysterious wise men from the east brought gifts to the Christ child.

- King Herod did not want the people to support an infant king so he ordered his soldiers to kill all boy babies in Bethlehem.

- Jesus' family escaped to Egypt to avoid the wicked decree.

- After Herod died, the family of Jesus returned to Palestine and settled in the town of Nazareth.

- At age 12 or 13, Jesus' knowledge of God astounded the Jewish religious leaders.

- John the Baptist urged people to prepare for the coming Messiah.

- John baptized Jesus, and God sent the Holy Spirit in the form of a dove that settled on Jesus.

- The Devil tempted Jesus in the wilderness. After Jesus sent the Devil away, angels came to comfort Jesus and give him food.

- At first, Jesus was very popular. He did amazing things, he taught, and he drew large crowds.

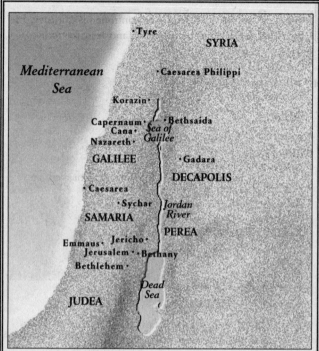

The ministries of Jesus

- Jesus healed the sick, comforted the brokenhearted, and told people how to enter the kingdom of God.

- Jesus denounced the religious leaders of the day because of their hypocritical faith.

- Jesus told his hearers that the only way to God the Father was through faith in himself.

- Jesus fed thousands of people with a few loaves of bread and two fish!

- The Pharisees and other leaders rejected Jesus' claims and teachings.

- Jesus trained his 12 disciples to continue his ministry. He told them about his coming death and resurrection.

- The religious leaders plotted to kill Jesus.

- Judas Iscariot, one of the 12 disciples, betrayed Jesus to the hostile leaders in Jerusalem.

- Jesus was nailed to a wooden cross to die among criminals.

- Jesus rose from the grave and appeared to many of his followers.

- As the disciples watched Jesus ascend into heaven, an angel appeared and told them that they would see him return in the same way.

The Life and Ministry of Jesus

Between 6 and 4 B.C.	Birth
Between A.D. 6 and 8	Visit to the Temple
Between A.D. 26 and 27	Beginning of Ministry
A.D. 28–29	Galilean Ministry
A.D. 29	Training of Disciples
A.D. 29	Later Ministry: Judea and Perea
Between A.D. 30 and 33	Death

Events During the Ministry of the Apostles

- After Jesus' ascension, his disciples replaced Judas (who had killed himself after betraying Jesus) with Matthias to round out the group of 12.

- On the Day of Pentecost, the risen Christ sent the Holy Spirit to the church to equip them for their worldwide task of spreading the good news of salvation.

- The young church lived in close community. They shared everything they had with each other, and took care of the poor among them.

- A couple in the church, Ananias and Sapphira, tried to deceive the community of believers about the proceeds from a property they had sold. God struck them dead for lying.

- The apostles and early Christian leaders were persecuted for their faith.

- Stephen, an ordained deacon in the early church, was stoned to death because of his preaching.

- Before his conversion, Saul of Tarsus was an aggressive enemy of the church. On his way to Damascus to attack Christians there, God confronted him. As a result, Saul gave himself to Christ and began a new life as a Christian.

- Filled with the Holy Spirit, Paul began to preach about Jesus in the Jewish synagogue. The Jewish leaders drove him out of Damascus.

- Peter was the primary leader of the apostles. He performed many miracles, he was a great preacher, and God used Peter to bring salvation to the Gentiles.

- James, one of the apostles, was martyred in Jerusalem.

- Peter was miraculously delivered from prison.

- The Holy Spirit called Paul and Barnabas to be missionaries, and the church ordained them for this work of preaching, teaching, and healing.

- The church expanded from Antioch to Rome through Paul's missionary journeys. Along the way, Paul was stoned, imprisoned, and shipwrecked.

- At the end of his third journey, Paul was imprisoned in Jerusalem because of a speech he made there.

- On the way to Rome to stand trial, the ship carrying Paul wrecked on the island of Malta. Paul was bitten by a poisonous snake there but was not harmed.

- Once in Rome, Paul lived for two years in a rented house, preaching to leading Jews and whoever visited him.

- At this point, the church was becoming a distinct organization. Starting in Jerusalem, it had grown and expanded all the way to Rome.

Bible Chronology: From Creation to the Time of Christ

The Beginning: Creation

1056 years after Creation	Noah and the Flood
2166 B.C.	Abraham and the beginning of a nation
1915	Joseph
1450	The Exodus
1399	Joshua and the Promised Land
1069	Samson
1043	Saul*
1000	David
960	Solomon
931	The Kingdom divides
722	Kingdom of Israel destroyed
720	Hezekiah
610	Josiah
605	Daniel
586	The destruction of Jerusalem
458	Return from captivity
(400 years of silence)	
5 B.C.	Birth of Jesus

*Dates prior to Saul are approximate.

100 Important Events in the Bible

EVENT	REFERENCE
1. The Creation	Gen 1
2. The Fall of humanity	Gen 3
3. The first murder: Cain kills his brother Abel	Gen 4
4. Noah and the Flood	Gen 6–8
5. The Tower of Babel	Gen 11
6. The call of Abraham	Gen 12
7. Selling Joseph into slavery	Gen 37
8. Israelites enslaved in Egypt	Ex 1
9. Moses in the bulrushes	Ex 1–2
10. The call of Moses	Ex 3
11. The ten plagues	Ex 7–12
12. The Passover	Ex 12–15
13. The Exodus from Egypt: Crossing the Red Sea	Ex 12–15
14. The institution of the Sabbath	Ex 16
15. Giving the Ten Commandments and the law	Ex 20–24
16. Completing the tabernacle	Ex 40
17. The anointing of Aaron as first high priest	Lev 8
18. The Israelites: 40 years of wandering	Nu 14
19. Korah's rebellion	Nu 16
20. Water from the rock	Nu 20
21. The bronze snake	Nu 21
22. Moses' farewell	Dt 32–34
23. Joshua commissioned as leader	Jos 1
24. Rahab and the spies	Jos 2
25. Crossing the Jordan River into Palestine	Jos 3
26. The fall of Jericho	Jos 6
27. Achan's sin	Jos 7
28. Defeat at Ai	Jos 8

EVENT	REFERENCE
29. The conquest of Canaan	Jos 9–1
30. The land divided among the tribes	Jos 13–19
31. Joshua's farewell	Jos 23–24
32. Deborah and Barak defeat the Canaanites	Jdg 4–5
33. Gideon's fleece	Jdg 6–7
34. Samson and his strength	Jdg 13–16
35. The marriage of Ruth to Boaz	Ru 4
36. The call of Samuel	1Sa 3
37 Saul becomes king and is rejected	1Sa 10–15
38. Samuel anoints David as future king	1Sa 16
39. David kills Goliath	1Sa 17
40. The friendship of David and Jonathan	1Sa 20
41. The deaths of Saul and Jonathan	1Sa 31
42. David is crowned king	2Sa 2
43. David conquers Jerusalem and recovers the ark of the covenant	2Sa 5–6
44. David's adultery with Bathsheba and murder of Uriah	2Sa 11
45. David's song of praise and last words	2Sa 22–23
46. The anointing of Solomon	1Ki 1
47. The building and dedication of the Temple	1Ki 5–6, 8
48. Visit of the Queen of Sheba	1Ki 10
49. Israel is divided into two kingdoms: Israel (north) and Judah (south)	1Ki 12
50. Elijah and the prophets of Baal	1Ki 18
51. Elijah is taken up to heaven in a chariot	2Ki 2
52. Joash is delivered from Queen Athaliah	2Ki 11
53. Israel captured by Assyria	2Ki 17

EVENT	REFERENCE
54. King Josiah's discovery of the Book of the Law	2Ki 22–23
55. The destruction of the Temple	2Ki 25
56. The Babylonian captivity of the southern kingdom	2Ki 25
57. The return of the captives under Cyrus' decree	Ezr 1
58. The completion of the new temple under Zerubbabel	Ezr 6
59. Celebrating the rebuilding of Jerusalem's city walls	Ne 12
60. Esther, Mordecai, and the deliverance of the Jews	Est 4–7
61. Daniel in the den of lions	Da 6
62. Jonah and the large fish	Jnh 1–2
63. Birth of John the Baptist	Lk 1
64. Birth of Christ	Lk 2
65. Escape into Egypt	Mt 2
66. Jesus visits the temple	Lk 2
67. Jesus' baptism	Mt 3
68. The temptation of Jesus	Mt 4
69. Call of the 12 disciples	Mt 10
70. The Sermon on the Mount	Mt 5
71. The raising of Lazarus	Jn 11
72. Death of John the Baptist	Mk 6
73. Peter's confession	Mt 16
74. The Transfiguration	Mt 17
75. Triumphal entry into Jerusalem	Mt 21; Mk 11; Lk 19; Jn 12
76. Passover/Last Supper	Mt 26; Mk 14; Lk 22; Jn 13–14
77. Jesus in Gethsemane	Mt 26; Mk 14; Lk 22–23; Jn 18

EVENT	REFERENCE
78. Jesus' arrest and trial	Mt 26–27; Mk 14–15; Lk 22–23; Jn 18–19
79. Jesus crucified and buried	Mt 27; Mk 15; Lk 23; Jn 19
80. Resurrection and appearances	Mt 28; Mk 16; Lk 24; Jn 20
81. Giving the Great Commission	Mt 28
82. Jesus' Ascension	Ac 1
83 The coming of the Holy Spirit (Pentecost)	Ac 2
84. Peter and John heal a crippled beggar	Ac 3
85. Martyrdom of Stephen	Ac 7
86 Severe persecution of the church in Jerusalem	Ac 8
87. Philip baptizes the Ethiopian convert	Ac 8
88. Conversion of Saul (Paul)	Ac 9
89. Peter's vision	Ac 10
90. Establishing the church at Antioch	Ac 11
91. The death of James	Ac 12
92. The deliverance of Peter	Ac 12
93. Paul's first missionary journey	Ac 13–14
94. The Jerusalem Council	Ac 15
95. Paul's second missionary journey	Ac 15–18
96. Paul and Silas in prison	Ac 17
97. Paul's third missionary journey	Ac 18–21
98. Arrest of Paul, trials, and shipwreck	Ac 21–28
99. Paul's house arrest in Rome	Ac 28
100. The visions of John the apostle on Patmos	Rev 1

The Age of the Apostles

EVENT	DATE
The coming of the Spirit at Pentecost	30 A.D.
Death of Ananias and Sapphira	31
The murder of Stephen	32 or 33
Conversion of Saul (Paul)	33 or 34
Conversion of Cornelius	40
Paul and Barnabas in Antioch	42
Martyrdom of the apostle James	44
Paul's first missionary journey	47–49
The writing of Paul's letters	47–67
The Council at Jerusalem	49
Paul's second missionary journey	50–52
Paul's third missionary journey	53–57
Arrest of Paul in Jerusalem	57
Paul's trial before Festus	57
Paul's trial before Agrippa	59
The voyage to Rome	59
Paul's arrival in Rome	60

Paul's first Roman imprisonment	60–62
Martyrdom of James, Jesus' brother	62
Final Roman imprisonment of Paul	66
Jewish revolt against Rome	66
Destruction of Jerusalem by Romans	70

Biblical Blurbs from A-Z

Abraham's Test of Faith *(Gen 22)*

When Abraham's son Isaac was a young man, God did an extraordinary thing. He asked Abraham to offer up Isaac as a sacrifice. At that time, human sacrifice was practiced among some groups of people in the region—but never was permitted among God's people.

Abraham set off with Isaac to do as the Lord asked. As they came to the place of sacrifice, Isaac noted that they had fire and wood, but not the lamb of offering. With a heavy heart, Abraham told Isaac that God would provide the lamb.

As Abraham raised the knife to kill his son, God's angel stopped him in the nick of time. Instead of Isaac, a substitute offering was found—a ram in a thicket, caught by its horns. Abraham offered it as a sacrifice, Isaac's life was spared, and Abraham discovered that he was prepared to trust God absolutely.

Belshazzar's Feast *(Da 5)*

Belshazzar, the spineless and self-indulgent monarch of Babylon, decided to host a great festival. During the course of the extravagant gala at the palace, Belshazzar ordered that sacred vessels from the Jewish temple be brought in so that he and his guests could drink from them.

As soon as he did this profane act, a disembodied hand appeared and wrote a message on the royal wall. Deathly afraid, Belshazzar demanded an interpretation of the strange words from his enchanters and diviners.

However, only Daniel the prophet could interpret the message, which was from God and directed to the king. Daniel told Belshazzar that his days were numbered, he had been weighed and found wanting, and that his kingdom would soon be divided.

That very night Belshazzar was killed.

Crossing the Red Sea *(Ex 14)*

As soon as the vast group of Israelites left Egypt, Pharaoh immediately regretted his decision to let his slaves go. He sent an army to bring them back. When the Israelites saw the approaching Egyptian horses and chariots, they were terrified. How could they escape with an army at their heels and the way ahead blocked by water?

Moses told the people not to be afraid and to trust the deliverance of the Lord. As God commanded, Moses stretched out his hand over the sea, and a strong east wind blew back the water into two walls, and the Israelites walked across on dry land.

When they were safely on the other side, God told Moses to bring the waters back together. When Moses stretched out his hand over the seas, the waters flowed together again, drowning the pursuing Egyptian army.

That day the people of Israel celebrated the great deliverance God had given them.

David Kills Goliath *(1Sa 17)*

David left tending his father's sheep and made his way to the encampment where his three brothers were in King Saul's army. Battle lines were drawn between the Israelite and the Philistine armies. Goliath, the giant champion of the Philistine army, challenged the Israelite army to settle the dispute in single combat. The Israelites cringed at the sight of the warrior.

David volunteered to fight the giant. Instead of protective armor and the usual weaponry, the young shepherd chose a few stones and a sling to face the bold predator. Goliath was incredulous that David was the one sent to fight him. Undaunted by the giant's mockery, David hurled a stone and struck the Philistine on his forehead. Goliath fell to the ground. David ran to him, took the huge man's own sword and cut off his head. The courageous young shepherd knew that the Lord had given him the victory.

Dismayed by the death of their hero, the frightened Philistine troops fled in disarray, chased by the soldiers of Israel and Judah.

Elijah's Contest *(1Ki 18)*

Elijah told King Ahab to call the people of Israel to Mount Carmel to witness a contest between God and the 450 prophets of Baal (Queen Jezebel's pagan god). In this showdown, both sides would prepare an altar, then the deity who could call down fire to burn the waiting sacrifice would prove himself the true God.

The prophets of Baal went first. They prayed, danced, shouted, cut themselves with knives and swords, but nothing happened. They kept this up all day, but to no avail.

When evening came, it was Elijah's turn. He called the people to come close. He prepared the altar and doused it with water to make a miracle more difficult. Then Elijah called on the Lord. Fire came down and consumed the sacrifice and licked up all the water.

Amazed at the miracle, the people acknowledged the God of Israel as the true God.

Felix, the Compromising Governor (Ac 23–24)

Felix, the Roman governor of Judea, was corrupt and easily bribed. When the apostle Paul was falsely accused of breaking temple laws, he came before Felix to be judged. Without making a decision about Paul's case, Felix kept Paul in custody for the last two years of his governorship, hoping to be offered a bribe for the apostle's release!

Gideon's Fleece (Jdg 6)

God called Gideon to rescue Israel from Midianite oppression. Gideon started by destroying the pagan altar and building instead an altar to God. Then Gideon pulled together an army to follow him. However, this meek farmer turned judge still had doubts. Had God really called him? Would he be victorious?

To be certain, Gideon told God that he would put a wool fleece on the threshing floor overnight, and if it gathered dew while the floor remained dry, this would be a sign from God of Israel's deliverance. When Gideon got up the next morning, he squeezed enough water from the fleece to fill a bowl! However, not quite satisfied, Gideon asked the Lord to perform one more test. This time, Gideon requested that the fleece remain dry and that the floor be wet with dew.

Next morning when Gideon checked the fleece and the floor, the Lord had done exactly as the judge had asked.

Hannah's Hope *(1Sa 1–3)*

Hannah longed for a child. She was taunted by her husband's second wife because she had no children, and—to make matters worse—Hannah's culture considered childlessness a form of punishment for hidden sin.

For several years, during annual visits to the worship center at Shiloh, Hannah pleaded with God for a son. She promised that she would dedicate him to the Lord. During one visit, Eli the priest observed Hannah's emotionalism in the temple and thought she was drunk. Hannah explained her behavior and the needs of her heart to the listening priest. He told her that her request for a son would be granted by the God of Israel. Hannah left in peace.

After a while, Hannah and Elkanah had a son whom they named Samuel. When he was weaned, true to her vow, Hannah brought the young boy back to Shiloh to be dedicated to the Lord's service. There Samuel lived with Eli and learned from him.

Isaac's Favoritism *(Ge 27)*

Isaac and Rebekah had twin sons, Esau and Jacob. He favored Esau, while Rebekah preferred Jacob. This division of love produced such fierce competition that Jacob managed to take his brother's birthright. Aided by Rebekah, Jacob tricked an elderly, blind Isaac by dressing as Esau. Isaac then blessed Jacob with the birthright intended for Esau.

Jericho's Fall *(Jos 5–6)*

Although now an embattled city, Jericho would not easily fall to the Israelites. God told Joshua to follow an unusual ritual in order to conquer besieged Jericho. For six successive days the Israelite troops were to march around the city, blowing trumpets and carrying the ark of the covenant with them. The soldiers were commanded not to speak or shout. On the seventh day, the procession was to march seven times around the city. When the priests sounded one long note on their trumpets, the soldiers were to shout with all their might.

Joshua put these strange commands into action, and as the soldiers gave their final vigorous shout on the seventh day, the city walls collapsed. The troops were able to walk right in and take Jericho.

Korah's Rebellion *(Nu 16)*

Korah, a Levite, and his group of dissidents confronted Moses and Aaron. They accused the Israelite leaders of exalting themselves above the people. Korah's complaint was without merit and did not disguise his greed for power. Moses challenged Korah and his followers, charging them with rebelling against the Lord.

Korah and his company continued to dispute Moses' authority, and the rebellion was so serious that he and all his cohorts were killed by an act of God. They were all buried and burned alive—by earthquake and fire. However, Korah's own clan was spared.

Lazarus' New Life *(Jn 11)*

Lazarus and his sisters, Mary and Martha, were friends of Jesus. When Lazarus became seriously ill, his sisters sent for Jesus. Surprisingly, Jesus waited until Lazarus was dead before going to Bethany to visit his friends' household. The grieving sisters wondered why Jesus had not come sooner. (Lazarus had died four days earlier.) Jesus assured Martha that Lazarus would rise again. Martha took this as a reference to the final resurrection on the day of judgment. Jesus then identified his power over life and death. In a strong show of faith in the Gospel, Martha declared Jesus the Messiah and Son of God.

Going to Lazarus' tomb with the group of mourners, Jesus ordered the stone rolled away from the door. With deep emotion, Jesus prayed and shouted for Lazarus to

come out. As the people watched in amazement, Lazarus emerged, still wrapped in his burial cloths. Jesus told the people to loosen his cloths and let him go.

Mary's Visit by Gabriel *(Lk 1)*

Mary, the young virgin, was engaged to Joseph, a descendant of Abraham and David. The angel Gabriel visited Mary, startling her. The angel told Mary not to be afraid and announced to her that she would become pregnant; she would have a child who would be called Son of the Most High, and he would inherit the throne of King David and reign forever. Mary wondered how it could happen since she was a virgin. Gabriel explained that Mary would become pregnant by the power of the Holy Spirit. Mary believed and accepted the unusual tidings that would inevitably transform her life.

Naboth's Vineyard *(1Ki 21)*

Naboth's family plot adjoined King Ahab's winter palace, and the king wanted the vineyard for his garden. Naboth refused to sell the land of his ancestors to King Ahab, so

Queen Jezebel schemed to acquire the land for her husband. She had Naboth falsely accused of blasphemy, and the consequence of that was murder. Thus Naboth was taken outside the city and stoned to death. Through Jezebel's treachery, the land became the property of the crown.

Obadiah the Hero *(1Ki 18)*

Jezebel, the pagan wife of King Ahab, began killing off priests of the Hebrew God. This was part of her strategy to promote Baal worship in Israel. Obadiah, the head of the royal household of King Ahab of Israel—and a godly man—decided to do something about the horrifying massacre. He risked his life by safely hiding 100 priests in caves to keep Jezebel from killing them.

Another time, Obadiah again took his life into his hands when he agreed to take a message from the prophet Elijah to King Ahab. Elijah had a price on his head and all who protected him were to be killed as well. Once again Obadiah's courage paid off: The king agreed to meet with Elijah, and Obadiah was not harmed.

Phoebe's Helpfulness *(Ro 16)*

The apostle Paul spoke of Phoebe in glowing terms. In his letter to the Roman church, he commended her and asked the believers there to welcome her with open arms. Phoebe was a deacon or church worker in the port of Cenchreae, a village on Corinth's east harbor.

She was a woman of some means and social position in the community, and she was known for her helpfulness to Paul and to the church as a whole. No wonder Paul asked the Roman church to take care of "our sister Phoebe."

Queen of Sheba's Royal Visit *(1Ki 10)*

In Solomon's time, the rich kingdom of Sheba was ruled by a queen. She was fascinated by reports of Solomon's legendary wisdom and Israel's growing power and wealth. No doubt she thought it useful to establish ties with this burgeoning kingdom. She decided to pay King Solomon a visit.

The Queen of Sheba and her entourage set out by camel caravan for the long and arduous trek across deserts and mountains. Solomon graciously received the queen, who was amazed by the luxury of his surroundings. The Queen of Sheba asked the king many hard questions and cunning riddles, and found him easily able to answer them all. Impressed by his great wisdom, she presented him with lavish gifts—gold, precious gems, and spices. In return, Solomon made the queen gifts from the royal treasury, and a satisfied queen set out once more on the long journey home to her domain.

Rahab and the Spies *(Jos 2)*

Rahab the prostitute lived along the city wall of Jericho. When Joshua sent spies there to explore the territory, Rahab hid the Israelites in her home and protected their whereabouts from the soldiers. She had heard all about the Israelite God and was convinced that he was the true God.

Certain that Jericho would later be taken by the Israelites, Rahab asked the spies to reward her for helping them by sparing her family when the city was overthrown. The spies promised her safety if she tied a crimson cord in her window and had all her relatives in the house at the time of the attack. Rahab promised to do as they asked.

When the Israelites destroyed Jericho, they rescued Rahab and her family before destroying the city. Rahab became known as a great spiritual hero.

Saul's Conversion *(Ac 9)*

Saul, a brilliant Jew educated in Greek culture and born a Roman citizen, set out to get rid of Christians. He voted for Stephen's death and watched while he was murdered. He organized house-to-house searches and arrests, and

when some Christians escaped, he had orders to find them in Damascus and bring them to Jerusalem for trial.

On his way to Damascus, a blinding light from heaven stopped him in his tracks. Saul fell to the ground, and Jesus confronted him in a vision. In a moment, Saul's anger and enmity subsided and he gave himself over to the authority of the Lord.

Blinded by the vision, Saul had to be led into Damascus where he remained for three days without food or drink. God led the disciple Ananias to Saul and he laid hands on the new convert: Saul's sight returned, he received the Holy Spirit, and was baptized. Saul was also known in Greek as Paul.

Turning Water to Wine *(Jn 2)*

Jesus was at a wedding in Cana when they ran out of wine. His mother asked him to do something about it. Jesus may have been reluctant at first, but then he agreed. Standing there were six large water pots. Each held 20 or 30 gallons. Jesus told the servants to fill the pots with water. When Jesus commanded them to dip water out, it had already turned to wine.

Uriah's Untimely Death *(2Sa 11)*

Uriah the Hittite was a leading soldier in King David's army. While Uriah was away in battle, David committed adultery with Uriah's wife, Bathsheba. When she became pregnant, David sent for Uriah hoping that he would have relations with his wife and think that he was the father of the child. This plan failed. David then sent Uriah back to the scene of battle, and commanded that he be placed in an unprotected position at the forefront of the battle. David wanted to make sure that Uriah would die. After Uriah was killed, David married Bathsheba. Later, God punished David for this crime.

Vashti's Refusal *(Est 1–2)*

The beautiful Queen Vashti of Persia was ordered by her husband to appear before him. King Ahasuerus was having a feast and he wanted to show off his wife's beauty to his guests. The queen boldly refused. As a punishment for her disobedience—and as a warning to other women in the kingdom—the king divorced her and started a search for a new wife!

Wise Men From Afar *(Mt 2)*

Some time after Jesus was born, sages from the east followed a star and came to where the child was in Bethlehem. These Gentile astrologers recognized Jesus as the Messiah, and they wanted to worship him. They brought him rich gifts of gold, frankincense, and myrrh.

Before arriving in Bethlehem, the wise men stopped in Jerusalem and asked for the whereabouts of the young king. Herod told the sages to go and search for the child and then bring word to him so that he, too, could go and worship. (Secretly, the cruel and suspicious ruler planned to murder the young boy.) After the wise men had paid homage to Jesus, they were warned in a dream not to go back to Herod, so they went back to their country another way. And the life of Jesus was spared.

Xerxes 1 and the Feast of Purim *(Est 3–10)*

Xerxes 1 (King Ahasuerus) ruled over a vast Persian empire. After divorcing his first wife, he married Esther, the Jewish adopted daughter of Mordecai. Soon thereafter, Haman—the king's prime minister—hatched a plot to persecute the Jews in the region. However, influenced by Esther and Mordecai, an enlightened king later executed Haman and granted political freedom for the Jews—an event still celebrated as the Feast of Purim.

Young Jesus in the Temple *(Lk 2)*

When the Passover festival in Jerusalem was over, the family of Jesus started on their way back to Nazareth. After

a day's journey, Mary and Joseph realized that their 12-year-old son, Jesus, was not with them. So they returned to Jerusalem to look for him.

After a three-day search they discovered him in the temple among the religious leaders and teachers, who were amazed at his wisdom and understanding, and the depth of his questions.

The astonished parents quizzed Jesus about his behavior and whereabouts. "Child, why have you treated us like this?" they wanted to know. Jesus told them that he had to be in the temple of God.

Jesus then returned to Nazareth with his parents, and Mary treasured these early experiences with her godly son.

Zacchaeus—a New Man! *(Lk 19)*

Zacchaeus, chief Jewish tax collector for the Romans at Jericho, wanted to see Jesus when he came to the city. Being a short man, Zacchaeus had to climb a tree to get a glimpse of Jesus through the crowd. When Jesus passed by, he looked up and told Zacchaeus to host him at his house. The crowd, who viewed Zacchaeus as a traitor assisting the Roman oppressors, was outraged. Why would Jesus go to the house of a despised and dishonest tax collector?

After his encounter with Jesus, Zacchaeus was a changed man. He vowed to repay the poor and all those he had defrauded. Jesus underscored the tax collector's conversion by telling the crowd that salvation had come to a son of Abraham and his household that day.

THE LANGUAGE AND LITERATURE OF THE BIBLE

WE ALL KNOW THE BIBLE IS A powerful religious document that describes God's relationship with humanity throughout history; but the Bible can also be seen as an equally impressive work of literature. It is, after all, a collection of books, encompassing many authors and many different writing styles. The Scriptures have been passed down from generation to generation over literally thousands of years! And much can be learned about the people described in the Bible—their beliefs, values, and customs—by examining its words.

While banished to the remote isle of Patmos, John recorded his visions in the Book of Revelation.

Archaeology and the Bible

When we read the Bible, we form some kind of idea about the people, objects, and ideas that are mentioned. However, bringing our modern minds to the world of the Bible has its problems.

What kind of clothing did Abraham really wear? Was he dressed like a Bedouin Arab as some illustrations suggest? How about big Goliath? Many of us imagine a medieval warrior hidden within a chunky suit of armor. And what about Jesus? For many, the image of Jesus is influenced more by European art than a clear understanding of the way people looked who lived in the lands of the Bible. When we approach the Bible with accurate pictures in our minds, its people, places, events, and ideas will come alive. The language and literature of the Bible resonate richly when we understand the people and the places to which its timeless message is firmly rooted.

This is where the value of archaeology comes in. Archaeologists are people who study the past. They dig up ancient sites and study what they find there. They examine houses,

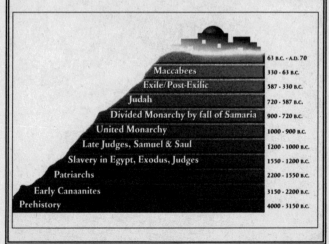

	63 B.C. - A.D. 70
Maccabees	330 - 63 B.C.
Exile/Post-Exilic	587 - 330 B.C.
Judah	720 - 587 B.C.
Divided Monarchy by fall of Samaria	900 - 720 B.C.
United Monarchy	1000 - 900 B.C.
Late Judges, Samuel & Saul	1200 - 1000 B.C.
Slavery in Egypt, Exodus, Judges	1550 - 1200 B.C.
Patriarchs	2200 - 1550 B.C.
Early Canaanites	3150 - 2200 B.C.
Prehistory	4000 - 3150 B.C.

implements, and other artifacts. They decipher inscriptions and evaluate the language, literature, monuments, art, and other aspects of human life. Their work is painstaking and time-consuming. Many years may pass from the time an archaeologist first digs into a ruin-mound (called a *tell*), studies the artifacts, and actually publishes the findings.

The results of the excavator's careful work satisfies our curiosity about life in Bible times and helps us gain a better understanding of the Bible itself. Fragments of ancient oil lamps can be glued together to give us an idea of what they looked like. Better still, by uncovering ruined towns of the ninth century B.C. we may not only discover the style of lamp used by Elisha's hostess, but we may also find out a lot of information about the kind of town the prophet visited (2Ki 4:8–10).

The tombs of kings and warriors provide valuable information about the lifestyles of ancient people. Graves in Jericho dating from about 1600 B.C. had grain and seeds left in them, giving us valuable evidence about the dietary habits of the time. Occasionally, a discovery may relate directly to a

Ten Quick Finds: Important Excavations in Palestine

SITES	DATES
Jerusalem	1867–70
Megiddo	1925–39
Jericho	1930–36
Lachish	1932–36
Qumran, Dead Sea Caves	1949–1967
Jericho	1952–58
Shechem	1956–73
Megiddo	1960, 1965–67
Ashdod	1962–
Ai	1964–72

passage of the Bible. Excavators may find an object or building mentioned in the text.

The study of the archaeology of the Near East is fairly recent. In 1865, the Palestine Exploration Fund was established to finance excavations. So far, only a few hundred mounds have been examined. They have provided valuable information, but much of the Palestinian ruins still wait to be explored. Although the hub of biblical archaeology is in Palestine and Israel (Canaan), it fans out from there to the Mesopotamian Valley, Egypt, Persia (modern Iran), and Asia Minor.

Even though there is still much work to be done, current findings give us a better knowledge of the biblical world.

Important Discoveries and the World of the Bible

- During excavations at Ur in 1929, Sir Leonard Woolley came across a thick layer of water-laid clay. He believed that he had found silt left by the Flood.

- Early Egyptian texts specify the quotas of bricks to be made by groups of laborers. One from the reign of Ramesses II mentions a group called Apiru; this group may have included the Israelites.

- The law-code of Hammurabi, king of Babylon (about 1750 B.C.) is similar to the laws concerning social life found in the Book of Exodus.

- Examples of shrines found in the tomb of Tutankhamen are similar to the tent-shrine (tabernacle) that Israel used in the Sinai Desert for the worship of God.

- Fragments of city walls and gateways at three cities have been identified from Solomon's time. They are Gezer, Hazor, and Megiddo. The style of pottery found in the ruins supports the dating.

- Extensive stables dating back to the tenth century B.C. were uncovered at Megiddo. Some archaeologists believe that they were built by Solomon and used by succeeding generations.

- The Moabite Stone, discovered in Transjordan in 1868, revealed the inscription YHWH (Israel's name for God). Mesha, king of Moab, had this monument inscribed and set up at Dibon about 840 B.C.

- The monument known as the Black Obelisk of Shalmaneser lists Ahab (874–853 B.C.) and other kings of the northern kingdom.

- Pottery fragments (known as *ostraca*) with writing listing payments of oil and wine as revenue were found at the excavation of Samaria. The fall of Samaria is described in the archaeological records of Sargon, king of Samaria.

- Clay tablets found near the Ishtar Gate in Babylon illuminate the last days of the southern kingdom (just before and after 600 B.C.). These tablets record the rations given by the king of Babylon to captive King Jehoiachin (2Ki 25:27–30).

- Tablets excavated at Nippur record evidence of the exiles in Babylonia and Egypt.

- A clay cylinder of Cyrus was discovered on which the edict of Cyrus and the return from Exile is recorded. The inscription concerns his sending displaced and captive people back to their original dwelling places.

- From the close of the Old Testament (425–400 B.C.) to the time of the New Testament, the rise of Alexander the Great and the spread of Greek culture is well documented in discoveries from practically every excavation of this period.

- Greek documents excavated in Egypt show that the New Testament was written in the Greek of everyday life, not classical Greek. One of the papyrus documents reveals that the word "daily" is at the head of a food shopping list. This was a list of food "just for the day."

- Recent discoveries in Jerusalem have revealed the wealthy lifestyle of some households at the time the city fell to the Romans in A.D. 70.

- Excavations made by Israeli scholars since 1967 demonstrate the richness of King Herod's palace.

- An inscribed stone found in the Roman theater at Caesarea names Pilate "Prefect of Judaea." The Gospels and Acts represent that title in Greek.

- The names of the dead were often scratched or written on the burial-chests found in the tombs of New Testament times. Many chests bear names that are familiar to us in the New Testament.

The Codex Syrus Sinaiticus contains one of the earliest known translations of the Gospels.

Egyptian Waste Paper

Archeological discoveries of throw-away papyrus documents from Egypt have proved to be extremely important for New Testament study. During the nineteenth century they were discovered in houses and rubbish dumps and sold to museums in large numbers.

The papyri cover all sorts of records, from tax receipts to books. The Greek language and alphabet were used for most of these documents, and the style of Greek is identical with the language of the New Testament. Consequently, the way language is used in the New Testament can be understood much better with the help of the papyri. For example, orders from government to local officials instruct them to get ready for the visit of a ruler. The word for the visit is "parousia," the same word used in the New Testament for the second coming of Christ. Readers would have readily pictured the coming of royalty.

Among the papyri are Egyptian census records that help illustrate Luke's account of the birth of Jesus. The documents also reflect the unpopular view of tax collectors that is depicted in the Gospels. Copies of famous Greek books have been found among the papyri. Similarly, Old Testament copies in Greek (the Septuagint) and copies of New Testament books have been recovered. A small recovered fragment belongs to a page of John's Gospel, copied about A.D. 130. This is the oldest known piece of a New Testament manuscript to survive.

The Dead Sea Scrolls

Mohammed was a shepherd boy who took care of goats in the valley of the Dead Sea. By chance he discovered a number of clay jars in one of the many caves in the area. Inside the jars were wads of cloth covered with pitch (a tarlike substance). These cloths were wrapped around manuscripts. This discovery was made in 1947.

Not knowing what the scrolls were, the boy sold them for next to nothing. Several years later, the true value of the discovery was realized. Archaeologists and shepherds searched the almost inaccessible caves. By the time they were finished, they had discovered more than 400 scrolls or books.

The books, mostly written in Hebrew or Aramaic, include copies of all Old Testament books (except Esther). The Isaiah scroll—dating from about 100 B.C.—was 1,000 years older than any other known manuscript of the Old Testament. The scrolls belonged to the library of a strict Jewish religious sect (probably the Essenes) at Qumran on the edge of the Dead Sea. The owners had placed their valuable manuscripts in jars and hidden them in caves when the Roman army invaded the area in A.D. 68. Fortunately, the dry heat of that location preserved the historic collection.

These important copies of the Scriptures provide valuable information concerning the text. The scrolls also tell us a lot about Jewish religious and political life in the New Testament period.

Readers and Writers

Besides scribes, there were others in ancient Israel who could read and write. Many inscribed objects found in Israel and Judah, especially from 750 B.C. and later, make it clear that it was not difficult to find ordinary people who were readers and writers. The discovery of alphabet letters written

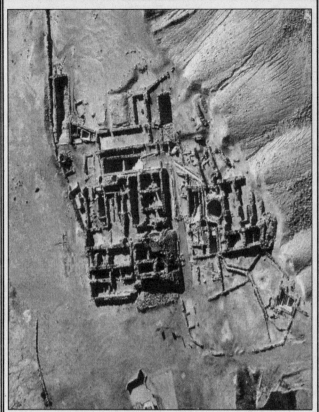

Qumran settlement

in order on potsherds and seal-stones seems to indicate the work of those learning to write. Teaching basic literacy skills was likely done in small groups in private homes.

The typical Jewish boy could read and write Hebrew (and perhaps Aramaic, as well). Literacy in Greek was not as widespread. By New Testament times, probably more children received a basic education in a school attached to the synagogue.

The Scribes

Professional scribes were important figures in biblical times. They had training, power, and authority in ancient Jewish society. The profession was not hereditary and was open to anyone who completed the training. The scribes came into existence when the nation developed a central government. As well as writers of documents (for example, copyists of the Bible: Jeremiah dictated his prophecies to the scribe Baruch), they could be counselors, secretaries of state, and tax officials of the king's court.

Scribes formed professional guilds, and they had special quarters in the temple or palace. They carried a writing case attached to the girdle, and probably sat in a public place to read or write documents for the majority of people who could neither read nor write.

After the Exile, scribes took on new functions. Increasingly they studied civil and religious law and decided how it should be applied. Their decisions became the oral law—the "tradition of the elders" spoken of in the Gospels. In fact, their opinions and decisions were considered to have equal authority with the written law of God by the Pharisees.

By the first century A.D., the scribes were a powerful group of Jewish leaders, and they—along with the Pharisees—were the target of some of the most critical words of Jesus.

How Bible Alphabets Compare to Ours

English: ABCDEFGHIJKLMNOPQRSTUVWXYZ

Hebrew: אבגדהוזחטיכךלמםנןסעפףצץקרששת

Greek: ΑΒΓΔΕΖΗΘΙΚΛΜΝΞΟΠΡΣΤΥΦΧΨΩ

Written Languages of Bible Lands

In an era of printouts and e-mail, it is hard to imagine what written communication was like in Bible times. Written materials were limited, and writing surfaces were different from what we know today. Papyrus and leather scrolls, as well as wooden and clay tablets, were used for permanent or important records. Bits of pottery, stone, clay, and metal were used for names, short messages, and texts. Kings everywhere would have their deeds carved on stone monuments and on the walls of buildings, and inscriptions were often engraved on tombs.

The discovery of written information is quite valuable. It provides us with the names of places, leaders, and other important people. We learn of invasions, wars, social life, and religious beliefs. Once the alphabet was invented, any aspect of human life could be kept on record—reading and writing was brought within the reach of everyone.

It is also clear that several ancient languages provided the basic framework for the Scriptures. A look at these languages will help give us a better understanding of the people who used them.

Sumerian

Writing was invented in Babylonia between 3500 and 3000 B.C. The first language to be written down seems to have been Sumerian. Archaeologists discovered tablets with this language at the ancient city of Sumer. Sumerian used wedge-shaped picture symbols (cuneiform) to represent words.

Akkadian

The oldest northeast Semitic language is called Akkadian. Akkadian texts from 2300 B.C. contain many Sumerian words and forms. The Akkadian language has helped Bible scholars understand the structure and historical variations in other Semitic languages.

Babylonian and Assyrian

These two dialects of Akkadian were written in a more simplified script. The stories of many Old Testament kings were written in these languages.

Eblaite and Amorite

Both of these languages lie in direct line behind biblical Hebrew. And even though archaeologists have uncovered thousands of tablets that contain material in these languages, research is still in the early stages. Scholars report that many of the names of places in Genesis appear on these texts (written in cuneiform).

Egyptian

The idea of writing was carried from Babylonia to Egypt. Egyptian clerks made up their own system of picture word-signs known as *hieroglyphs*. Egyptians used this writing system for inscriptions on buildings and other monuments until the fifth century A.D. After that, simpler handwriting forms were developed.

Ugaritic

The west Semitic language of the Canaanites, this language contains many words and expressions that are identical with those in the earlier parts of the Hebrew Bible.

Hebrew

This language has been written down since at least 1500 B.C. A dialect of Hebrew is still spoken and written today. Hebrew belonged to the Semitic group of languages and was written in a script from right to left. The word order is very different from English.

Over the centuries there were different dialects of Hebrew, and all of them have affected the copying of Old Testament manuscripts. For example, Genesis contains many Egyptian expressions as well as some Akkadianisms. Numbers, Joshua, Judges, and Ruth include very early Canaanite expressions, and some of the oldest Hebrew in the Old Testament.

Aramaic

Aramaic words, phrases, and sometimes entire passages (Da 2–7; Ezr 4–7) appear in the Old Testament. Of all the Semitic languages, Aramaic was most like Hebrew. The primary works of Jewish religious tradition were written in a dialect of Aramaic.

Aramaic became the common language of the Jews after the Exile. From that time, they began translating the Old Testament into Aramaic. In the New Testament several Aramaic words and expressions may be found. Aramaic was the language of Jesus and his disciples.

Greek

The written form of Greek has been around for nearly 3,600 years. The first written Greek was developed by the Mycenaeans. They derived their written language from the Hittite hieroglyphs. However, by 1000 B.C. the Greeks had adapted the simpler form of the West Semite script to their language and added all-important vowels—something missing from all Semitic scripts. Thus the Greeks were the first to have a written language that was based on an alphabet system.

The conquest of Alexander the Great spread a simple dialect of Greek (called *koine*) to the Mediterranean countries. This form of Greek was the language of the Greek Old and New Testaments. Modern Greek is different from the text of the New Testament.

Latin

As Rome became the hub of the ancient world, Latin spread to influence generations of Europeans. By 50 B.C., it was spoken, written, and understood from the coast of England to the Baltic Sea. Latin has influenced many languages, particularly English. It was the common language of western Christianity from 400 A.D. until the 1800s.

The Bible—a Library of Books

The Bible is not just one book. It is a collection—a library—of 66 books written over many centuries by more than 40 different writers. There are books of law, history, prophecy, poetry, wisdom, letters, and apocalyptic literature—written in a variety of literary styles.

The Pentateuch

The first five books of the Bible are known as the *Pentateuch*. (The Jewish name for them is the *Torah*, which means instruction or teaching.) These are the books of God's Law. God told Moses how the people of Israel should live, and Moses recorded these commands in the Pentateuch. A few scholars believe that there are four distinct strands to the writings of the Pentateuch. One writer used the name Yahweh for God, another used the term Elohim; there were also two other groups of writers—compilers who used their own skills, traditions, and purposes in compiling the books. Exactly when these writers lived is uncertain. Some parts of the five books are extremely old and seem to date back to oral or written records of Moses himself.

Although the five books are very different, they all tell the story of God at work, not just in creating the world, but in calling out individuals and a nation to obey him and to bless the whole world.

Books of The Pentateuch

Genesis	Numbers
Exodus	Deuteronomy
Leviticus	

Old Testament History

A large series of books from Joshua to Esther record what happened to the people of Israel from the time they conquered and settled the Promised Land, through the period of judges and kings, to the time of exile. This section spans approximately 800 years of Jewish history (from about 1200 B.C. to 400 B.C.). Ezra and Nehemiah describe the return of the Israelites from captivity. The Book of Esther tells the story of a Jewish queen and how she saved her people from destruction.

The primary purpose in providing this history was to show how God fulfilled his intentions for Israel. Thus the writers faithfully recorded disasters as well as blessings, the stories of good and bad kings, the actions and attitudes of obedience and disobedience on the part of God's people.

Books of Old Testament History

Joshua	1 and 2 Samuel	Ezra
Judges	1 and 2 Kings	Nehemiah
Ruth	1 and 2 Chronicles	Esther

The Wisdom Books

Job, Proverbs, and Ecclesiastes are known as books of Wisdom. This type of writing also appears elsewhere in the Old Testament, particularly in the Book of Psalms. Wisdom literature is also found in the writings of some of Israel's neighbors.

The three Wisdom books are quite different from each other in subject matter. Job focuses on the meaning of suffering, Ecclesiastes dwells on the apparent meaninglessness of life, and Proverbs is a series of sayings—practical advice on how to behave in everyday life. All three books, however, do have aspects in common since all are concerned with behavior and daily living. God is the central figure within each book; but he is in the home rather than in the temple. A core teaching in the wisdom poems of all three books is that we find true knowledge when we obey God and his laws.

Books of Wisdom

Job	Proverbs	Ecclesiastes

Poetry

Psalms, the Song of Solomon, and Lamentations are known as the poetic books of the Bible. Besides poetry, this body of literature includes hymns, prayers, and songs. The Book of Psalms is the largest collection of Old Testament poetry. Jewish scholars put this book in a section of the Bible they call the *Writings*.

The song poems of Psalms express profound emotion—from great ecstasy to utter despair. Recurrent themes are lifting praises to God, warning Israel of the consequences of sin, personal spiritual struggles, and prophetic words. After the Exile, the Psalms became Israel's psalter.

The theme of the Song of Solomon is the delightful expression of love between a young husband and his bride. This collection of six songs is in the form of a dialogue between the man and the woman, and is set in the countryside in spring.

Jewish scholars also include Lamentations in the Writings. The book is made up of five poems, four of which are written as acrostics based on the letters of the Hebrew alphabet. The writer expresses the writer's personal lament over the fall of Jerusalem. The book also voices the nation's collective despair concerning the collapse of their holy city. The writer holds out a thread of hope to those who put their faith in God's unfailing mercy. The Book of Lamentations, written in a beautiful style, reflects a long tradition of ancient Near Eastern lament poetry.

Books of Poetry

Psalms	Song of Solomon	Lamentations

The Prophetic Books

This last section of the Old Testament consists of 16 books. All are called by the name of the prophet whose words they contain. Isaiah, Jeremiah, Ezekiel, and Daniel are known as "major prophets." The other 12 are called the "minor prophets." The prophets were good interpreters of history. Their words reflect the social and religious conditions of their age. God told the prophets to be his servants; they were to take his words to the people, and they were given special abilities to carry out their tasks.

Biblical prophetic literature consists of four categories: First, the prophets communicated messages of faith, advising God's people to trust in God alone. Second, they urged people to know and practice God's word. These prophets based their teachings on the law of Moses, and they emphasized messages of obedience. Third, the prophets gave messages of hope, encouraging faithful ones about the future. Fourth, God's messengers taught the people that Yahweh was Lord of all creation. The prophets proclaimed messages on the lordship of God.

Books of the Prophets

Isaiah	Amos	Habakkuk
Jeremiah	Obadiah	Zephaniah
Ezekiel	Jonah	Haggai
Daniel	Micah	Zechariah
Hosea	Nahum	Malachi
Joel		

New Testament History

The four Gospels are more than biographies of Jesus. They do not tell us much about his early years, but they do focus on the last week of his life and what happened in the days following his death. The word "gospel" means "good news," and these four books (Matthew, Mark, Luke, and John) concentrate on telling the good news—that Jesus, the promised Redeemer, had come to bring salvation to all who would put their trust in him.

For 30 years after Jesus' ascension, the apostles spread the good news about him. At the same time, stories, records, sayings, and word-of-mouth memories about Jesus were being collected. Eventually they were written down by the writers of the Gospels. The first three books have a considerable amount of material in common. The fourth, John's Gospel, is different in its approach. The four Gospels give us a comprehensive picture of Jesus and his ministry. Each account has something unique to bring to the whole.

The Acts of the Apostles completes New Testament history. The author, Luke, writes in a careful, detailed manner, with the touch of an accurate historian. He tells the story from Jesus' ascension into heaven, to the coming of the Holy Spirit, and the growth of the Christian movement from a group of 200 to a great community of believers that spread across the Roman Empire.

Books of New Testament History

Matthew	Luke
Mark	John
Acts	

The Letters

Much of the New Testament consists of letters that we call *epistles*—a common form of writing among ancient Greeks. The New Testament letters provide penetrating insight into the faith and life of the early church.

The apostle Paul wrote several of the epistles, and they are unique compared to letter styles found outside of biblical literature. Paul's letters include proclamation and exhortation that turns them into written sermons. Before launching into the main part of his letters, Paul bestows a rich blessing on his readers. Usually the body of his epistles focuses on practical and spiritual matters in the life of the church. Paul closes each letter with notes of greeting, a doxology (expression of praise), and a benediction (blessing).

The Book of Hebrews, included among the epistles, is part letter, theological essay, and sermon all blended together. This epistle makes frequent reference to the Old Testament and applies Old Testament passages to main doctrinal points.

Besides Paul, other followers of Jesus wrote general letters to the churches scattered throughout the Roman empire. Each writer had a particular style and emphasis, and in some cases, the words were directed to a particular church or group of Christians.

Books of Letters

Romans	Titus
1 and 2 Corinthians	Philemon
Galatians	Hebrews
Ephesians	James
Philippians	1 and 2 Peter
Colossians	1, 2, and 3 John
1 and 2 Thessalonians	Jude
1 and 2 Timothy	

Apocalyptic Literature

This type of writing includes religious works that abound in visions of God or revelations from God concerning the depravity of the present age. Throughout the Old Testament there are certain passages that are apocalyptic in nature, for example sections in Joel, Amos, Zechariah, and Daniel 7–12.

Apocalyptic Writing—Between the Testaments

Apocalyptic literature was a type of religious writing that developed between the testaments and had its roots in Old Testament prophecy. The word *apocalyptic* implied an unveiling or revelation and referred to the hidden purposes of God, the end of the age, and the final fulfillment of God's kingdom spoken about in these writings.

In Old Testament apocalyptic literature, the writers encouraged God's people to fight against, or flee from the forces of evil. However, apocalyptic literature between the testaments was far more passive in its approach: readers and hearers were warned not to struggle against the enemy; God would ultimately prevail against evil.

The apocryphal book, 2 Esdras, contains some visions and revelations of the early Jewish rabbis, and includes chapters that predict the rejection of the Jews. It speaks of a Jewish book of visions of the future ascribed to Ezra. The Dead Sea Scrolls also contain apocalyptic material from this period.

In the Book of Daniel, the prophet presents God and evil opposing each other. In the end, God will triumph, and in the future age, the righteous will be resurrected and the wicked will be judged. Daniel sets forth his themes through visions, revelations, and symbols; this symbolism and the use of numbers, animals, and inanimate objects makes the literature difficult to interpret.

In the New Testament, apocalyptic writing is found in Matthew, 1 Thessalonians, and the Revelation to John. Revelation highlights the Son of Man, the second coming of Christ, the final glory of the kingdom of God, and the last judgment. The literary style of Revelation is similar to the writing of Old Testament prophets.

Apocalyptic writing was designed to reveal its message to insiders in terms that an outsider could not understand. Writers of this genre could encourage readers to stand against pagan governments, and predict destruction without fear of reprisal.

Revelation emphasizes contrasts in terms of conflict, actions, location, and time: God is pitted against Satan; a new Jerusalem will be established and Babylon will be destroyed. The writer speaks of heaven and earth, land and sea; and there is a distinction between time and eternity. These contrasts communicate the sense that good and evil vie for supremacy in this world, and we cannot hope for peace until the day of Christ's triumph.

Books of Apocalyptic Literature
Revelation

Ten Quick Facts About Bible Literature

• Three ancient sources—the Rosetta Stone, the Behistun Rock, and the clay tablets of Ugarit—have helped to make clear the ancient languages of Bible times.

• Hebrew wisdom literature centered around almighty God.

• Wisdom for the Egyptians centered on the individual.

• Some of the Bible books existed in spoken form long before they were written down.

• The shorter prophetic books in the Old Testament are called "minor" only because of their length, not because they are less important than the "major" prophetic books.

• Like authors everywhere, the Bible writers had their own perspective, and the way they pass on a story tells us a lot about their point of view.

- The *chiasm* was one of the writing styles of the Bible. It worked like this: the writer wrote down each idea in sequence, in ascending order. Then the ideas were presented again in inverted form, in descending order. This style resembled climbing to the top of a mountain then going down the other side. The following example shows the chiasmatic order of thoughts:

First idea	For my thoughts
Second idea	are not your thoughts,
Second idea	nor are your ways
First idea	my ways, says the Lord. (Isa 55:8)

- Jesus told parables to help ordinary people understand what God's kingdom was like.

- Poetry is not limited to the Old Testament. The Gospels and Letters contain flowing poetic language. Mary's Magnificat (Lk 1:46–55) is steeped in Old Testament imagery, and there are poetic fragments in Paul's writing.

- Miracle stories are prominent in the Gospels.

Significant Bible Themes

The language and literature of the Bible are the means to express its unique teachings and major themes. From Genesis to Revelation significant topics, ideas, and images on the life of faith are presented and underscored. Some are very familiar, others less well-known—and all are found within the pages of Scripture:

1. God's covenant with Abraham (Ge 12:2–3; 15:18; 17:1–8)
2. The Passover (Ex 12:11–14)
3. The Ten Commandments (Ex 20; Dt 5)
4. The Day of Atonement (Lev 16; Heb 7–9)
5. The Day of the Lord (Isa 2:12; Jer 30:7; Eze 7:19; Ob 15; Zec 14:1; Rev 16:14)

6. The "I am" claims of Jesus (Jn 6:35; 8:12; 10:7; 10:11; 11:25; 14:6; 15:1)
7. The Sermon on the Mount (Mt 5; Lk 6)
8. The Beatitudes (Mt 5; Lk 6)
9. The Lord's Prayer (Mt 6:9–13; Lk 11:2–4)
10. The Parables of Jesus (Mt 5:14–15; Mk 12:1–9; Lk 10:30–37)
11. The Kingdom of God (Mic 4:6–7; Mt 5:1–20; Lk 7:18–23)
12. The Miracles of Jesus (Mt 8:2–3; Mk 5:1–15; Lk 18:35–43; Jn 6:19–21)
13. The Lord's Supper (Lk 22:19)
14. The Fruit of the Spirit (Gal 5)

Writing Styles of the Bible

The Bible is noted for its profound prayers, poems and hymns, wise sayings, warm greetings, farewells, and blessings. These samples portray deep content and expressive language:

Hezekiah's Prayer

When King Hezekiah prays to God, he speaks openly and simply. He is seriously ill and wants to live, so he begs God for help:

"Remember now, O Lord, I implore you, how I have walked before you in faithfulness with a whole heart, and have done what is good in your sight." (2Ki 20:3)

Nehemiah's Prayer

Concerned for Israel's sins, Nehemiah approaches God in grand tones, appealing to his power and faithfulness:

"O Lord God of heaven, the great and awesome God who keeps covenant and steadfast love with those who love him and keep his commandments; let your ear be attentive and your eyes open to hear the prayer of your servant that I now pray before you day and night for your servants, the people of Israel . . ."(Ne 1:5–6)

Biblical Poetry

The songs and poems of the Hebrews reflect the whole range of human feelings. Word patterns and rhythms are flexible, and the thoughts are drawn from the depths of experience. In the Psalms we find the writers pouring out their hearts to God:

Psalm 51

Have mercy on me, O God,
    according to your steadfast love;
according to your abundant mercy
    blot out my transgressions. (Ps 51:1–2)

Psalm 117

Praise the Lord, all you nations!
    Extol him, all you peoples!
For great is his steadfast love toward us,
    and the faithfulness of the Lord endures forever.
Praise the Lord! (Ps 117)

Many of the Psalms were probably used as hymns in worship. And some psalms have a call and response pattern as if they were used in liturgy. Psalm 24 is an example of a liturgical psalm with its call:

Psalm 24

Who is this king of glory?

and the response:

    The Lord, strong and mighty,
    the Lord mighty in battle . . .
    The Lord of hosts,
    he is the king of glory. (Ps 24:8, 10)

Biblical Songs

Songs of praise are recorded throughout the Bible. Moses and his sister broke into song and danced when God preserved the Israelites from the Egyptians. Deborah the judge sang a triumphant song after victory over Sisera. Perhaps one of the best known songs of Scripture is Mary's canticle of praise known as the Magnificat:

Mary's Song of Thanksgiving
My soul magnifies the Lord,
    and my spirit rejoices in God my Savior,
for he has looked with favor on the lowliness of his servant.
    Surely, from now on all generations will call me blessed;
for the Mighty One has done great things for me,
    and holy is his name.
His mercy is for those who fear him
    from generation to generation.
He has shown strength with his arm;
    he has scattered the proud in the thoughts of their hearts.
He has brought down the powerful from their thrones,
    and lifted up the lowly;
he has filled the hungry with good things,
    and sent the rich away empty.
He has helped his servant Israel,
    in remembrance of his mercy,
according to the promise he made to our ancestors,
    to Abraham and to his descendants forever. (Lk 1:47–55)

Biblical Wisdom

The wisdom literature of the Bible is godliness in everyday clothing. Its pithy sayings and wise proverbs are as varied as life itself. Underneath all the good advice is the belief that the first step in wisdom is reverence for God:

Wise Sayings
The fear of the Lord is the beginning of wisdom,
    and the knowledge of the Holy One is insight. (Pr 9:10)

Proverbs includes a wealth of instruction on life at home:

Better is a dry morsel with quiet
    than a house full of feasting with strife. (Pr 17:1)

Train children in the right way,
    and when old, they will not stray. (Pr 22:6)

Some friends play at friendship
    but a true friend sticks closer than one's nearest kin.
    (Pr 18:24)

Well meant are the wounds a friend inflicts,
    but profuse are the kisses of an enemy. (Pr 27:6)

In the poetry and wisdom of Ecclesiastes, there is a sense of the futility of life without God. But even though there is a gloomy tone throughout the book, the writer ends on an optimistic note:

This is what I have found out: the best thing anyone can do is to eat and drink and enjoy what he has worked for during the short life that God has given. (Ecc 5:18)

Greetings

During the apostle Paul's day, there was a well-known Greek letter form that was similar in some ways to the structure of the New Testament epistles. In the popular Greek form, the standard greeting was ordinary and colorless. In his letters, Paul created a rich new salutation:

Grace to you and peace from God our Father and the Lord Jesus Christ. (Eph 1:2)

In his short letter, Jude varies the wording of his greeting:

May mercy, peace, and love be yours in abundance.
(Jude 2)

Farewells

Closing greetings are another unique characteristic of New Testament letters. In typical Greek letters, the farewell was usually a single word but Paul expanded his into notes of greeting, an expression of praise, and a benediction:

Greet every saint in Christ Jesus. The friends who are with me greet you. All the saints greet you, especially those of the emperor's household.

The grace of the Lord Jesus Christ be with your spirit. (Php 4:21–23)

Greet one another with a holy kiss. All the saints greet you. The grace of the Lord Jesus Christ, the love of God, and the communion of the Holy Spirit be with all of you. (2Co 13:12–13)

Blessings

Besides benedictions, the Bible is known for its remarkable blessings. Prophetic blessings were often bestowed on individuals, family members, or the nation as a whole. Aaron and the priests pronounced this special blessing on the Israelites. It is a benediction that is familiar to many:

The Lord bless you and keep you;
the Lord make his face to shine upon you, and be
gracious to you;
the Lord lift up his countenance upon you, and give you
peace. (Nu 6:24–26)

Before he died, Moses blessed the clans of Israel. They were about to enter the Promised Land without him. Their valiant departing leader set before them God's covenant promises, and he reminded them to be obedient to God in order to experience his blessing:

Happy are you, O Israel! Who is like you,
a people saved by the Lord,
the shield of your help,
and the sword of your triumph!
Your enemies shall come fawning to you,
and you shall tread on their backs. (Dt 33:29)

Fascinating Facts from Aleph to Taw

What do aleph-taw, alpha-omega, and A-Z have in common? They are all the first and last letters of the alphabet in three languages—Hebrew, Greek, and English respectively. Here are 20 other intriguing and factual stories from the world of biblical language, writing, and literature:

A is for Ox

Very early alphabets used pictures of everyday objects to represent the sounds of the first letters of these words. The first letter of the Hebrew alphabet is aleph, derived from alpu "ox," and so the Hebrew "A" was a line drawing of an ox head.

Blessings from A to Z

In Jewish tradition, God blesses Israel from "aleph to taw." These Hebrew letters are the first and last in the Hebrew alphabet, so the expression means that God blesses Israel completely. By striking coincidence, the list of blessings found in Leviticus 26:3–13 begins with aleph and ends with taw.

Covenants, Commands, and Codes

The Mosaic Law contains 613 specific commandments that regulate most aspects of people's lives and worship—from circumcision to food laws. The concept of covenant was familiar to people living in the time of Moses. Archaeologists have discovered records of Hittite covenants dating from 1400 to 1200 B.C.

Did Adam Speak Hebrew?

Adam's words recorded in the Scriptures are in Hebrew, but he likely did not speak this language. Although Hebrew goes back beyond 2000 B.C., we cannot trace its roots all the way to early Bible people such as Adam, Noah, or Abraham.

Early Paper

Our word "paper" comes from papyrus—an early inexpensive material used as a writing surface. Papyrus was made by stripping long papyrus reeds of their bark and laying them next to each other in rows. Another layer was laid crosswise across the top. The layers were soaked with glue and water, then pounded into a sheet. It was finally smoothed with pumice.

Familiar Greek Words

Many English words have their roots in Greek words used in the New testament. Theos (God) and logos (word, study) gives us theology (the study of God). Anthropos (man) gives us anthropology (the study of humanity). Other words include angelos (angel) and ethnosis (nation).

God's Writing

The Bible tells us that the Ten Commandments were "written with the finger of God" (Ex 31:18). In fact, this is emphasized later when the writer says: "The tablets were the work of God, and the writing was the writing of God, engraved upon the tablets." (Ex 32:16)

How to Write on Clay

In ancient times, even before Abraham, clay was a popular writing surface. Wet clay was touched with the tip of a sharp pointed reed to make impressions. Soft clay tablets were used for writing, and afterwards baked hard. Broken fragments of pottery (shards) might also be used. Assyrian and Babylonian scribes used a wedge-shaped stylus to make cuneiform characters on their clay documents. Thousands of these artifacts have survived, providing scholars with valuable information about people in Bible lands.

It's Carved in Stone!

The most important documents in ancient times were laboriously carved into stone so they would remain permanently on record. The Ten Commandments were written on two stone tablets. Hammurabi's Law Code was engraved on a stele (a type of stone marker) eight feet high. At the top, Babylon's King Hammurabi is shown receiving the symbols of authority from the god Marduk.

Joseph's Robe

There have been many stories, plays, and even a Broadway musical about Joseph and his famous coat. It is usually depicted in gorgeous colors and fancy design. Indeed, Joseph's gift from his father Jacob has taken on a legendary life of its own. Yet the best Bible translations simply describe the garment this way: "... and he [Jacob] had made him a long robe with sleeves." (Gen 37:3)

King Mesha's Inscription

Moabite king Mesha carved a message on a large black basalt stone. It had 34 lines of text and dates to 830 B.C. It tells of his conflicts with the Israelite kings Omri and Ahab. Mesha says of Omri:

"As for Omri, king of Israel, he humbled Moab many years, for Chemosh [the Moabite god] was angry with his land."

Leviathan and Behemoth

Although people are fascinated by these mysterious creatures of the Bible, they disagree on the meaning of leviathan and behemoth (Job 40:15–24; 41). Some think they refer to imaginary monstrous beasts, or ancient animals that are now extinct. Others think that behemoth was an elephant or a hippopotamus, and that leviathan was a whale or a crocodile. Even though scholars cannot agree on the identity of

these creatures, they are wonderfully described in the Scriptures!

mrhdlttllmb

This is the nursery rhyme "Mary had a little lamb," written without any vowels, word divisions, or punctuation. The Old Testament was originally written without any of these, and readers had to supply these themselves in order to make sense of the text.

Not All the OT Is in Hebrew

While most of the Old Testament was written in Hebrew, several chapters in Ezra and Daniel (and even one verse in Jeremiah) were written in Aramaic.

Old Hebrew Inscription

The earliest object with a Hebrew text written on it is a limestone tablet containing a farmer's calendar. It was used in Gezer, a biblical city, almost 3,000 years ago. It reads in part:

"His two months are (olive) harvest,

His two months are planting (grain)."

Psalm 119—Poetic and Precise

Psalm 119 is the longest psalm—176 verses in all, consisting of 22 eight-verse sections. Each section begins with a successive letter of the Hebrew alphabet, and each verse within that section begins with the same letter. In this stylized, formal psalm, the writer expresses delight in God's law.

Q and the Synoptics

Matthew, Mark, and Luke are sometimes called the synoptic Gospels. The word "synoptic" means "able to be seen together." It is possible to look at these three books side by side and compare their contents. Much of the material is shared and seems to come from a common source.

Q is the first letter of the German word for source (Quelle). It is the name given to the unknown document from which scholars think Matthew and Luke took their sayings of Jesus (which do not appear in the Book of Mark). Q may have been written in Aramaic in about A.D. 50.

Revival of a Language

Hebrew began to die out as a spoken language toward the end of the Old Testament period. Nehemiah was distressed to find Jews who had married foreign women and whose children could not even speak "the language of Judah" (Hebrew).

After that, Hebrew was kept alive only among the rabbis in the synagogues for more than 2,000 years. Then—about 100 years ago—Eliezer Ben-Yehuda, a Lithuanian Jew, proposed and worked tirelessly for its revival as a spoken language. Modern Hebrew is based upon biblical Hebrew and Talmudic Aramaic, and it has traces of Yiddish, German, and Russian.

Strange Meditations

The Hebrew word for "meditation" (hagah) is also used to describe the coo of a dove, the growl of a lion, the plotting of evil rulers, as well as the reading of the Bible. These things are all something done audibly. Thus, when Jews were instructed to meditate on God's word (Psalm 1:2), this meant that they should recite it aloud to themselves.

Tablets of Clay

More than 4,000 clay tablets were discovered in the 1920s at ancient Nuzi, east of the Tigris River. These date to the middle of the second millennium B.C. The texts give a wide-ranging picture of everyday life at that time, including things such as land ownership, the position of slaves and women, prices and sales of goods, occupations, legal customs, and family law. Many intriguing parallels are found between Genesis and the Nuzi documents.

Fun Facts from Genesis to Revelation

There are many fascinating figures and facts about the books, chapters, verses, and authors of the Bible. Bible readers everywhere are curious about Bible statistics. Commonly asked questions include: Which are the longest books in the Bible? What are some of the best-loved Bible passages? Who are the Bible authors? What is the significance of numbers in the Bible?... and the list goes on. These fact-filled records will answer some of these questions:

20 Important Topical Chapters

1. God's covenant with Abram	Gen 15
2. The Ten Commandments	Ex 20
3. God's faithfulness	Jos 15
4. The friendship of David and Jonathan	1Sa 20
5. The heavenly shepherd	Ps 23
6. Confession of sin	Ps 51
7. Thanksgiving for God's goodness	Ps 103
8. The virtues of God's Law	Ps 119
9. Wisdom	Pr 8
10. Ode to a capable wife	Pr 31
11. The majesty of God	Isa 40
12. An invitation to abundant life	Isa 55
13. The Beatitudes	Mt 5
14. The Lord's Prayer	Mt 6
15. Pentecost	Ac 2
16. Justification	Ro 5
17. Directions about marriage	1Co 7
18. The gift of love	1Co 13
19. The meaning of faith	He 11
20. Hearing and living the Word	Jas 1

Authors of the Books of the Bible

AUTHOR	BOOK
1. Moses	Genesis, Exodus, Leviticus, Numbers, Deuteronomy
2. Possibly Joshua, Phineas, Eleazer, Samuel, Jeremiah, or one of Joshua's elders	Joshua
3. Uncertain	Judges
4. Uncertain	Ruth
5. Samuel likely wrote only part of 1 Samuel	1 and 2 Samuel
6. Possibly Ezra, Ezekiel, or Jeremiah	1 and 2 Kings
7. Possibly Ezra	1 and 2 Chronicles, Ezra
8. Nehemiah	Nehemiah
9. Attributed to Mordecai (by Josephus)	Esther
10. Uncertain	Job
11. Attributed to many authors: David, Solomon, Asaph, and the sons of Korah among them	Psalms
12. Solomon and other wisdom writers	Proverbs
13. Solomon or a Jewish sage	Ecclesiastes
14. Possibly Solomon	Song of Solomon
15. Isaiah	Isaiah
16. Jeremiah	Jeremiah
17. Attributed to Jeremiah	Lamentations
18. Ezekiel	Ezekiel
19. Daniel	Daniel
20. Hosea	Hosea
21. Attributed to Joel	Joel

AUTHOR	BOOK
22. Amos	Amos
23. Obadiah	Obadiah
24. Attributed to Jonah	Jonah
25. Micah	Micah
26. Nahum	Nahum
27. Habakkuk	Habakkuk
28. Zephaniah	Zephaniah
29. Haggai	Haggai
30. Zechariah	Zechariah
31. Malachi	Malachi
32. The apostle Matthew	Matthew
33. John Mark	Mark
34. Luke	Luke, Acts
35. The apostle John	John
36. The apostle Paul	Romans, 1 and 2 Corinthians, Galatians, Ephesians, Philippians, 1 Thessalonians, Philemon, Colossians, 2 Thessalonians, 1 and 2 Timothy, Titus
37. Unknown	Hebrews
38. James, the brother of Christ	James
39. The apostle Peter	1 and 2 Peter
40. The apostle John	1, 2, and 3 John
41. Jude	Jude
42. The apostle John	Revelation

Bible Statistics

	OLD TESTAMENT	NEW TESTAMENT
1. Books	39	27
2. Chapters	929	260
3. Verses	23,214	7,959
4. Longest book	Psalms	Luke
5. Shortest book	Obadiah	3 John

Numbers: Signs and Symbols in the Bible

NUMBER   MEANING AND REFERENCE

1. One   Unity and absolute singleness:

"There is one body and one Spirit...one Lord, one faith, one baptism, one God and Father of all, who is above all and through all and in all." (Eph 4:4–6)

2. Two   Can represent both unity and division:

a) "After this the Lord appointed 70 others and sent them on ahead of him in pairs to every town and place where he himself intended to go." (Lk 10:1)

b) "Enter through the narrow gate; for the gate is wide and the road is easy that leads to destruction, and there are many who take it. For the gate is narrow and the road is hard that leads to life, and there are few who find it." (Mt 7:13–14)

3. Three   Sometimes associated with God's mighty power:

a) "Jesus answered them, 'Destroy this temple, and in three days I will raise it up.'" (Jn 2:19)

b) "Go therefore and make disciples of all nations, baptizing them in the name of the Father and of the Son and of the Holy Spirit, . . ." (Mt 28:19)

4. Four   One of the symbols of completion in the Bible:

"After this I saw four angels standing at the four corners of the earth, holding back the four winds of the earth so that no wind could blow on earth or sea or against any tree." (Rev 7:1)

5. Five   An expression of grace:

a) "Taking the five loaves and the two fish, he looked up to heaven, and blessed and broke the loaves, and gave them to the disciples, and the disciples gave them to the crowds. And all ate and were filled; . . ." (Mt 14:19–20)

b) ". . . and five were wise." (Mt 25:2)

6. Six   Closely associated with humanity:

a) "So God created humankind in his image, in the image of God he created them; male and female he created them . . . And there was evening and there was morning, the sixth day." (Gen 1:27, 31)

b) "Six days you should labor and do all your work." (Ex 20:9)

7. Seven   Divine perfection:

a) "And on the seventh day God finished the work that he had done, and he rested on the seventh day . . . God blessed the seventh day and hallowed it, . . ." (Gen 2:2–3)

b) "The promises of the Lord are promises that are pure, silver refined in a furnace on the ground, purified seven times." (Ps 12:6)

8. Eight   May refer to a new beginning:

"... and it shall be a sign of the covenant between me and you ... every male among you shall be circumcised when he is eight days old, ..." (Gen 17:11–12)

9. Nine   The number of blessing:

"... the fruit of the Spirit is love, joy, peace, patience, kindness, generosity, faithfulness, gentleness, and self-control ..." (Gal 5:22)

10. Ten   Represents law and government:

The Ten Commandments (Ex 20:3–17)

11. Twelve   Linked to the divine purpose of God:

a) "Then Jesus summoned his twelve disciples and gave them authority..." (Mt 10:1)

b) "It [the holy city Jerusalem] has a great, high wall with twelve gates, and at the gates twelve angels, and on the gates are inscribed the names of the twelve tribes of the Israelites.... And the wall of the city has twelve foundations, and on them are the twelve names of the twelve apostles of the Lamb." (Rev 21:12, 14)

12. Thirty   Sometimes associated with sorrow:

"The Israelites wept for Moses in the plains of Moab thirty days; then the period of mourning for Moses was ended." (Dt 34:8)

13. Forty   The number of testing and trial:

a) "...I will send rain on the earth for forty days and forty nights;... " (Gen 7:4)

b) "And your children shall be shepherds in the wilderness for forty years, ..."(Nu 14:33)

c) "Then Jesus was led up by the Spirit into the wilderness to be tempted by the devil. He fasted forty days and forty nights, and afterwards he was famished." (Mt 4:1–2)

14. Fifty   Celebration and ceremony:

a) "And you shall hallow the fiftieth year and you shall proclaim liberty throughout the land to all its inhabitants. It shall be a jubilee for you: . . . ." (Lev 25:10)

b) "After this Absalom got himself a chariot and horses, and fifty men to run ahead of him." (2Sa 15:1)

15. Seventy   The number associated with committees and judgment:

a) "So the Lord said to Moses, 'Gather for me seventy of the elders of Israel, whom you know to be the elders of the people and officers over them; bring them to the tent of meeting, and have them take their place there with you. I will come down and talk with you there; and I will take some of the spirit that is on you and put it on them; and they shall bear the burden of the people along with you so that you will not bear it all by yourself.' " (Nu 11:16–17)

b) "Seventy weeks are decreed for your people and your holy city: to finish the transgression, to put an end to sin, and to atone for iniquity, to bring in everlasting righteousness, to seal both vision and prophet, and to anoint a most holy place . . ." (Da 9:24)

c) "For thus says the Lord: 'Only when Babylon's seventy years are completed will I visit you, and I will fulfill to you my promise and bring you back to this place. . . .' " (Jer 28:10)

d) "After this the Lord appointed seventy others and sent them on ahead of him. . . ." (Lk 10:1)

It's Not in the Bible

People attribute all manner of sayings, numbers, and things to the Bible that are not found anywhere in it. Here's a chance to get the facts straight:

1. The Bible does not say Eve sinned by eating an apple. It says that the woman ate a fruit from the forbidden tree.

2. All animals did not come to Noah in twos. Some came in sevens.

3. The Bible does not say that Jonah was swallowed by a whale. It says a large fish.

4. The Bible does not say that there were three wise men who visited the child Jesus. It only names the three gifts that they brought, and doesn't number the men.

5. Jesus did not just feed five thousand with the loaves and fish. The Bible says that besides about five thousand men, there were women and children who also ate.

6. The Bible does not say that money is the root of all evil. It says the love of money is a root of all types of evil.

7. Hezekiah is not a book in the Bible. He was, however, a king of Judah for 29 years.

8. The maxim "God helps those who help themselves" is not found anywhere in the Bible.

Popular Bible Phrases

There are favorite Bible phrases that are familiar to many of us. We may not even be aware that some expressions that we regularly use actually come from the Bible! Many well-known Bible phrases are part of church liturgy, Christian hymns, songs, and inspirational material.

PHRASE	REFERENCE
1. abide in him	1Jn 2:28
2. all is vanity	Ecc 12:8

PHRASE	REFERENCE
3. balm in Gilead	Jer 8:22
4. Bless the Lord, O my soul	Ps 103:1
5. Blessed are the peacemakers	Mt 5:9
6. call on the Lord	2Ti 2:22
7. children of God	Jn 1:12
8. Do not be afraid	2Sa 13:28
9. do not throw your pearls before swine	Mt 7:6
10. Do not worry about anything	Php 4:6
11. eye for eye, tooth for tooth	Ex 21:24
12. faith, hope, and love abide	1Co 13:13
13. Fight the good fight	1Ti 6:12
14. For everything there is a season	Ecc 3:1
15. For God so loved the world	Jn 3:16
16. give thanks	1Ch 6:18
17. Give us this day our daily bread	Mt 6:11
18. go in peace	Lk 7:50
19. God is love	1Jn 4:16
20. God loves a cheerful giver	2Co 9:7
21. Grace be with you	Col 4:18
22. Hear the word of the Lord	2Ki 7:1
23. I am the way, and the truth, and the life	Jn 14:6
24. Jesus began to weep	Jn 11:35
25. kingdom of God	Mt. 6:33
26. Lamb of God	Jn 1:29
27. let justice roll down like waters	Am 5:24
28. Let my people go	Ex 5:1
29. Love your enemies	Mt 5:44
30. My soul magnifies the Lord	Lk 1:36
31. my thoughts are not your thoughts	Isa 55:8
32. O God	Gen 32:9
33. O Lord my God	Ps 7:1
34. Out of the mouths of babes and infants	Ps 8:2
35. Owe no one anything	Ro 13:8

PHRASE	REFERENCE
36. Peace be with you	Jn 20:19
37. Praise the Lord!	Ps 150:1
38. pray without ceasing	1Th 5:17
39. prepare the way of the Lord	Isa 40:3
40. Pride goes before destruction	Pr 16:18
41. rejoice and be glad	Ps 40:16
42. sackcloth and ashes	Est 4:1
43. salt of the earth	Mt 5:13
44. Search me, O God	Ps 139:23
45. Spirit of the living God	2Co 3:3
46. Thus says the Lord	Ex 4:22
47. Trust in the Lord	Pr 3:5
48. word of the Lord	Gen 15:1
49. you of little faith	Mt 6:30
50. Your sins are forgiven	Mt 9:5

Bible Factoids

The wonderful literary world of the Bible is filled with unusual bits of information and curious trivia. As you travel through this section, you will find out who Beliar was, how to say Shibboleth, and what's not new under the sun.

Heavenly Books

In many passages, the Bible refers to books kept in heaven. Moses pleads with God to blot him out of the "book that you have written" (Ex 32:32) for the sake of Israel's forgiveness. The books of Daniel and Revelation both speak of the day that "the books were opened" (Da 7:10 and Rev 20:12).

Malachi speaks of a "book of remembrance" that was written about those who feared the Lord (Mal 3:16).

Book Burning in the Bible

King Jehoiakim of Judah burned the Book of Jeremiah strip by strip as it was read to him (Jer 36:23). On another occasion, a number of magicians at Ephesus—who were newly converted as a result of Paul's preaching—brought their books of magic together and burned them publicly (Ac 19:19).

What's a Parbar?

Many words in the Bible occur only once or twice, and scholars have no real idea what they mean. Parbar is one. The word is used in 1 Chronicles 26:18, and it probably means "colonnade" or "court."

Can you say Shibboleth?

How do you say shibboleth? If you were an Ephraimite and couldn't pronounce the first h, you would say "Sibboleth." And if you said "Sibboleth" you would be seized by the Gileadites and killed immediately! This is what happened to 42,000 Ephraimites at the fords of the Jordan. There the men of Gilead determined who were Ephraimites by the way they said this tricky word—which is pronounced SHIB-uh-leth (Jdg 12:1–6).

Under the Sun

The author of Ecclesiastes uses the phrase "under the sun" more than 25 times as he expresses a weariness with life. He says:

What has been is what will be, and what has been done is what will be done; there is nothing new under the sun. (Ecc 1:9)

Who Was Beliar?

Beliar (or Belial) was not originally a name, but it developed into a name for Satan in Jewish literature between the Testaments. The apostle Paul used the word in this way when he asked "What agreement does Christ have with Beliar?" (2Co 6:15)

Eat Your Words

On two occasions, Bible characters ate a scroll that contained God's words. The prophet Ezekiel (Eze 2:8–3:2) and also the apostle John (Rev 10:9–10). They both said that God's words tasted as "sweet as honey."

THE EVERYDAY WORLD OF THE BIBLE

THE BOOKS OF THE BIBLE are filled with breathtaking images and events—from angels and holy miracles to horrific visions of destruction and demons. It is important to remember, however, that day-to-day life for the Israelites and early Christians wasn't always as dramatic as those moments recorded in Scripture. What was this everyday world like? How did the average person live, work, and worship during the writing of the Bible? The answers to these questions will help us see that the Bible is populated with ordinary people; people who had many of the same feelings and concerns that we have today.

Jesus often used common, familiar tasks—such as the preparation of bread—to illustrate his teachings.

People at Home

In Bible times, the home was at the hub of people's lives. Birth, marriage, and death all took place there, and it was often the center of social activity, a workplace, and somewhere to eat and sleep as well. Several generations might live under the same roof.

Back then, there was variety in housing from place to place and period to period. Just as the Native American tepee is different from the twentieth-century urban town house, so too was the bedouin tent in the time of the patriarchs different from the flat-roofed house in Capernaum during the time of Jesus.

Tent Dwellings

Tents were the most common dwellings in the ancient world. They were constructed by setting poles in the ground and stretching a covering of skin over them. The covering was fastened to stakes driven into the ground. Sometimes occupants used curtains to divide their tents into rooms, and they used mats or carpets to cover the ground. The sides of the tents could be folded back or even taken down to let fresh air circulate through during the heat of the day.

These dwellings, often made of goatskin, were the homes of the patriarchs. For hundreds of years, Abraham and his descendants lived in tents—in Canaan, in Egypt, and then in the desert. These tent dwellers moved around from place to place with their flocks and herds in search of fresh pasture and water. Their portable, practical homes were easily taken down, bundled up, and moved to a new site. When the Israelites conquered the Canaanites, they took over their towns and homes, and copied their style of building.

The Courtyard House

The typical house in Palestine during the time of the patriarchs was built off the side of a courtyard. The simplest house had one small room and a circular, stone-lined pit inside the house for storing grain. Houses were built together and sometimes back-to-back. Entire terraces of these small homes (no bigger than an average bathroom or kitchen today) have been excavated. Surprisingly, these cramped quarters provided shelter for entire families. Larger homes have been discovered, however. One found at Megiddo, dating from 1600 B.C., had nine rooms with a door to each room—a luxury in those days.

Brick Homes

Most average homes in Palestine were made of stone, but down in the Jordan Valley homes were built of bricks because there was so much rich mud available there. At first oval mud bricks were made by hand, but once wooden molds were designed and made, the mud bricks became rectangular in shape. After the mud bricks were baked, they were white or pale red in color.

The roof of the house was made by placing wooden beams across the brick walls, covering the beams with brush, and finally mud or clay. Long timbers were too expensive for ordinary homes, so most rooms were fairly narrow.

The Four-Roomed House

When the Israelites moved back into Palestine after Joshua's victories, they began building four-roomed houses. This became the standard pattern of homes for centuries. The design was simple: You entered a courtyard from the street. On one side there were one or two rooms for storage; on the other side, a cattle barn. At the end was a large room for living and sleeping. The roof was flat, and strong enough for work, rest, or play by family members.

Rooftop Living

To get to the roof of a typical Israelite house, people climbed an outside staircase or even a wooden ladder propped against the wall. The roof was surrounded by a parapet, required by Jewish law to safeguard against falling to the ground below. A variety of activi-

Rooftops were a neccessary part of small, crowded Israelite homes

ties took place at this topmost level. This was the place to do weaving and washing. In the hot sunny weather, figs, dates, and flax were set out and dried. Prayer and meditation took place here (Ac 19:9–16), and it was the ideal location to make public announcements (Mt 10:27). Festivals and celebrations were often set up on the roof, and many families celebrated the week-long Feast of Tabernacles at the top of the home.

New Testament Homes

Besides the typical Israelite house, there were other types of dwellings in Jesus' day. When Jesus ate his last supper with his closest followers in a large upstairs room (Lk 22:12), it was likely in one of Jerusalem's wealthier homes.

To enter a home like this, you had to pass through a door that was usually kept locked. This door opened into a porch furnished with seats or benches. On the other side of the porch there was a short flight of stairs leading to the rooms and the open court. This courtyard area was the center of the Jewish home. It let in light and air to surrounding rooms. The floor was paved with tile or rock. Sometimes homeowners built the court around a fountain or well (2Sa 17:18). The courtyard was used for celebrations and other social gatherings (Est 1:5). The room surrounding this area opened onto the court, and in later centuries, many of these rooms had balconies or galleries that faced this central area.

A stairway led from the court to the upstairs rooms, and to the roof. The upper rooms were often quite large and nicely furnished. Paul preached his last sermon in this type of setting. Some of the crowd may have been next to the wall lying on cushions beside the window casement. It would have been easy for Eutychus, asleep in this position, to have fallen to the street below (Ac 20:7–12).

The master's quarters were downstairs and faced the entrance. This was the most lavish area in the house. His reception area was smartly furnished with a raised platform, a square table, and a couch on three sides (used as a bed at night).

Some of these homes had one or two rooms built over the porch or gateway of the house. This structure was called the *alliyah*, and it was used as guest rooms, a place to rest or meditate, or for storage. Steps connected the alliyah to the street and to the central court of the house. Jesus likely referred to such an area when he spoke of praying privately (Mt 6:6).

In ancient houses, windows were small rectangular holes facing the street (or inside—facing the open court). Sometimes a porch was built along the front of the house, carefully enclosed with latticework. This porch window was only opened for festive events and other special occasions.

Doors in these houses were not hung on hinges. Wooden doors were fixed to heavy posts that turned on stone sockets. Often the main door of the house was equipped with a lock and key made of wood or metal. Some of these ancient keys were huge and were clearly seen when carried in public (Isa 22:22).

How Houses Were Built

When the Israelites moved into Palestine, most people built their own houses or moved into the ones left there by the Canaanites. But as society expanded and became more complex, the need for public buildings and large dwellings grew. As workers became more skilled, they became specialists in stone building, brick-laying, and carpentry.

Many homes throughout Bible times were built out of large, rough stones—limestone, basalt, and sandstone. Smaller stones were used to fill the gaps between the larger stones, and the rough walls were covered with mud plaster.

Floors were usually hardened mud, and they were covered with straw mats. In wealthy homes, floors might be paved with stone slabs and covered with plush carpets.

Building materials were readily available in Palestine. The wealthy could easily obtain stone, brick, and the best timber for their homes. They used hewn stone and marble, cedar paneling, and gold, silver, and ivory for ornamental work.

Many wealthy landowners had "winter homes" and "summer homes." The latter were built partly underground, paved with marble, and constructed to bring in cool currents of air. They were a delightful sanctuary during the hot and humid summer months.

Homes of the Poor

The homes of the poor were one-room huts with mud walls. These walls were strengthened with reeds or stakes, but they were still not very secure and often became the breeding ground for snakes and vermin (Am 5:19). The family and animals occupied the same room, although family members sometimes slept on a platform above the animals. The windows were small holes high in the wall, and to keep intruders out, the doors of these homes were made very low. A person had to stoop to enter and leave the home.

Furnishings

If someone from the time of Jesus were to visit you, he or she would be amazed at the number and variety of furnishings in your home. Even the best-furnished house in Palestine would have appeared empty to us today. Here is a typical inventory of household furnishings back then:

Mats and Rugs

In the average home, straw mats were used as a floor covering or for seating. Poor people may well have had only a skin or mat on the floor to use for eating, sitting, and sleeping. The wealthy homeowner, on the other hand, would have had beautiful rugs, skins to recline on, and cushions of rich fabric.

Stools, Tables, Benches, and Chairs

Long before the time of Jesus, the rich Shunammite woman furnished the prophet Elisha's room with a bed, a table, a stool, and a candlestick (2Ki 4:10–13). This was more than would be available in an ordinary home. In wealthy homes, the owner would have a bench in his quarters. Some people in Bible times owned and sat on finely designed chairs. Examples of these have been discovered in

the tombs of the wealthy of Jericho. In ancient times, a table was a circular piece of leather placed on the floor mat. In the New Testament period, a three-sided couch (known as a *triclinium*) was introduced by the Romans. It extended around three sides of a rectangular table, and it was used for reclining at meals. It was likely in this setting that Jesus and his disciples observed the Jewish Passover feast, the Last Supper.

Beds

At night, family members would put down thick, coarse mattresses to sleep on, and cover themselves with quilts made from goat hair. Pillows may have been made from goatskin stuffed with feathers, wool, or some other soft material. In the morning, bedding would be rolled up and put away. Even from Old Testament times, wealthy families had bedsteads made of ivory, wood, or other expensive materials (Am 6:4), and they stored their bedding in expensive trunks.

Pots, Pans, and Storage Bins

Most household utensils during Bible times were made of earthenware or terra cotta. Later on, wealthy homes sometimes had kitchenware made of metal. There were flat-based bowls and "dipper juglets" in Abraham's day, and a "pilgrim flask" was used as a drinking vessel by soldiers and travelers. There were particular jars for storing flour and olive oil, and pots for carrying and storing water. There were cooking pots, and bowls and cups for serving food and drink.

When Jesus washed the disciples' feet (Jn 13:5), he probably used a large container called a *krater*, around since the time of the kings. This type of container had two or four handles, and was usually hung on wall pegs.

Every house had stone or clay storage bins for animal fodder as well as food for the family. Fire for cooking was made on the earth floor or sometimes in an earthenware pot.

Lamps

Lamps were common in Bible times. Light was important because homes were very dark. Olive oil, pitch, or wax were used and wicks were made of cotton or flax. Poorer Israelites made their lamps of clay, while the well-to-do had lamps of bronze and other metals. Lamps were left burning all night for a sense of security and for safety—a thief would be less likely to break into a well-lit house. For the Jews, the lamp was a significant symbol of the life and dignity of the family (Jer 25:10).

Comfort at Home

In our society, many of us are protected from summer's heat and winter's cold by the touch of a thermostat that controls a central cooling and heating system in our homes. The Israelites were not so fortunate. During the summer, the average Old Testament home was stuffy and alive with insects. When it was cold, the house was filled with smoke from the smoldering fire built in a hole in the earth floor. In the rainy seasons, the roof and walls of the house leaked. Clearly, home was not always a comfortable or comforting environment.

From Solomon's day, however, wealthy families began to emerge, and for them life was quite different. Their homes were built differently—they had more space and greater amenities. During the time between the Testaments, wealthy people were adding bathrooms to their homes, with tubs set into the tiled floors. By New Testament times, rich people living in Palestine built their homes in the Roman style, with two rectangular courtyards each surrounded by rooms.

Food and Drink

Jesus encouraged his hearers not to worry about food, drink, and clothing. He knew that for ordinary people these were basic concerns. Cereal crops, fruit, and vegetables were staples in the Hebrew diet, but they were subject to drought and pests (such as locusts). Some mutton and goat's meat were eaten, and fish was an important food in New Testament times. Here is a list of some basic Bible time staples:

	FOOD	REFERENCE
1. Grains:		
	barley	Jn 6:9
	corn	Gen 41:35
	millet	Eze 4:9
	wheat	1Sa 6:13
2. Fruit:		
	almonds	Gen 43:11
	figs	Jer 24:1–3
	grapes	Dt 23:24
	melon	Nu 11:5
	olives	Dt 8:8
	pomegranates	Nu 13:23
	sycamore	Am 7:14
3. Vegetables:		
	beans	2Sa 17:28
	cucumbers	Nu 11:5
	garlic	Nu 11:5
	gourds	2Ki 4:39
	leeks	Nu 11:5
	lentils	Gen 25:34
	onions	Nu 11:5

	FOOD	REFERENCE
4. Meat and Fish:		
	calf	Lk 15:23
	goat	Gen 27:9
	lamb	2Sa 12:4
	oxen	1Ki 19:21
	quail	Ex 16:13
	sheep	2Sa 17:29
	venison	Gen 27:7
	fish	Jn 6:11
5. Various Foods and Drinks:		
	cheese	2Sa 17:9
	curds	Isa 7:15
	eggs	Lk 11:12
	honey	Mt 3:4
	locusts	Mt 3:4
	milk	Gen 18:8
	wine	Jn 2

Meals

In the typical Israelite home, there was no breakfast. A snack might be eaten on the way to work, and the midday meal was usually bread, olives, and maybe fruit. In the evening, the family sat on the floor to eat dinner, which was usually a vegetable stew from a common pot eaten with bread. The Hebrews were a hospitable people (He 13:2) and welcomed guests to their homes. Even in their nomadic past, travelers would be invited to stay with the clan in their tents. Flat loaves of bread and milk were always part of the meal.

In wealthy homes, more food was available and in greater variety. At mealtimes, people reclined on couches around a table as they enjoyed appetizers and a number of main courses, followed by pastries and fruit for dessert.

Food Laws

In the Old Testament, strict food laws were laid down for all Jews. They were generally as follows:

1. Animals that chew their cud and have divided hoofs could be eaten.
2. Pork could not be eaten. It was considered unclean.
3. Only fish with fins and scales could be eaten.
4. Scavengers and many other birds were not eaten.
5. Blood had to be drained from a carcass before it was cooked.
6. Meat and milk dishes were not to be cooked or eaten together.
7. Meat that had been offered to idols could not be eaten.

The gecko, crocodile, and lizard were all off-limits, but locusts, crickets, and grasshoppers were just fine for snacks or meals! Although the reasons for these strict diet laws are not fully clear, they were likely given to protect the health of the Israelites, and to set this group apart as the people of God (Lev 11).

Drinks

Drinking water was not readily available in the Palestine area. Local wells provided fairly safe water, which was collected in earthenware jars. However, water collected from the roof in the family cistern sometimes contained impurities that were not fit to drink. Even during Roman times, when water was brought to the towns by aqueduct or by pipeline, maintaining sanitary conditions was a concern.

Other liquids had to be found to quench thirst. Milk from the family goat was popular, and people drank fresh juice from newly picked grapes. Since grapes grew well in the Mediterranean climate, and had to be fermented so that it would keep, wine was naturally the most common drink.

Ten Quick Food Facts

- The Israelites did not have sugar. Honey from wild bees was the main sweetener.

- Fig cakes were especially practical for taking on a long journey.

- Butter was hardly used because it would not keep; but cheese and yogurt were popular.

- Salt was used for preserving food. Small fish were dried, salted, and eaten with bread.

- Many vegetables were eaten raw.

- It was not until the time of the Romans that a divided oven was invented, with the fire separate from the cooking area.

- Most people ate with their fingers (although a spoon was used for something like soup).

- Before the time of the apostles, a Jew could not eat at the home of a non-Jew because of Jewish food laws.

- Flat loaves of barley bread were probably the most common type of bread.

- Although wine was a common, everyday drink, intoxication was always condemned.

Family Roles

Family life in Bible times was quite different from family life as we know it today. Back then in the Hebrew culture, family—grandparents, parents, children, relatives, and even servants—formed a unique social unit that was defined along patriarchal lines. This group could be very large (as in the case of Abraham's family). In the extended family setting, the grandfather had complete authority, and when he died, the eldest son took over by right of gender and birth. Each family member had a clearly defined role in the home and in the community, and every stage of life was marked by appropriate ceremonies to affirm social position and place.

Birth

Children were considered a gift from God (Ps 127), and a big family was a sign of God's special blessing. A childless family was perceived as having displeased God in some way, and "barren" women were looked on with disfavor, even ridicule.

Among children, boys were valued most. In a male-dominated culture, boys were needed to carry on the family name and continue the work of the land. Girls were necessary workers, but considered less important.

At birth, salt was rubbed into the baby's skin to make it firm, and the infant was wrapped in tight cloths to make the limbs grow straight. The name of the infant was carefully chosen to reflect something about the child's character. Babies were not weaned until they were two or three years old.

When a boy was eight days old, he was circumcised by his father or rabbi. The firstborn son was considered to belong to God in a special way and had to be bought back (redeemed) a month after circumcision by a payment to the priest (Ex 13:13).

After giving birth, in order to be considered "clean" again a mother had to sacrifice a pigeon and then a lamb. In New Testament times, money was deposited in the offering boxes of the temple to "redeem" a firstborn son—a tradition that began during the Exodus, when Israelite freedom cost the Egyptians the lives of their sons.

Growing Up

For Israelite children, play, work, and education were all closely tied to the home. Parents taught children their first lessons and prayers, and the entire family attended worship on the sabbath and festival days. Schooling for boys started when they were about six. Girls, however, were not formally educated. The rabbi of the local synagogue gave moral and religious instruction based on the Torah, and the boys learned largely by repetition. In later times, there were also Roman schools throughout the empire where pupils studied philosophy, mathematics, literature, rhetoric, astronomy, and architecture.

Work was an important part of the growing years. Children had to help in the fields, workshop, or kitchen as soon as they could manage the simplest task. Of course, there was opportunity to play as well. Children in Bible times enjoyed toys and games. Rattles, dolls, and dollhouses have all been uncovered by archaeologists—even board and dice games, ball games, and target games!

At 13, during New Testament times, a boy became a man in a special ceremony called the *Bar Mitzvah* ("son of the law"). After his coming of age, the boy was regarded as a responsible member of Israel in home, community, and in the synagogue.

Twenty Famous Bible Couples

NAMES	DESCRIPTION	REFERENCE
1. Adam and Eve	the first couple	Gen 3:20
2. Abraham and Sarah	father and mother of Israel	Gen 11:29
3. Jacob and Rachel	father of Israel's 12 tribes, parents of Joseph and Benjamin	Gen 29–30
4. Amram and Jochebed	parents of Aaron and Moses	Ex 6:20
5. Moses and Zipporah	lawgiver and his Midianite wife	Ex 2:21
6. Boaz and Ruth	great-grandparents of King David	Ru 4:13

NAMES	DESCRIPTION	REFERENCE
7. Elkanah and Hannah	parents of Samuel	1Sa 1:1–2
8. Nabal and Abigail	surly farmer and his clever wife	1Sa 25:3
9. David and Bathsheba	parents of Solomon	2Sa 12:24
10. Ahab and Jezebel	evil rulers over Israel	1Ki 16:30–31
11. Ahasuerus and Esther	Persian king and his Jewish queen	Est 2:16
12. Haman and Zeresh	cruel Persian official and his wife	Est 5:14
13. Hosea and Gomer	faithful prophet and his promiscuous wife	Hos 1–3
14. Zechariah and Elizabeth	parents of John the Baptist	Lk 1:5
15. Joseph and Mary	legal father and actual mother of Jesus	Lk 1:27
16. Zebedee and Salome	parents of James and John	Mt 4:21
17. Herod Antipas and Herodias	ruler of Galilee and his evil wife	Mt 14:3
18. Ananias and Sapphira	died after lying to the apostles	Ac 5:1
19. Aquila and Priscilla	godly couple who assisted Paul	Ac 18:2
20. Felix and Drusilla	Roman governor of Judea and his Jewish wife	Ac 24:24

Marriage

People in Israel married at an early age. To be married at 13 was not uncommon, and marriages were arranged by parents. In Old Testament times, marriages were arranged within the same clan—and often to a first cousin!

A man was allowed to have more than one wife, and by the time of the judges and the kings, men could have as many wives as they could afford. This arrangement, motivated by economic and political reasons, often created domestic strife. In the Israelite community after the Exodus, most marriages were monogamous, and such a marriage was viewed as ideal.

Since the bride was considered a working asset, she had to be paid for. The fee (called the *mohar*) was paid to the girl's father. In return, the young woman's father gave the couple a dowry. At the binding ceremony of betrothal, gifts were exchanged between the couple. On the day of the wedding, in the evening, the bridegroom and his party went in procession to the bride's home, where she was waiting, veiled and in her wedding dress. A blessing was given, then the bridegroom took the bride through the village to his own home. Friends went in torchlight procession to the new home. The marriage celebration and feast that followed sometimes lasted as long as a week.

Polygamists in the Bible

Husband	Number of Wives	Number of Concubines	Reference
Lamech	2		Gen 4:19
Abraham	1	1	Gen 16:1–3
Esau	3		Gen 26:34; 28:9
Jacob	4		Gen 29:15–35; 30:4, 9
Gideon	many	at least one	Jdg 8:30–31
Elkanah	2		1Sa 1:1–2
Saul	1	1	1Sa 14:50; 2Sa 3:7
David	8		1Sa 18:27; 25:42–43; 2Sa 3:2–5; 11:27; 12:8
Solomon	700	300	1Ki 11:3
Ahab	many		1Ki 20:7
Rehoboam	18	60	2Ch 11:21
Abijah	14		2Ch 13:21
Joash	2		2Ch 24:1–3

Death and Burial

A death in the household is always a tragedy, and in Bible times elaborate mourning rituals followed such an event. The body was prepared for a quick burial because of the hot climate. It was washed and clothed, then wrapped in special grave cloths, with a linen napkin bound around the head. The body was then put on a wooden stretcher (a *bier*) and carried to the place of burial. Family and friends—and even hired professional mourners—made a great public display of sorrow: Weeping, wailing, tearing clothing, wearing ashes, and fasting were all part of the seven-day mourning ceremonies.

Ordinary Israelites buried their dead in common graves or caves. Some caves were large enough for all the members of the family. Wealthy families could afford to have tombs specially hewn out of rock and sealed with a boulder. Graves were painted white to draw attention to them. They were not to be touched, as any contact with the dead made a person "unclean."

Clothing and Fashion

In Bible times, the type of dress that was worn was affected by climate and the availability of materials. Over the centuries, five basic items of clothing evolved:

1. In Old Testament times, a simple, everyday tunic—called a *kethon*—was made of animal skin. Later on, this basic item was made out of linen and silk and worn by the wealthy.

2. Shem and Japheth, Noah's sons, took an outer garment—the *simlah*—to cover their father's nakedness (Gen 9:23). The simlah was like a large sheet with a hood. It was first made of wool, but camel's hair was used later. A type of coat, the simlah was used for additional warmth, and the poor used it as daily wear and as a covering at night.

3. For special occasions, the Israelites wore the *beged*. They believed that this article of clothing gave honor to the wearer. After temple rituals priests wore the beged, and Rebekah dressed Jacob in this garment when he went before his father Isaac to receive his blessing (Gen 27).

4. The *lebhosh* was a garment used for general wear, but it eventually became an outer garment for everyone in Israelite culture. It was possible for the lebhosh to be made out of sackcloth (for mourning), while a decorative lebhosh could be worn as royal apparel.

5. In Bible times, the wearer of an *addereth* (an outer cloak) was a person of importance. Today, this is a common garment in Palestine that everyone wears.

Even in the Garden of Eden, fabric and clothing were important. After Adam and Eve realized they were naked, they made loincloths of fig leaves to cover themselves. Then God made the pair coverings of skin before sending them out of the garden (Gen 3). Later, a variety of fabrics were used to make clothes:

Linen: This was made from the flax plant and was one of the most important fabrics for the Israelites. It could be made coarse, thick, fine, or delicate. The Egyptians had a wide reputation for their fine linen.

Wool: Sheep's wool was the principal material for making clothes.

Silk: This was a fabric of great value because of its quality and the vivid colors available.

Sackcloth: The dark color and coarse texture of the goat's hair material made it ideal as a ritual sign of mourning and repentance. Sackcloth material was also used to make grain sacks.

Cotton: Although it is possible, we are not certain whether the Israelites used cotton for making clothes. Both Syria and Palestine grow cotton today.

Making and Caring for Clothes

Preparing fabrics and actually making clothes were considered women's work. There were a number of steps in making any garment:

- **Distaff Spinning:** Jewish women would attach wool or flax to a rod or stick called a distaff, and then use a spindle to twist the fibers into thread (Ex 35:25–26).

- **Weaving:** After raw materials were spun into thread, the thread was used to make cloth. The warp (lengthwise thread) was attached to a wooden beam on the loom, and the weaver stood while working. Various types of woven fabrics were made this way, including woolen garments, linen, and the embroidered clothing of the priests (Ex 28:4, 39).

- **Tanning:** In the Jewish community the tanner's trade was not considered respectable. This line of work involved drying animal skins to make garments. Lime, the juice of particular plants, and the leaves or bark of certain trees were used to tan the skins.

- **Embroidering:** The Jews were noted for their fine needle-work, but it was different from embroidery as we know it today. Cloth was woven with a variety of colors, and then a design was sewn onto it (Ex 26:11). In another method, embroidery was done by weaving gold thread or designs right into the fabric. This type of fine work was only done on garments worn by the priests.

- **Dyeing:** From early on in Bible history, the Israelites were familiar with the art of dyeing. Many natural colors were used for clothing, particularly red. Purple goods were highly valued (Ac 16:14), but that often meant anything that had a red hue to it.

Clothes were cleaned by washing the garments, which often included stamping on them and beating them with a stick in a tub of water. Niter, soap, and chalk were used for cleaning (Jer 2:22). Garments were often cleaned by a fuller, who did business on the outskirts of town (where water was available, and where the offensive odor of the cleaning business would not bother townsfolk).

What People Wore

The Israelites were not influenced by the dress of surrounding countries, and fashions tended to remain the same from one generation to the next. Although some of the clothing for men and women looked quite similar, women were forbidden to wear anything that belonged to a man, and men were forbidden to wear a woman's garment (Dt 22:5).

The poor had little clothing—even using their outer garment as a covering at night. The rich, on the other hand, had an extensive and colorful collection of apparel. The following is a sampling of the Israelite wardrobe:

Men's Clothing

1. **Inner garment:** close-fitting and made of wool, linen, or cotton and worn by both sexes
2. **Girdle:** a belt or band used to secure the inner or outer garment
3. **Outer garment:** coat, robe, or mantle made of linen or goat's hair
4. **Purse or scrip:** both were used to carry necessities
5. **Sandals:** a sole of wood or leather fastened with straps of leather and worn by both sexes
6. **Robes of honor:** very thin, fine garments worn over colorful tunics
7. **Mourning garments:** made of goat's hair material and worn next to the skin in times of deep sorrow
8. **Winter clothing:** fur robes or skins; cattle skins were worn by the poor
9. **Rings:** worn as a seal or token of personal authority
10. **Phylacteries** (see next page)
11. **Headdress:** worn on special occasions

Women's Clothing

1. **Inner garment:** described as a coat, robe, or tunic
2. **Girdle:** used to secure the the outer garment
3. **Outer garment:** longer than a man's; the front could be tucked over the girdle to make an apron
4. **Veil:** worn to show modesty and to indicate an unmarried state
5. **Sandals:** never worn indoors
6. **Anklets:** often made of gold, these made a tinkling sound when the woman walked
7. **Mourning garments:** ashes were placed on the head when wearing sackcloth

8. **Winter clothing:** fur robes or skins
9. **Earrings:** worn by Hebrew and Egyptian women
10. **Cosmetics and perfume:** henna was used as a cosmetic stain; frankincense, myrrh, aloes, and spikenard were sources of perfume
11. **Headdress:** used to some degree; hair ornaments may have been worn

Amulets and Phylacteries

In ancient times, idolatrous people wore magical charms to protect themselves from evil spirits. These amulets—earrings worn by women, or pendants worn around the neck by men—had sacred words or the figure of a god engraved on them. Another kind of amulet had words written on a scroll that was rolled tightly and sewn up in linen.

To counter this pagan practice, Israelite men began wearing phylacteries. One type was worn on the forehead and was called a frontlet. It had four compartments, and in each compartment there was a piece of parchment that contained a passage from the Law. All four pieces of parchment were wrapped in animal skin in a small bundle and then tied to the forehead.

A second type of phylactery was made of two rolls of parchment on which the words of the Law were written in special ink. The parchment was enclosed in leather and worn on the arm. Some men wore their phylacteries at evening and morning prayers, others wore them only in the morning. Phylacteries were not worn on the Sabbath or on other holy days.

The Pharisees were known to make their phylacteries larger than normal so that everyone would see them and marvel at such holy men!

Village, Town, and City Life

In early Old Testament times, village life centered around a farming settlement. The lifeblood of the community was animals and crops, and villages grew up near a stream or brook that would provide water year round.

When Abraham settled in Canaan, each family was given a plot of land. This was a gift from God (Isa 34:17), and each family was expected to utilize the land in the following ways: live on it, grow crops, maintain animals, and perhaps bury family members there. Each parcel of land was supposed to be kept within the family and not casually bought and sold.

Every 50 years marked a time of Jubilee, when land that had been mortgaged or sold was returned to the family. This helped equalize social standing between rich landowners and poor laborers.

By the time of the kings, however, a wealthy class of rulers and officials began to emerge. They bought up a lot of land and oppressed the poor. Estates took the place of family farms. When people lost their land, they had to hire themselves out as farm laborers. Life in the village changed. Bigger and better homes were built for the wealthy and grouped together in a certain part of town. Within the same community, the very poor suffered tremendous hardship, thus the prophets cried out against injustice (Mic 2:2).

Fifty Well-Known Bible Places

PLACE	DESCRIPTION	REFERENCE
1. Aceldama	known as Potter's Field and purchased with the money that bought the betrayal of Jesus	Ac 1:19
2. Alexandria	home of Apollos	Ac 18:24–26
3. Ararat	mountainous land in western Asia	Jer 51:27

PLACE	DESCRIPTION	REFERENCE
4. Ashdod	one of five main Canaanite cities	Jos 11:22
5. Athens	capital city of Greece	Ac 17:15–34
6. Babylon	capital city of the Babylonian Empire	Ne 7:6
7. Baca	a valley of Palestine where many balsam trees are found	Ps 84:6
8. Beautiful Gate	a part of the east gate of Jerusalem where Peter and John healed a lame man	Ac 3:2
9. Bethany	where Lazarus was raised from the dead	Jn 11
10. Bethel	located north of Jerusalem, this is an important biblical site	Gen 13:3
11. Bethlehem	birthplace of Jesus	Jn 7:42
12. Cana	a village of Galilee where Jesus performed his first recorded miracle	Jn 2:1
13. Canaan	the name of Palestine, the land given to Abraham and his offspring	Gen 11:31
14. Capernaum	main area where Jesus ministered	Mt 4:13
15. Carmel	a town in the mountains of Judah	Jos 15:55
16. Cenchrea	a harbor east of Corinth	Ac 18:18
17. Chebar	the Jewish exiles, including Ezekiel, lived along its river banks	Eze 1:3

PLACE	DESCRIPTION	REFERENCE
18. Cities of Refuge	six cities of the Levites were set aside as sanctuaries for criminals: Bezer, Kedesh, Shechem, Golan, Ramoth-Gilead, and Kirjath-arbu	Dt 4:41–43; Jos 20:7–9
19. Corinth	the church in this city received two letters from Paul the apostle	Ac 18:1
20. Damascus	city connected with Paul's conversion	Ac 9:1–18
21. Decapolis	group of ten cities forming a Roman district on the plain of Esdraelon and the upper Jordan Valley	Mt 4:25
22. Elim	a resting place for the Israelites after they crossed the Red Sea	Ex 15:27
23. Ephesus	visited by Paul during his second missionary journey	Ac 18:19
24. Galatia	a district of central Asia Minor	Ac 16:6
25. Gath	a Philistine city, home of Goliath	1Sa 17:4
26. Gomorrah	a depraved city that was destroyed	Gen 19
27. Haran	a Mesopotamian city	Gen 11:31
28. Hebron	a city of refuge	Jos 20:7
29. Helbon	a village of Syria near Damascus	Eze 27:18
30. Hermon	this mountain marks the northeast boundary of Palestine	Dt 3:8

PLACE	DESCRIPTION	REFERENCE
31. Israel	the northern kingdom of the Jews in Israel	2Ch 35:18
32. Jericho	where Jesus met Zacchaeus	Lk 19:1–10
33. Jerusalem	capital of the southern kingdom of Judah, 30 miles from the Mediterranean Sea and 18 miles west of the Jordan River	2Sa 5:5
34. Judah	the southern kingdom of Israel	2Ch 13:8
35. Lydda	a town on the Plain of Sharon	Ac 9:32
36. Masada	where David hid from Saul	1Sa 24:22
37. Nain	a village in Galilee	Lk 7:11
38. Nazareth	where Jesus grew up	Lk 2:39–40
39. Nineveh	ancient capital of Assyria	Jnh 1
40. Rome	the church in this city received a great theological epistle from Paul the apostle	Ro 1:7
41. Samaria	capital of the northern kingdom	1Ki 16:24
42. Sea of Galilee	a large lake in northern Palestine	Jn 6:1
43. Salt Sea	also known as the Dead Sea or East Sea, it is the body of water at the southern end of the Jordan Valley	Nu 34:12
44. Shechem	ancient political and religious center	Gen 12:6–7

PLACE	DESCRIPTION	REFERENCE
45. Sodom	a depraved city that was destroyed	Gen 19
46. Tarsus	birthplace of Paul	Ac 9:11
47. Thessalonica	Paul established a church here	Ac 17:1–9
48. Thyatira	home of Lydia	Ac 16:14
49. Tyre	city of Ezekiel's great prophecy	Eze 26
50. Ur	birthplace of Abraham	Gen 11:27

Villages, Towns, and Cities

The difference between village and town life in Bible times is in fortification. Villages were settlements without walls. Towns were walled settlements that were built on top of a hill or mound and near a good water supply. Towns were usually built in fertile areas, or at a strategic junction of trade routes. Unprotected villages often surrounded fortified towns.

Old Testament towns were often very small, about six to ten acres, with about 150–250 houses inside its walls, and about 1,000 residents. Walled towns began to develop when nomadic tribes or clans started to settle down. The chief of the clan became the "king" of his own territory. There was no central government, and kings of different towns often had conflicts.

Town life was extremely cramped. Houses were small, joined together, and streets were narrow. The main open space in town was the fortified gateway. Here, cattle and human traffic came and went, disputes were settled, and workers, merchants, town elders, and others all gathered for meetings, business, and trade.

From the time of King Solomon, towns grew into cities as they expanded in size and importance. Government became large and central. In Jerusalem, the capital, Solomon installed an administrative cabinet with diverse responsibili-

Jerusalem

ties. Besides being the government center, Jerusalem also became the religious capital. A magnificent temple was built there, and Solomon constructed palaces and a number of other large buildings at this site.

The great cities of New Testament times were different from early fortified towns. With the coming of the Greeks and Romans, towns and cities were planned carefully. In some locations, particularly Samaria and Caesarea, streets were made wider and paved, piped water was brought in from aqueducts, shops and public baths were built in central locations, and effective drainage for waste water and sewage was put in place.

Jerusalem in Jesus' day was a bustling, heavily populated city. It boasted a dazzling white limestone and gold temple built by the Herods, many other grand buildings, and streets crowded with people buying and selling. On market days, shops and stalls sold everything from sandals and cloth to luxury goods offered by merchants. Besides seven different markets, there were many shops and restaurants to serve the needs of possibly a quarter of a million people living in the city—a far cry from the small farming settlement of earlier times.

Farmers, Shepherds, and Fishermen

The work of farmers was mostly done by hand, even though they did use simple machinery—a wooden plow pulled by an ox, a wooden sickle to cut the stalks of grain, and a pronged fork to winnow the fresh corn. Besides growing and harvesting grain, other major crops included grapes, olives, and figs. Crops were planted after the autumn rains had softened the ground.

Shepherding was also important. The shepherd was usually in charge of a mixed flock of sheep and goats that he had to feed and protect. It was important to watch for wild animals, including lions and jackals, that inhabited the Jordan Valley area. The flock was important because wool and goat hair were used for clothing, goats were important for milk, and both animals were a significant source of meat.

The Israelites were poor sailors, so there was little fishing in Old Testament times. But by the time Jesus was in Galilee, there was a thriving fishing industry. The Lake of Galilee was full of fish. Using a cast net or a dragnet (a large net used from the boat), fishermen were able to pull in a good catch. Some fish were sold right away, others were salted. The work of fishing was often dangerous because the lake could become stormy without warning because of sharp climatic changes.

Working Life

In Bible times, much of the history of the Israelites was lived out in an agricultural setting. Work tended to reflect this type of environment, the most important occupations being farming, shepherding, fishing, and village carpentry and crafts. Besides these, the Bible notes several other occupations:

OCCUPATION	REFERENCES
Baker	Gen 40:1
Barber	Eze 5:1
Brick maker	Gen 11:3
Carpenter	2Sa 5:11
Cook	1Sa 8:13
Coppersmith	2Ti 4:14
Cupbearer	Gen 40:2
Embalmer	Gen 50:3
Embroiderer	Gen 28:39
Engraver	Ex 28:11
Fuller	2Ki 18:17
Gardener	Jer 29:5
Gem-cutter	Ex 28:4
Jeweler	Ex 28:17–21
Mason	2Ki 12:12
Mariner	Eze 27:9
Military officer	Ac 10:1
Musician	2Sa 6:5
Painter	Jer 22:14
Perfumer	1Sa 8:13
Physician	Gen 50:3
Porter	2Sa 18:26
Potter	Isa 64:8
Refiner	Mal 3:3
Silversmith	Ac 19:24
Smith	1Sa 13:19
Spinner	Ex 35:25
Stonecutter	Ex 31:5
Tailor	Ex 39:1
Tanner	Ac 9:43
Tax collector	Mt 9:10
Tentmaker	Ac 18:3
Toolmaker	Gen 4:22
Weaver	Ex 28:32
Worker in metal	Ex 31:3–4

Village Artisans

From early Bible times, various village crafts were practiced. Carpenters made farm tools and furniture for the home. Stonecutters shaped blocks and bricks for building. Potters used a wheel and a primitive oven to make clay utensils for the home. The tanner preserved the skins of animals to make various useful items—among them, sandals, girdles, and goatskin bottles for water.

The Work of Women

The woman in Bible times was ruled by her husband. She had low status, few rights, and did much of the hard work. Every day she had to bake bread and collect water from the local spring or well. Both jobs involved many steps of back-breaking effort, from grinding grain into coarse flour to carrying heavy water pots home on her head or shoulder. She might also have to make cheese or yogurt from milk. There might be spinning and weaving to do, and clothing to be made. During the harvest, women sometimes worked in the fields and helped crush the grapes and olives in the presses. The long workday ended with the preparation and eating of the evening meal when the whole family gathered together.

Sickness and Health

Medical practice in biblical times was basic and, for the Hebrews, based on the health and hygiene laws given in the Pentateuch. Unlike surrounding tribes who mixed medical practice with superstition, magic, and sorcery, the Hebrews trusted God for good health and believed that sickness indicated spiritual disobedience or lack of faith (Job 4:8).

Along with their religious responsibilities, local priests were expected to fulfill medical duties. The Book of Leviticus describes both religious and medical purification rites, including cleansing after childbirth and for leprosy (12, 13). Prophets also had a role in medical care. Elisha purified the water of Jericho, and helped in the cure of Naaman the Syrian and the son of the Shunammite woman (2Ki 4–5).

Various ailments are mentioned in the Bible, including physical and mental disabilities. By New Testament times, doctors were at work, trained in medical schools that taught basic anatomy and medical care. Excavations have revealed collections of surgical instruments. The role of the ancient pharmacist was probably more important than that of the doctor. He prepared the oils, ointments, and potions for the sick, the spices for embalming, the incense and oils for the temple, and cosmetics for everyday use.

Ten Quick "Medical" Cures

- Myrtle, saffron, myrrh, and spikenard were used in personal hygiene.

- Olive oil and "balm of Gilead" were used for wounds and sores.

- Wine mixed with myrrh was used as a painkiller.

- It was believed that mandrake roots would help a woman to conceive children.

- Broken arms or legs were bound up tightly.

- A hole was bored in the skull to relieve pressure.

- Skilled midwives helped mothers give birth.

- A poultice (heated mixture) of figs was applied to boils.

- Honey was sometimes mixed with oil and applied to a wound.

- Frankincense and myrrh were often used to help stop bleeding.

Justice and the Law

In Israel, there was no real separation between civil and religious law. Priests, Levites, and elders worked toward the same goals and shared the administration of justice. In the Old Testament, the gate of the city or town was the place where grievances were aired, local quarrels settled, and cases tried. During New Testament times, the high court was the Sanhedrin, a body of 70 men who met in the temple. The authorities in Rome allowed them to pass any sentence under Jewish law except the death penalty.

Trade and Commerce

Even from the time of Abraham, the buying and selling of land took place. It was a practice that was disapproved of, so there were laws to protect the property rights of families. There were traditional customs connected with purchasing property. In the Book of Ruth, the seller took off his shoe and gave it to the buyer! When Jeremiah bought some land, there was a deed of contract and a copy was stored inside a clay jar.

Marketplaces for local trade developed around the gates of towns and cities. Animals were sold there, as well as the merchandise of potters and smiths. Visiting foreign merchants also set up their stalls at the community gates.

Eventually, international trade developed as Israel expanded and experienced the growth of industries. As Israel conquered new territories, trade routes opened up; also, political leaders had an interest in buying luxury goods and creating wealth. All these factors contributed to a brisk import and export industry:

EXPORTS	IMPORTS
olive oil	tin, lead, silver, copper
honey	peacocks, apes
nuts	timber
aromatic gum	linen

EXPORTS
myrrh
wool
cloth
woven garments
wines

IMPORTS
purple dyed cloth
gems, gold, ivory
spices
algum wood
cotton, silk
apples, cheese
baskets
slaves

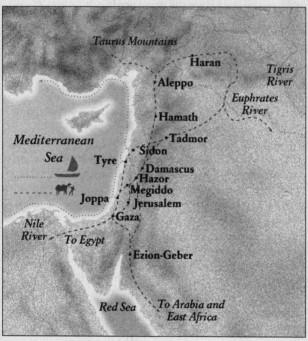

Main trade routes of Israel by land and sea

Israel was positioned close to the Mediterranean sea and between Asia Minor, Egypt, and Arabia. The Israelites took advantage of this location in their use of trade routes by land and sea. In Jerusalem's markets, however, goods were expensive and taxes were high. Jewish rabbis enforced strict business rules.

In earlier times, trade was done by bartering, then gold and silver were introduced, and eventually money. Although not actually coins, a shekel or talent was a weight of gold or silver. Trading involved shekels and talents, which had to be weighed and measured. In New Testament times, however, there was a regular banking system, and money changers handled currencies of various countries.

Weights, Measures, and Money

When we read about weights, measures, and money in the Bible, we are confronted with terms and amounts that are foreign to our world of ounces, gallons, kilometers, and dollars. It is also hard to compare purchasing power across the centuries. Measuring distances back then was quite different from the way we approach and understand it today. In comparing ancient measures with modern equivalents, it is important to note that this table is simply a rough approximation.

TERM	BIBLICAL EQUIVALENT	MODERN EQUIVALENT
1. Bath	ephah (dry measure)	38.5 pints
2. Beka	½ shekel	0.25 ounces
3. Bushel	8 quarts	15 pints
4. Cab	¼ seah	3.5 pints
5. Cor	Homer	48.5 gallons
6. Cubit		17.5 inches
7. Daric		$5
8. Denarius	a day's wage	one penny

TERM	BIBLICAL EQUIVALENT	MODERN EQUIVALENT
9. Didrachma	½ Jewish shekel	32 cents
10. Drachma		16 cents
11. Farthing		¼ cent
12. Fathom		6 feet
13. Finger span		¾ inch
14. Furlong		202 yards
15. Gerah		¹⁄₄₀ ounce
16. Hin	⅙ bath	6 pints
17. Homer	10 baths	90 gallons
18. Koros		114 gallons
19. Log		0.5 pint
20. Measure		9 gallons
21. Mile (milion)		1,618 yards
22. Mina	50 shekels	1.6 pounds
23. Mite		⅛ cent
24. Omer	¹⁄₁₀ ephah	38.5 pints
25. Pace		1 yard
26. Palm		3 inches
27. Pot		1 pint
28. Pound (litra)		7.5 pounds
29. Quadrans		¼ cent
30. Quart		1.7 pints
31. Reed	6 cubits	8 feet, 9 inches
32. Saton		21 pints
33. Seah		13 pints
34. Shekel (common)		0.4 ounce
35. Shekel (royal)		0.5 ounce
36. Shekel (temple)	½ or ⅓ shekel	0.2 ounce
37. Span	½ cubit	9 inches
38. Talent (light)	3,000 shekels	66 pounds
39. Talent	125 libra	88 pounds

Getting Around in Bible Times

Journeys were commonplace in the Bible. Abraham moved from Ur to Canaan, the Israelites wandered around in the desert for several years, and the travels of Paul on land and sea are on record as well. These are just a few of many journeys we read about in the Scriptures. How did people move from one place to another? This is what travel and transport looked like back then:

- **On Foot.** In Bible times most people walked from one place to the next.

- **Animals.** The working animal of the Bible was the donkey. It was the chief means of transport for the average citizen all through biblical history. After about 1000 B.C. camels were used, especially in international trade. Horses were also used in New Testament times.

- **Caravans.** To protect themselves against marauders, traders traveled together in a caravan—donkeys, camels, goods, and men—along the main trade routes of the Mediterranean world.

- **Vehicles.** In the Old Testament, horse-drawn chariots were used by armies and nobility. Carts drawn by donkeys were used on farms. In New Testament times, when roads were much better, a variety of chariots were popular. People who could afford it traveled in litters on the narrow city streets. Litters were couches with a framework that had curtains to conceal the traveler. The litter rested on poles that were carried by men or sometimes by horses.

- **Roads.** The Romans built a system of excellent roads connecting the provinces to Rome. Some sections still remain in fine condition today. Even so, they did not go everywhere and many journeys had to be made on the old, unsurfaced roads, worn down by many travelers over the centuries.

- **Inland Waterways.** Besides the Nile, the Tigris, and the Euphrates, no other rivers in Bible lands were used for travel and transport. Barges with sails were used on the Nile to bring corn to the seaport.

- **Travel by Sea.** The seafaring nations of the Old Testament were the Egyptians and the Phoenicians, who dominated travel in the east Mediterranean Sea. During this period, Israel had limited success in maritime trade. By the time of Jesus, Rome controlled the Mediterranean. The Gospels record several times when Jesus crossed the Sea of Galilee by boat, and in Acts Paul's Mediterranean journeys are well documented.

War and Warriors

War was very much a part of the history of Israel—even though God's law protected life and spoke out against murder. From early on, every man was expected to be a soldier to help defend God's "holy people" from the pagan tribes that often attacked them. Sometimes Israel's battles and skirmishes were seen as God's way of punishing them for wrongdoing and faithlessness.

Even then, the everyday life of the Israelite family was ordinary and routine, jolted only here and there by the attack and invasion of warriors. Here is a quick look at the facts about war during Bible times:

- The tribes of Israel rallied together to resist and defeat desert tribes who constantly raided Israel.

- When Saul was appointed king, he chose 3,000 men as the first permanent army of Israel.

- King David was a military genius. Under him, the Israelites learned new methods of warfare, and he was the first king to have a bodyguard of great warriors.

- For a long time the army was made up entirely of foot-soldiers.

- The kings built fortresses to protect the land.

- Soldiers usually went to war in spring, when food was available.

- War was rarely declared; the element of surprise was important.

- The ram's horn, called a *shofar*, was blown to gather troops.

- Israelites often consulted oracles and prophets before facing battle.

- Before battle started, the priest offered a sacrifice to God.

- When Israel was plundered by desert tribes, the invaders rode in on camels, destroyed crops, and took cattle and captives.

- An attack on a city often took place just before dawn.

- From the city walls, defenders of a city hurled down burning arrows, boiling oil, and stones in an attempt to keep the attackers at bay.

- After a city was taken, soldiers were usually free to take what they wanted. The walls were broken down and the city was burnt.

- Wars were sometimes settled by a single combat.

- The New Testament was not written against a background of war. The Mediterranean world was at peace under Roman government.

- At times, Jews rebelled under Roman authority; these rebellions were quickly crushed.

- Companies of Roman soldiers were stationed within the provinces (for example, Caesarea) to keep the peace.

Social Life

Although the people in Bible times had to work hard to live, they did have times for social activities. For a start, God had ordered one day in seven—the sabbath—to be set aside from ordinary work. It was a time to rest, relax, and worship him. The wealthy had slaves and servants to do the hard labor so that there was more time for them to choose to do as they pleased. The religious festivals not only provided an opportunity to celebrate God; they also were welcomed as holidays and fun festivities for everyone.

Children then played as children do today. Of course, there was no knowledge of video games and the like, but dolls and board games were common. Children played outside, in the market, and at weddings—even funerals (Mt 11:16–17). Children also played ball and target games, and marbles were popular in Egypt.

Casting lots—dice games—were popular with adults, although the religious leaders strongly disapproved of gambling. Shooting with bows and arrows was also a pastime, and children practiced with slings and stones. Wrestling was a favorite Bible sport, and in Babylon they wrestled while holding on to the opponent's belt.

During the time of the Greeks, public entertainment became very popular. People even made a living at it. The Sadducees enjoyed this kind of recreation while the Pharisees believed it to be wrong. King Herod built a stadium for gladiators, and an amphitheater for chariot racing in Jerusalem. Greek games and athletics were also performed in the stadium, including footracing and boxing. In his writings, Paul the apostle uses the strict training and conditioning of an athlete as an example of living the Christian life effectively (1Co 9:24–27).

Music and dancing were also an important part of the social—and especially the religious—life of the Israelites.

Everyday Life in the Bible—30 Quick Facts

1. Children were taught to respect their mother even though she had low status in the society.
2. The skeletal remains of loved ones were sometimes removed from graves and stored in stone chests called *ossuaries*.
3. When putting on shoes, the right sandal was always put on and taken off before the left.
4. The Israelites of the Old Testament normally grew their hair long.
5. In the Old Testament, the days of the month were marked by putting a peg into a bone plate that had three rows of ten holes.
6. As a sign of mourning, men shaved off their beards.
7. Even though Israelite society was patriarchal, family life was not always oppressive to women.
8. The four biggest problems for farmers were locusts, wild animals, invading armies, and the lack of water.
9. Measurements of distances in the Old Testament were based on a day's journey or even a bowshot.
10. There were 12 months in the calendar, with five days added at the end of the year.
11. In later Bible times, the day started at dusk. A whole day became an evening and a morning.
12. Merchants had two sets of weights: one when they were buying, the other when they were selling. Sometimes they used the weights dishonestly and cheated their customers.
13. In Old Testament times, slavery was accepted in Israel; in New Testament times, there were both Jewish and non-Jewish slaves in Palestine.
14. It was common for Israelite farmers to live in a village or fortified town near the farm they owned.
15. Canaanite and Philistine pottery was far more artistic and decorative than Israel's pottery.
16. Only Roman citizens could wear the Roman toga.

17. In Egyptian schools for adults, many subjects were taught and discipline was strict—no wine, women, or music.

18. The Jews disapproved of Greek athletes because they practiced and competed in the nude!

19. Cavalry and chariots for war were introduced in Israel under Solomon.

20. Since the streets were not clean in most towns, the Romans made pavements and stepping-stones so pedestrians could avoid dirt and mud.

21. When the clans of Israel settled in permanent homes, the normal family unit became smaller—father, mother, and children.

22. Israelite children kept pets, such as birds.

23. Soldiers did not wear sandals. They wore high-topped leather shoes that laced up to the knee.

24. When he was a boy, Jesus probably went to a synagogue school, where he learned the Torah.

25. Leaven (to make the bread rise) was used to make round, flat loaves. The unleavened bread of Bible times was much like today's pita bread.

26. If someone fell into debt in Israel, he could sell some property—or even himself—into service to repay the debt.

27. An important part of Jewish family life was the blessing of the children by their parents. Today, many Jewish children are blessed at the sabbath meal.

28. The Israelites were taught to make tassels for the corners of their outer garments. They would tie a blue thread to each tassel to help remember God's commandments.

29. The Romans constructed amazing aqueduct systems for cities throughout their empire. Jerusalem's aqueducts brought water into the city from as far away as 25 miles.

30. Execution by crucifixion was usually reserved for the lower classes in Greek and Roman societies. It was a slow, excruciatingly painful, and humiliating death.

RELIGION AND WORSHIP IN THE BIBLE

ROM THE WRITING OF THE Ten Commandments to the teachings of Jesus, the Bible reveals how God helps to guide humanity with his holy hand. In return, his people have strived to show their love and thanksgiving to the Lord. The Israelites built great temples and offered burnt sacrifices to prove their faithfulness. Early Christians humbly prayed together in homes to express their personal commitment to God. Worship—whether by song, poetry, or feast—is at the heart of the Bible. This chapter examines some of the traditions and practices of Jewish and Christian religions.

After his death and resurrection, Jesus ascended to heaven to continue his holy mission.

Israel at Worship in the Old Testament

The Israelites loved and worshiped God. They were thankful to him for his goodness to them, and they stood in awe of his great power. At times they were disobedient, turning away from him, his laws, and his leading. Yet they always came back to him in repentance, with renewed hearts ready to worship. Indeed, religion was at the core of the nation's life, and the Israelites responded to the living God in many ways and at many places throughout their history. How did this journey begin?

First Glimpses of God

The first clear act of worship is recorded in Genesis. The children of Adam and Eve brought two types of offering to God. Cain brought the fruit of the ground and Abel brought an animal offering. God responded to their actions, accepting Abel's offering and rejecting Cain's (4:2–7). This distinct interaction between God and these two established a pattern in worship—that is, God is vitally involved with his people.

Israel's religion really began when Abraham was called by God to leave his nomadic life, move to a new land, and become the founder of a great people. Abraham obeyed God, and the seed of the nation Israel was born. In his dialog with God, Abraham learned that God honored and wanted animal sacrifices and the worship of his fledgling people.

As God had promised, the new nation continued to grow from Abraham's progeny: Jacob (Abraham's grandson) and his 12 sons formed the clans of Israel. They were a nation on the move, and wherever they settled they built altars (and sometimes stone monuments) and offered sacrifices to God (Gen 8:20). Certain trees and wells were marked as sacred because they were tangible reminders of the hand of God at work in their lives at particular times (Jos 24:26; Gen 16:14).

Worship during this time was often spontaneous. God acted and spoke when he chose, calling a few of his people to worship him at any given time. Altars were outdoors, exposed to the weather, affecting the time of the ceremonies.

The Ten Commandments

1. ...you shall have no other gods before me.
2. You shall not make for yourself an idol, ...
3. You shall not make wrongful use of the name of the Lord your God, ...
4. Remember the Sabbath day, and keep it holy.
5. Honor your father and your mother, so that your days may be long in the land that the Lord your God is giving you.
6. You shall not murder.
7. You shall not commit adultery.
8. You shall not steal.
9. You shall not bear false witness against your neighbor.
10. You shall not covet your neighbor's house; you shall not covet your neighbor's wife...or anything that belongs to your neighbor.

Exodus 20 and the Law

The Ten Commandments were God's covenant with his people. However, in Israel's law books, Exodus to Deuteronomy, there are three major collections of laws. The first follows the Ten Commandments in Exodus (21–23) and deals with moral, civil, and religious laws. In Leviticus (17–26), the second collection, known as "holiness" laws, focuses on worship rituals. The third collection, in Deuteronomy (12–25), underscores the detailed commands given in Exodus and Leviticus, and spells out the duties of the king. Given in the form of a sermon by Moses, the third set includes encouragement to the people to keep the Law.

The purpose of the Law was to direct the nation in how to live in relationship with God and others. It was not intended to be an impossible list of do's and don'ts, but was there to provide guidance as its name in Hebrew *torah* (meaning "instruction") suggests.

The Law reflects God's holy, just, and good character. He wanted his chosen people to imitate and reflect his character. Indeed, on several occasions God told Israel to be holy in the same way that he was holy (Lev 11:45; 19:2; 20:26).

Worship During the Time of Moses

Worship and religion changed during the time of Moses and extended far into Jewish history. God revealed his holy and personal name *Yahweh* (usually translated "the Lord" and sometimes "Jehovah") to Moses and directed him in leading the Israelites out from Egypt. Leaving Egypt meant that God's people had started a new chapter in their knowledge and worship of God. Now they began worshiping God together as a group, and the whole idea of united worship was an innovative concept for this called-out people.

When Moses climbed to the top of Mt. Sinai, he received from God much more than the Ten Commandments. Once again God revealed himself and his name, and here he revealed the core of Old Testament religious teaching. When Moses came down from the mountain, the people were awed by God's glorious presence—the cloud, the trumpet sound, the thunder and lightning—and they willingly agreed to keep the new covenant with the Lord their God.

While on the mount, Moses received a plan for an enclosed worship center for the people. This place of worship would be distinctly different from the altars fashioned under the open sky. When it was put together, the tabernacle became the place where the Israelites worshiped God on their journey from Egypt to Canaan. Each time the Israelites camped, the newly ordained priests—Aaron, his sons, and men from the clan of Levi—set up the tabernacle for worship. This center of Israel's religious life was a constant reminder that God was always with them. The "tent of meeting," as the tabernacle came to be called, was the dwelling place of God and the place where he met with his people.

The Tabernacle—a Mobile Worship Center

The tabernacle was a large tent supported by a frame of acacia wood. Inside was draped with colorful violet, purple, and scarlet tapestries that were sewn together into two sets of five curtains. The walls of the tabernacle were made of goat-hair coverings. The roof was made of rams' skins, dyed red.

Inside, the tabernacle was divided into two rooms. The smaller, inner room was called the *holy of holies* and could only be entered by the high priest once a year. An embroidered linen curtain separated this sacred place from the larger room, called the *holy place*. The entrance to this room was covered by another linen curtain.

The ark of the covenant stood in the holy of holies. It was a rectangular box made of acacia wood and overlaid with gold. The covenant box contained the two stone tablets of the Ten Commandments, a golden pot of manna, and Aaron's rod. On top of the box was the *mercy seat*, a slab of gold with a cherub at each end.

In the holy place, there was an incense altar in front of the curtain. It was made of acacia wood, overlaid with gold, and decorated with horns. The seven-branched lampstand— the only source of light in the tabernacle—was also in this room, along with a table for the Bread of Presence.

The tabernacle was erected in a courtyard, which itself was enclosed by a screen of linen curtains. There was an entrance on one side with an embroidered linen curtain drawn across it. Within the tabernacle courtyard was an altar made of acacia wood and lined in copper. A huge bronze basin called the *laver* was used by the priests for washing their hands and feet each time they were about to enter the tabernacle or offer a sacrifice.

When the Israelites pitched camp, the tabernacle was erected at the center, with the priests' tents around it, and beyond that the many tents of the 12 tribes. In the Bible, we learn that it was set up at Shiloh soon after the Israelites entered Canaan, then it was moved to Nob, and on to Gibeon. Solomon brought it to his temple, but beyond that we have no knowledge of its whereabouts.

The Age of the Kings

During this period, the Israelites developed a deep sense of regal splendor. They liked the idea of having kings rule over them, but they understood that these earthly rulers were a pale reflection of their heavenly king—the Lord God whom they worshiped. It was in this age that God made a new promise to his people that the dynasty of King David would never end. In this assurance lay the hope of a coming Messiah.

When King Solomon built the temple in Jerusalem, worship and religion finally took place in a permanent home.

Solomon's temple

From this point on, Jerusalem became the center of worship (although there were unapproved temples and false altars set up in other places). Solomon's temple was patterned after the tabernacle in its layout. It was a place known for its beauty. The cedar paneling, which lined the stone building, was covered with gold. Although not a large structure by today's standard, the temple was likely the largest building the Israelites had constructed up to that time. A detailed account of how the temple was built and furnished is given in 1Kings 5–7.

After the temple was completed, King Solomon held a grand dedication service. All the religious leaders and the people of Israel were there. Numerous animals were sacrificed, the ark of the Lord was placed in the inner sanctuary, and the cloud of God's glory filled the temple. It was a wonderful moment in Israel's religious history, and King Solomon himself led the worship, his hands spread out to heaven (1Ki 8).

The Prophets

The prophets' job was to keep Israel true to the faith God had given his people. They spoke out fearlessly about false religion, empty rituals, and wrong behavior. This group was called to touch the conscience of Israel when the nation strayed from the Lord: They warned of God's punishing hand, encouraged repentance, and offered God's hope for a bright future.

Jeremiah prophesying.

These messengers of God were appointed by him for a particular task and place, and they were given a particular message. In their ministry they saw visions; they preached sermons; they used parables, drama, and poetry to get God's message across—often to a hostile audience.

From the time of Samuel, the prophets came and went at crisis points in Israel's history. Their tasks were many and varied. It was through Samuel that God appointed Saul—and later David—as Israel's leaders. Through Elijah, God successfully challenged Israel's rampant worship of the Canaanite gods Baal and Asherah, and the work of their pagan prophets in the land of Israel. Through Elijah, and his successor Elisha, many miracles of healing were performed.

The Exile was a crisis point in Israel's history, and many prophets spoke out before, during, and after this period. The wayward Israelites had broken faith with God countless times, and after several warnings and calls to repentance delivered by the prophets, God allowed his beloved Israel to be taken captive.

Who's Who Among the Prophets

The words and actions of some of the prophets were second-hand accounts recorded in the Scriptures by others. Some prophets, however, wrote their own stories. This partial list of biblical prophets includes both writers and nonwriters with a brief description of their ministry.

1. Amos	spoke out against social injustice and unrighteousness	Am 5:24
2. Anna	a prayer warrior who foretold the coming of Jesus, the Messiah	Lk 2:36–38
3. Deborah	predicted the victory of Barak over the Canaanites	Jdg 4:4–9
4. Elijah	opposed Baal worship in the time of Ahab and Jezebel	1Ki 17–2Ki 2
5. Elisha	Elijah's successor who performed many miracles and predicted the salvation of Samaria	2Ki 2–13
6. Enoch	prophesied before the Flood about God's judgment of sin	Jude 14–15
7. Ezekiel	foretold the siege of Jerusalem	Eze 4–5
8. Gad	told David about the kind of judgment that would fall upon him for his sin in taking a census of the people	2Sa 24
9. Hosea	declared God's great, forgiving love for unfaithful Israel	Hos 11:8–9

10. Huldah	predicted the prosperous reign of King Josiah	2Ch 34
11. Isaiah	spoke out against outward worship that was not rooted in right, holy living	Isa 6:5–9
12. Jeremiah	predicted captivity and disaster, but also the promise of restoration for Jerusalem	Jer 13–17; 30–33
13. Joel	offered the hope that if Israel repented there would be a coming day of God's blessing	Joel 2:28, 32
14. Jonah	a rebellious prophet; God gave Jonah a second chance and showed mercy to the people of Nineveh	Jnh 3
15. Nathan	condemned King David for his adultery with Bathsheba	2Sa 12
16. Zechariah	prophesied about the promise of blessing for Jerusalem and the coming Day of the Lord	Zec 8, 14

Lessons Learned During the Exile

Captivity in Babylon was hard for the Israelites. Their city and temple were destroyed, and they were taken thousands of miles away from Jerusalem to a new land. It's no wonder they sat down by the rivers of Babylon and wept when they remembered home (Ps 137).

Even then, God's people used this time of hardship wisely. They rediscovered who they were as the people of God, and they renewed their relationship with him. Many

Israelites saw this period as a time of purification and discipline for the nation.

After 70 years, small groups of Israelites returned home from captivity to rebuild the temple in Jerusalem. Those who returned (probably less than 75,000) were determined to follow the Law in serving God. They returned to strict observance of the Sabbath, to the ritual of circumcision, and to following the Jewish food laws.

Priests Who Made a Difference

1. Melchizedek	a great king-priest who offered bread and wine to the war-weary Abraham	Gen 14
2. Aaron	head of the priesthood and in charge of national worship	Ex 28
3. Eli	the temple priest at Shiloh who raised Samuel	1Sa 1–4
4. Zadok	loyal high priest in David's court who also anointed Solomon king	2Sa 15
5. Jehoiada	high priest who saved Joash from the murderous Queen Athaliah	2Ki 11–12
6. Azariah	high priest who stopped King Uzziah when the arrogant ruler tried to take over the duties of a priest	2Ch 26
7. Hilkiah	high priest who cleared the temple of all traces of Baal worship during the reign of Josiah	2Ki 22–23

8. Jeshua	Judah's first high priest following the Exile	Ezr 2
9. Ezra	outstanding priest, teacher, and scribe during the rebuilding of Jerusalem's walls	Ezr 7
10. Eliashib	high priest who rebuilt the Sheep Gate in Jerusalem during the days of Nehemiah	Ne 3; 13

The Work of Priests

The priests were considered the most "holy" group within Israel. They were the ones in charge of the tabernacle and temple, and only they could offer sacrifices. Priests were originally appointed from Aaron's family (the brother of Moses), and the priesthood continued through his descendants. Within this group, the "high priest" was the only individual allowed to enter the holiest place once a year, on the Day of Atonement. Subordinate to the priests were the Levites, the tribe set apart for religious duties. They had to be supported by the other clans, who gave a tenth of all their harvests and livestock for the work of God.

Most of the work of priests and Levites centered around tabernacle and temple sacrifices and worship. A group from the Levites formed the temple choirs and may have composed some of the Psalms in the Bible. The priests and Levites were also responsible for deciding when to go out to battle in the name of God. But perhaps the most important task of these religious leaders was to teach the people the Law of God. Unfortunately, the prophets often had to scold these messengers of God for failing to teach true knowledge of God.

What the Priests Wore

The high priest wore elaborate and splendid robes of gold, blue, purple, and scarlet. He wore an *ephod* (similar to a waistcoat) with shoulder straps. Each shoulder strap had an onyx stone engraved with the names of six of the tribes of Israel; these were carried before the Lord whenever the high priest entered the tabernacle or temple.

Attached to the ephod shoulder straps by rings and gold chains was a breastplate made of linen in gold, blue, purple, and scarlet. It had four rows of stones, each representing one of the 12 tribes. The breastplate was a double square into which the *Urim* and *Thummim* could be placed. These were sacred stones that the priest used to determine God's will for the people. If the Thummim was picked from the pouch in response to a question, the answer from God was "yes"; if the Urim was selected, the answer was "no."

Under the ephod, the high priest also wore a blue or velvet robe with bells attached to the skirts, which made a wonderful sound as he moved about the house of the Lord. He also had a coat and turban made of fine linen. Affixed to the turban was a plate of pure gold on which was engraved "Holy to the Lord."

Compared to the garb of the high priests, the clothing of the other priests seemed almost ordinary. The main distinctive item was the sash each priest wore, which was decorated according to his rank.

Sacrifices and Their Purpose

The practice of sacrificing offerings to the Lord was an ancient and basic part of Jewish religion and worship. The Book of Leviticus spells out the details and purpose of the sacrifices. Here are five basic facts:

Cain and Abel each made offerings to the Lord.

1. A sacrifice was always made to God alone; he deserved the best that could be offered.
2. Sacrificing was a way given by God for humans to make peace with him.
3. Sacrifices were for everyone.
4. Sacrifices could not take away sin. They were an act of obedience and a mark of repentance. Direct pardon could only come from God.
5. Often, the death of an animal was seen as a substitution for the person who brought the sacrifice. Wrongdoing that deserved death could not be atoned for by sacrifice, but after repenting of sin and obtaining God's forgiveness, the sacrifice was offered as a sign of sorrow for sin.

TYPES OF SACRIFICES

• **Burnt offering:** A whole animal—except for the skin, which went to the priests—in perfect condition was sacrificed. The blood of the animal was sprinkled on the altar to dedicate the sacrifice to God.

- **Grain offering:** This offering of flour, grain, or baked cakes along with oil and frankincense was a goodwill offering to God. Part of it was burnt on the altar, the rest was a contribution to the priests.

- **Offering of well-being:** This offering was similar to a burnt offering, except here only the fat (the best portion as far as the Israelites were concerned) was burnt on the altar. The meat was shared by the family offering the sacrifice. Since God shared in the sacrifice too, it was considered a friendship meal with him.

- **Offering for sin:** When someone sinned against another person or against God, this sin defiled the holy place of the tabernacle or temple, which then had to be cleansed. The blood of the animal was sprinkled about to symbolize that the contamination had been removed by the death that had taken place. Some of the meat was given to the priest. When he ate the meat without incident, the worshiper took this as a sign that God had accepted his act of repentance.

Festivals

Religious festivals played a significant part of Jewish life and were connected to the seasons and the farmer's year. Most of the festivals and holy days existed from Israel's earliest history, but the celebration of Purim and Hanukkah began to be observed much later. After the seventh century B.C., these festivals were held only in Jerusalem. Crowds of pilgrims would descend on the city for these annual events of thanksgiving and reflection. There would be rejoicing, feasting, music, sacrifices, and occasions to honor God for all his blessings.

The Calendar and Festivals

CALENDAR		FARMER'S ALMANAC	FESTIVALS
Month 1	Nisan	Barley harvest	Passover, Unleavened bread, Firstfruits
Month 2	Iyyar	General harvest	
Month 3	Sivan	Vine tending	Weeks, Pentecost
Month 4	Tammuz	First ripe grapes	
Month 5	Ab	Summer fruit	
Month 6	Elul	Olive harvest	
Month 7	Tishri	Ploughing	New Year, Trumpets, Day of Atonement, Tabernacles or Booths
Month 8	Heshvan	Grain planting	
Month 9	Kislev		Dedication or Lights
Month 10	Tebeth	Spring growth	
Month 11	Shebat	Winter figs	
Month 12	Adar	Pulling flax	Purim

- **Passover and Unleavened Bread:** One of the most important Jewish festivals, it served as a reminder of the time God rescued the Israelites from Egypt, and spared the lives of firstborn Jewish children. Celebrated in the Jewish month of Nisan (March/April), celebrations began in the evening when each family sacrificed a lamb and ate unleavened bread at the Passover meal. This remains one of the most important Jewish festivals today (Ex 12).

- **Firstfruits:** Celebrated during Nisan, this ceremony was held on the last day of the Festival of Unleavened Bread. The first sheaf of the barley harvest was given to God (Lev 23:9–14).

- **Weeks:** This festival took place seven weeks (or 50 days) after Passover and it marked the end of the grain harvest. It was celebrated during the month of Sivan (May/June). Later on it became known as Pentecost (from the Greek word "fiftieth"). People celebrated God's gifts at harvest, and the priest offered animal sacrifices and two loaves of bread made from new flour (Lev 23:15–21).

- **Trumpets:** On the first day of Tishri (September/October), the seventh month of the Jewish year, the trumpets sounded for a special celebration. It marked the beginning of the most solemn month of the year and was a day of rest, worship, and offerings. After the Exile, it became a religious festival (known as Rosh Hashanah) to mark the New Year (Nu 29:1–2).

- **Day of Atonement (Yom Kippur):** Also commemorated during the month of Tishri, this marked a national day of mourning for Israel. The nation confessed their sin and asked for God's forgiveness. The priests offered a sacrifice for their own sin, and a second sacrifice for the sin of the people. This was the only time of year when the high priest (dressed in white linen) entered the inner sanctuary, the most holy place of the tabernacle or temple. There he sprinkled blood from the sacrifice. Then, after laying his hand on a live goat (a "scapegoat"), the high priest let it go free in the desert as a sign that the sin of the people had been taken away (Lev 16).

- **Tabernacles or Booths:** This week-long festival, held during the busy month of Tishri, was a popular and joyful celebration marking the end of the fruit crop harvest. Water was poured out and prayers offered for the coming season. Part of the festivities included camping out in gardens and on rooftops in tents or huts made from tree branches as a reminder of the time when Israel lived in tents in the desert (Lev 23:39–43).

- **Dedication or Lights:** Celebrated today as Hanukkah during the month of December (Kislev), this festival honored the cleansing and rededication of the temple by Judas Maccabaeus in 164 B.C. after it had been desecrated by Antiochus IV Epiphanes, the Syrian ruler. During the festival, lamps were placed in houses and synagogues each evening (1Mac 4:52–59).

- **Purim:** This festival—celebrated during Adar (February/March)—traced its roots to the time when Esther and her cousin, Mordecai, saved the Jews from massacre during the reign of the Persian King Xerxes (Ahaseurus). The name of the celebration refers to the lots cast by Haman, the king's hateful chief minister, to decide the day of the bloodbath (Est 9).

Besides annual festivals, Israel regularly had other celebrations, the most important being the Sabbath. This was commemorated every seventh day and was set apart for rest, remembering God's goodness, and serving him (Isa 58:13–14).

The appearance of the new moon marked the beginning of each month, and at this time trumpets were sounded and sacrifices were made. This helped the Israelites remember that God had created an ordered world. On this monthly public holiday there were special meals and religious instruction (Nu 10:10).

Every seventh year was designated as a time of rest for cultivated land. Thus fields lay fallow seven years after they were sown. Anything that grew in the seventh year could be harvested by the poor. This was a reminder to Israel that the land ultimately belonged to God, not to them (Lev 25:1–7).

The year of Jubilee occurred every 50 years. The Law intended this to be a time when land and property were returned to original owners, slaves would go free, debts would be canceled, and the land allowed to lie fallow. The law of Jubilee was a wonderful idea but difficult to enforce. It finally came to be looked on as a time that only God himself could bring about. It was a time promised by the prophet Isaiah and declared by Jesus to have arrived (Isa 61:1–2; Lk 4:16–21).

Fasts

Part of Israel's religion included fasting. Praying and fasting were often done together as a sign of repentance. Fasting means having nothing to eat or drink. Other rituals connected with fasting included tearing clothing, wearing sackcloth and ashes, and remaining unwashed.

However, only one day annually was set apart for a national fast in the Old Testament laws. This was the Day of Atonement. During the Exile, special fasts were held to mourn the destruction of the temple. After this period in Israel's history, two other fasts were held to remember the siege of Jerusalem and the final capture of the city.

Music and Worship

Music was an important part of everyday life among the Israelites and surrounding cultures. Social functions were not complete without music, and it played an important role in festivals, weddings, funerals, and even war. Although Hebrew music tended to be rhythmic rather than melodic, music-making developed to serve the specific needs of the people. For example, the shofar was an ideal instrument for sounding signals or alarms; lighthearted social occasions called for the lilting tones of the pipe; and some psalms were put to set tunes.

Even though God directed the development of Israel's religious and social life, music, like other aspects of its culture, was influenced by surrounding societies. King Solomon married an Egyptian woman whose dowry included 1,000 musical instruments! (It is likely she brought her own musicians to the new culture to play these instruments in the traditional Egyptian manner.)

Those who ministered in the temple took care, however, to avoid using music and instruments associated with pagan worship. The prophet Amos judged those "who sing idle songs to the sound of the harp" (Am 6:5). Even back then, there were definite ideas about music suitable for worship.

Music served as an accompaniment to many religious rituals prescribed by God. There were singers and musicians who took part in temple worship. Only certain instruments were allowed in the temple orchestra, and the singers were males from Levite families.

The Psalms—religious songs—were written to be sung, and many of them carry notes regarding tunes and musical directions. The term *selah*, included in many Psalms, probably marked some kind of musical interlude. Some Psalms were jubilant songs that encouraged worship with the backing of a full orchestra (Ps 16); other Psalms were written for processions to sing to celebrate a victory or pilgrimage (Ps 68:24); still others were probably sung as pilgrims wended their way up to Jerusalem for religious festivals and worship (Ps 120–134).

Beyond temple worship, music was a part of other religious functions, and instruments not allowed in the temple were used at these events, particularly feast days. Music often led the festivities, and music, dancing, and singing were part of the celebration. Women singers and musicians were allowed to take part in these events.

Musical Instruments of the Day

INSTRUMENT	DESCRIPTION

A. Percussion Instruments

1. Bells — Tiny, pure gold bells were fastened to the hem of the high priest's robe. They made a sound when they touched each other.

2. Cymbals — Made of copper, they were the only percussion instrument in the temple orchestra.

3. Rattler-sistrum — A handle was attached to a small U-shaped frame, and small objects were strung on bars stretched across the frame to make a noisemaker.

4. Timbrel — Similar to a tambourine, it was carried and beaten by the hand.

5. Gong — Made of metal, it was used for weddings and other celebrations.

B. Stringed Instruments

1. Harp — Lavishly made, it was used in the temple orchestra.

2. Lute — This three-stringed triangular instrument was usually played by women.

3. Lyre — A small type of this harplike instrument (kinnor) produced a pleasing sound, and was used in secular and sacred settings. Skilled artisans made lyres of silver or ivory and decorated them extravagantly.

4. Trigon — Probably borrowed from the Babylonians, this was not a common instrument in Israel.

INSTRUMENT	DESCRIPTION
C. Wind Instruments	
1. Clarinet	A primitive version of today's clarinet, this instrument was popular at banquets, weddings, and funerals.
2. Flute	A big pipe with a mouthpiece, the biblical flute produced a sound rather like an oboe. Because of its sharp, penetrating sound, this instrument was often used in processions.
3. Pipe	This was used both in the temple for religious celebrations and for social events. (Some Bibles use the terms *organ* and *flute* to refer to the pipe.)
4. Shophar, Shofar	This instrument, best understood as a "ram's horn," was used to give signals and announce special events. (Some Bibles use *trumpet*, *cornet*, and *horn* to translate the Hebrew word shophar.)
5. Trumpet	Bones, shell, or metals were used to make trumpets. These instruments were often used in pairs, and their high, shrill sounds announced battles and ambush, and called people to assemble for various secular and religious events. Similar to the shophar, trumpets were used by the priests.

Religion Between the Testaments— Ten Quick Facts

- Under Persian rule, the temple at Jerusalem was maintained on a lavish scale (Ez 1; 6:1–12).

- During the age of the Greeks, Jewish religion (Judaism) was strongly influenced by Greek culture (Hellenism).

- Two parties arose among Jews with regard to Greek religion: those who embraced the foreign ways (Hellenists), and conservative Jews (Hasidim), who strongly believed that Hellenism and Judaism were mutually exclusive.

- With the support of some leading Jewish families, Antiochus IV Epiphanes transformed Jerusalem into a Greek city. He forbade the practice of Jewish religion and desecrated the temple.

- Judas Maccabaeus built a new altar to replace the one defiled by Antiochus, and the temple was rededicated in 164 B.C. (1Mac 1–4)

- From 165–63 B.C. Judea was an independent state ruled by the Hasmonean priest-kings.

- By the time of Jesus, the Roman conquest had long taken place and Judea was a Roman province.

- At this time, Jewish religious belief turned toward the future. Many hoped for the coming of the warrior Messiah who would rid the Jews of hated foreign rule.

- This was an era when Jews studied and debated ideas about the resurrection, angels, demons, and other apocalyptic themes.

- The Law was studied as never before, and a variety of religious groups came into being.

Jewish Religion in the New Testament

The world to which Jesus came was in the hands of the Romans, and although they encouraged Greek culture, they allowed the Jews to practice their own religion. During this time, the temple in Jerusalem was still at the heart of Israel's worship. Pilgrims trekked there for the great annual festivals, sacrifices were offered there, and it was the center of religious instruction.

Jews agreed on the authority of the Torah (the Law) and the importance of temple sacrifices, yet a number of groups within the nation had different ideas on the way these beliefs should be worked out in everyday life.

Jewish Worship in the Synagogue

The synagogue probably came into being during the Exile when the Jews were without the temple and far away from Jerusalem. By the time of Jesus, the local synagogue was an important place for prayers and Scripture readings on the Sabbath. The synagogue itself was a plain, practical building that served as the local school, the center for local government, as well as a place for worship.

Inside each synagogue was a chest in which the scrolls of the Law were kept. During services, the religious leaders sat in front of the chest facing the people. The men sat in one section, the women in another. The synagogue was regularly attended by Jesus, and it was a popular place during the ministry of the apostle Paul.

Jewish Religion and Everyday Life

The practice of Jewish religion in New Testament times was not very different from the past. Festivals, sacrifices, and fasting were basic components, as were tithing, food laws, and rituals concerning uncleanness. In the home, Jews were expected to pray 18 benedictions each morning, afternoon, and evening; and the father of the household said a blessing before every meal.

After the Exile, some Jews settled in different parts of the Persian Empire. In New Testament times, there were probably more Jews living in Alexandria than Jerusalem. The Jews that moved away from Palestine were known as the Jews of the Dispersion (or Diaspora). Synagogue worship kept their faith alive, but their language was Greek and they used the Septuagint (the Greek translation of the Old Testament) as their Scriptures. They were less strict than their counterparts in Palestine, influenced as they were by the local culture.

Herod's Temple

When the Jews returned to Jerusalem to rebuild Solomon's temple, which had been destroyed earlier, they completed the work in 515 B.C. Although it was in use for 500 years, little is known about this second temple (Zerubbabel's). We do know that it was desecrated by the Syrians, then restored and rededicated under Maccabean rule three years later (an event still remembered at the Jewish festival of Hanukkah).

In 20 B.C., King Herod the Great started to build yet another temple in Jerusalem. He wanted to impress the Roman world and win the hearts of the Jews. Ten years later the main construction was complete, but work continued for many years following. This third temple, although built on the same plan as Solomon's, was the most extravagant ever seen. It was a dazzling, gigantic structure, with special areas for Jews and non-Jews, a court designated for women, and the Court of Israel for Jewish men. Herod's temple was destroyed by the Romans at the time of the Jewish rebellion in A.D. 70, and its treasures were taken back to Rome.

Jewish Sects During the New Testament

The Hasidim

These were faithful followers of the Law who resisted the influence of Greek ideas and culture into the Jewish way of life. Many of them joined the sects of the Essenes and the Pharisees.

The Pharisees

The Pharisee sect grew out of the Hasidim of an earlier time. As well as the Torah, the Pharisees accepted the oral law that had grown up around it and tried hard to live up to a multitude of burdensome rules. They expected others to do the same and were contemptuous of "sinners" who did not abide by their strict codes. The Pharisees (meaning "separated ones") wanted above all else to avoid "uncleanness" so they devoted themselves to keeping each minute detail of every ritual and moral commandment. Besides this preoccupation with the letter of the law, the Pharisees also believed in apocalyptic teaching, angels, and the resurrection.

The Sadducees

Most Sadducees were members of influential priestly families. They had political standing and believed in working along with the ruling power. They accepted only the first five books of the Bible as their Scripture, and would not accept the oral law that was embraced by the Pharisees, or any beliefs that were not taught in the Torah. They did not believe in angels, demons, the resurrection, or apocalyptic predictions of the last days. They did, however, emphasize the sacrifices at the temple and the role of the priests.

The Essenes

This small sect had emerged in the second century B.C. to protest Greek influence on Jewish religion. The Essenes were even stricter than the

Pharisees about keeping the Law. Disillusioned with Jewish society and—in their view—the nation's loose interpretation of the Law, they formed their own monastic communities. There they studied the Torah and made careful copies of it as they waited for the coming of the Messiah. The Jewish settlement at Qumran (near the Dead Sea) was probably an Essene commune.

The Zealots

These nationalists (similar in spirit to the Maccabean revolutionaries) firmly believed that only God was their authority. They refused to pay taxes to the Romans and prepared themselves for the war that would usher in God's kingdom. They led several guerilla revolts against the Roman authorities.

Unfortunately, one of their revolts ended with the Roman destruction of Jerusalem in A.D. 70.

The Scribes

Originally, scribes wrote down the words of others. Then they became copyists and explainers of the Law. By the time of Jesus, they had become official interpreters of the Law and decided how it should be applied to everyday life. The scribes were an influential group of people, many of whom belonged to the Sanhedrin (the supreme Jewish court).

The Herodians

Although they were not officially a religious sect, the Herodians are believed to have been both religiously and politically active during the time of Christ. They were a party of influential Jews who supported the dynasty of Herod (and, therefore, the rule of Rome). The Herodians were united with the Pharisees in their opposition to Christ, and they tried to trick Jesus into making anti-Roman statements.

The Life and Message of Jesus

Jesus made an impact on the Jewish world from the moment he was born (about 5 B.C.). Angels announced the event, a bright star or comet appeared to mark the occasion, and shepherds came to honor him. When Jesus was presented in the temple soon after birth, Simeon, devoutly religious, and Anna, a prophet, were expecting him. They blessed the baby and praised God for the coming of the promised Messiah.

Some time later, wise men from the East hurried to Judea to worship the young king of the Jews. The ailing King Herod was threatened by news of the boy's arrival and decreed that all Jewish male toddlers were to be killed. Joseph and Mary, the parents of Jesus, safely whisked him out of Herod's reach.

After Herod died, the family of Jesus moved to Nazareth, where Jesus grew up. At 12 years of age, Jesus amazed the teachers of the law at the temple. Clearly, he had an understanding of the content and meaning of the Scriptures far beyond his young years. Even then, Jesus knew that he was unique and that God had called him to do special business.

When he was 30, Jesus began his ministry. This period was marked by unique events, just as his birth had been. Jesus was baptized by John the Baptist in the Jordan River, and God opened up the heavens, sent the Holy Spirit down on Jesus like a dove, and blessed his "Son, the Beloved" (Mt 3). Then Jesus spent 40 days of fasting in the wilderness. He was tempted by the devil, but resisted—appealing to the truth of the Scriptures to withstand the attack. The devil left in defeat, and angels came to take care of Jesus. From this point on, the ministry of Jesus began in earnest.

The Teachings of Jesus

- The core of the message of Jesus was that the "kingdom of God" (the rule of God in people's lives) had arrived (Lk 17:21). This message was for everyone for the asking, even the poor and the beggars on the street.

- Jesus told people to repent (turn away from their sins) and believe in the good news that he came to bring (Mk 1:15).

- Jesus taught that he was the way to God. In order to have eternal life, people were to put their trust in him, the Son of God. Jesus even declared that "The Father and I are one" (Jn 10:30).

- Jesus brought joy to religious life (Mt 6:16–18).

- Jesus pronounced blessings ("beatitudes") on the hungry, poor, and just. Those whose lives depend on God are happy and blessed, and the kingdom of God belongs to them.

- Much of Jesus' teaching was given in the form of stories known as parables. These were vignettes about everyday life—each tied to a spiritual truth or principle.

The Parables of Jesus

	MATTHEW	MARK	LUKE
Lamp under the bushel basket	5:14–15	4:21–22	8:16
Houses on rock and sand	7:24–27		6:47–49
Unshrunk cloth on an old cloak	9:16	2:21	5:36
New wine in old wineskins	9:17	2:22	5:37–38
Sower, seeds, and soils	13:3–8	4:3–8	8:5–8
Tiny mustard seed	13:31–32	4:30–32	13:18–19
Weeds	13:24–30		
Yeast (leaven)	13:33		13:20–21
Treasure hidden in a field	13:44		
One pearl of great value	13:45–46		
Net thrown into the sea	13:47–48		
One sheep that went astray	18:12–13		15:4–6
King and his slaves	18:23–24		
Landowner and his laborers	20:1–16		
Man and his two sons		21:28–31	
Landowner and his tenants	21:33–41	12:1–9	20:9–16
Wedding banquet and guests	22:2–14		
Sign of the fig tree	24:32–33	13:28–29	21:29–30
Ten bridesmaids	25:1–13		

	MATTHEW	MARK	LUKE
Talents (or Pounds)	25:14–30		19:12–27
Sheep and goats	25:31–46		
Seed and harvest		4:26–29	
Creditor and debtors			7:41–43
Good Samaritan			10:30–37
Friend in need			11:5–8
Rich fool			12:16–21
Watchful servants			12:35–40
Faithful slave			12:42–48
Fig tree without fruit			13:6–9
Places of honor at the banquet	14:7–14		
Great dinner and the reluctant guests			14:16–24
Estimating the cost			14:28–33
Lost coin			15:8–10
Prodigal son			15:11–32
Dishonest manager			16:1–8
Rich man and Lazarus			16:19–31
Master and slave			17:7–10
Widow and the unjust judge			18:2–5
Pharisee and tax collector			18:10–14

- According to the Gospels, Jesus performed more than 30 miracles, including bringing the dead back to life.

- Jesus selected 12 disciples to learn from him and to carry on his ministry after him (Mt 10).

- Jesus taught his hearers to approach God personally, as a

child approaches his or her earthly Father. This was a revolutionary idea to many people.

- Jesus taught his followers how to pray (Lk 11:1–4).

- Jesus treated women and children with unique dignity and
  respect.

- Jesus regularly attended the local synagogue and went to
  the festivals in Jerusalem.

- Jesus did not bring a new system of laws; he came to fulfill
  the Law, establish a new covenant, and bring the hope of
  salvation (Mt 5:17).

- Jesus was crucified by the Roman authorities (Lk 23).
  Three days later he rose from the dead and made several
  public appearances before his ascension to heaven
  (Lk 24).

- New believers were expected to follow Christ's example:
  meet with other converts, pray, study the Scriptures, and
  speak to others about him.

- The Lord's Supper was instituted by Jesus so that his followers would remember his death when they shared bread
  and wine together (Lk 22:14–20).

Christian Worship in New Testament Times

The early believers were a close-knit company of people
committed to Jesus, the Son of God, whom they deemed
supremely worthy of honor and praise. The new
Christians—as the followers of Christ came to be called in
the Book of Acts (11:26)—drew much from their Jewish
background for their forms of worship. They also created
new practices. They met in the temple for fellowship and
worship, but they also met in the homes of believers for the
same purpose.

It soon became clear to the early Christians that temple
sacrifices were no longer necessary; the death of Jesus was

the final and complete sacrifice for sin. Christians began to break away from temple worship, especially when they came into conflict with practicing Jews. However, for decades many Jewish Christians continued to attend the synagogue, and the apostle Paul often preached and worshiped there—until he was forced out!

Other elements of New Testament worship were unique to the first Christians; some were new interpretations of old rituals. The following are the most significant practices:

- The Jewish Passover ritual is reflected in the Lord's Supper practiced by Christians. At first, this "breaking of bread" was part of an actual meal that took place in homes. Eventually it moved from homes to a special building and was no longer part of a meal.

- The synagogue service, with its prayer, Bible reading, and sermon became the model for early Christian services.

- The Christian rite of baptizing new converts came from a Jewish practice that developed during the time between the Testaments. Non-Jews who became converts to Judaism were baptized in water as a sign of cleansing. John the Baptist baptized many people as a sign of their repentance and inward cleansing by God. Christian baptism was regarded as a symbolic death, burial, and resurrection reflecting the work of Christ on behalf of the believer.

- Prayer was an important part of the life of the early church. Many of these prayers were spontaneous, but they reflected the language and spirit of the Old Testament.

- The New Testament church had a set of beliefs not only expressed in the New Testament writings, but also in their spoken words and songs of worship. Some of their early creeds and statements of faith were short and simple. For example, "Jesus is Lord," and "one Lord, one faith, one baptism." One early statement of faith is a creed in the form of a hymn (1Ti 3:16), and an even more detailed confession of faith is expressed by Paul in his letter to the Philippians (2:6–11).

- New terms and words were introduced into the language of New Testament religion:

Marana tha: These two Aramaic words meaning "Our Lord, come!" were addressed to Jesus, calling him "Lord," the Jewish term reserved for God alone (1Co 16:22).

abba: An intimate term of endearment, this Aramaic word implies "dear father" or "dad." Jesus encouraged his disciples to use this term when addressing God, their heavenly father (Mk 14:36).

Amen: This Hebrew word (meaning "so be it") was used in temple and synagogue services at the end of prayers. It underscored the certainty of the words that were said whether it was a blessing, a request, or an expression of praise (Ro 9:5; 15:33; Gal 1:5; 6:18).

The Young Church

Just before the ascension of Jesus, he gave his disciples some last instructions about the work before them, and he promised to send the Holy Spirit in his place to be their helper. The Book of Acts recounts the story of how the good news spread from Jerusalem to the surrounding lands and on to the capital of the Roman Empire mainly through the work of Peter and a new convert who became the apostle Paul. This period was highlighted by unique events and remarkable teaching:

- Jerusalem was packed with pilgrims for the festival of Pentecost. The dramatic coming of the Holy Spirit was experienced and witnessed by many at this time.

- As the new Christian church grew and flourished, they were persecuted for their teaching and beliefs by the religious authorities, particularly the Sadducees.

- Empowered by God, the apostles performed many miracles.

John and Paul heal a lame man.

- The apostles were called "heralds" because they proclaimed God's message for all to hear.

- The gospel spread to Africa through an Ethiopian official who became a convert after Philip explained the good news about Jesus.

- Cultural and religious prejudice between Jews and Gentiles was a fixed and deep gulf up to this point. Through a pointed and explicit vision from God, Peter was given a clear call to take the gospel to non-Jews. This was a revolutionary step, and it transformed religion and worship in the history of the church.

- Paul's contribution to the Christian church was outstanding. He was the primary apostle to non-Jews, and he traveled hundreds of miles, always breaking new ground with his preaching and teaching. He was imprisoned, beaten, and poorly treated because of his faith. But he always clung joyfully to his hope in Christ. Paul's letters to the early church provided the theological framework for the Christian faith for all believers.

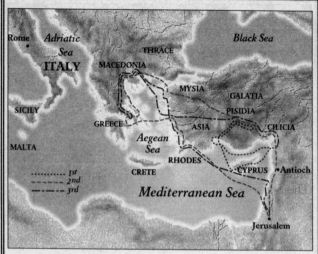

Paul's missionary journeys

The Religious Beliefs of Other Groups in Bible Times

Israel's religious faith was unique compared to the beliefs practiced by surrounding nations. Yahweh, the God of the Hebrews, revealed himself to his people, and he was to be the only God they served. In ancient times, monotheism was an uncomfortable concept, and time and again Israel was attracted to the paganism of the groups around them.

The Religion of Egypt

The Egyptians worshiped many gods at local shrines and in their great temples. They believed in life after death, and every care was taken to prepare for this new life by putting provisions in the tomb where the carefully embalmed body of the dead person was laid. The Pharaoh, Egypt's king, was the intermediary between the gods and the people. Priests played an important role in the religious life, and magic was a significant part of faith and practice.

Baal, Astarte, and the Religion of the Canaanites

According to Canaanite belief, the god Baal controlled the forces of nature, and his wife, Astarte, ruled over love and war. El, the chief of gods, was a shadowy figure at the time of the Israelite conquest of Canaan. The Canaanite gods were notoriously brutal and capricious. They interfered in human affairs only to delight themselves, with no thought of the consequences. In fact, the gods were considered no more or less than reflections of those that worshiped them.

Bronze statuette of Baal

The Canaanites had rich temples for their gods, with priests, choirs, and temple servants. There were altars for sacrifices and altars for incense, and there were pillars in the temples thought to be the homes of gods or spirits.

Even though the Canaanites and Hebrews shared several words for sacrifices, priests, and common expressions for other religious issues, the two systems of belief were extremely dissimilar. Worship of the Canaanite gods was not demanding, without rules of conduct, and without any apparent joy and happiness. On the other hand, the Israelites had strict laws and rituals, and one God who demanded total loyalty. Hebrew worship expressed joy and delight in the one whom they served.

Assyrian and Babylonian Religion

Like other groups in the ancient world, the people of Babylon and Assyria worshiped the great powers of the universe and also had favorite local gods. These deities were in control of everything but they were unpredictable. Anu was the chief god, and Enlil, his son, ruled over the earth's surface. Ishtar, the wife of Anu, was far more prominent in religious life than her husband.

Marduk (Bel) was the patron god of Babylon, and eventually he became the king of all the gods. The national god of Assyria was Ashur, and he came to be identified with Enlil as Assyria increased in power.

Babylonian religion was a mix of demons and evil spirits, divination and omens, and the ghosts of the underworld. Worship centered around the local temple or shrine, and animals and goods were offered as presents to the gods. A priest performed the rites on behalf of the worshiper. In spite of the fact that this religion included many myths about creation, the history of the world, and the role of the gods, Babylonian religion offered minimal information about the future. It was a set of beliefs that offered little hope.

Persian Religion

These beliefs were based on the life of herders, and the gods reflected nature and the world of ideas and speech. Worship rituals included the sacrifice of animals and imbibing intoxicating drinks. The prophet Zoroaster encouraged everyone to worship Ahura-mazda as the supreme deity. Zoroaster's ideas influenced the Persian kings and many other people—even influencing Jewish thought.

The Religion of the Greeks and Romans

The supreme god of Greece was Zeus. He ruled all the other gods, who lived on the mountain Olympus. When the Romans conquered the Greeks, they took over their gods, giving them Roman names. Zeus became the Roman god Jupiter; his wife Hera became the Roman Juno.

Although the ordinary person worshiped many gods, it had little effect on daily life. In the final analysis, belief and behavior were not really important to the Greek or Roman. What was important was good citizenship and loyalty to the state. By the time of Julius Caesar, educated Romans often had little use for the gods. Some, like the Greeks, turned to philosophy or new religions to find deeper meaning in life. Those who wanted a more personal faith turned to the "mystery" religions or foreign cults. One of these, Mithraism, proved to be a serious rival to Christianity.

In their vast empire, the Romans were tolerant of other religions so long as they did not prove to be a threat to the state. Judaism was allowed, and—at first—Christianity was tolerated. As time passed, however, Christians were required to compromise their faith, and they were persecuted when they resisted.

Statue of Artemis from Ephesus

The apostle Paul was constantly challenging the early church to remain true to the gospel they had been taught. The Roman world was filled with so many eclectic religious beliefs and philosophies that it was not difficult to confuse the truth. In fact, at Lystra Paul and Barnabas were

The people prepare to offer sacrifice to Paul and Barnabas at Lystra.

mistaken for Hermes and Zeus (Ac 14:12–13), and in Ephesus a great temple was built in honor of Artemis, an eastern fertility god with a Greek name.

In spite of the various religions and philosophies of the day, Judaism survived, and the spread of Christianity continued throughout the world.

Religion and Worship—Ten Quick Facts

- The temple at Ur (whose ruins are more than 4,000 years old) tells us that religion was important in ancient times.

- Covenants were popular in Moses' day. However, God's covenant was in a class by itself—he promised Israel unequaled benefits and blessings!

- Moses was so angered by the Israelites for worshiping a golden calf (fashioned by Aaron for the people), he ground the idol to powder, mixed it with water, and made the Israelites drink it!

- Shechem and Shiloh were important worship sites for the tribes of Israel. Shrines in these places housed the ark of the covenant at various times during the period of the judges.

- The Philistines—who gave their name Palestine to the whole country of Canaan—worshiped the Canaanite deities of Dagon, Ashtoreth, and Beelzebub.

- The Stoic philosophy in Paul's day emphasized the importance of reason, harmony with nature, and virtue over pleasure.

- Founded by Epicurus, the Epicurean philosophy stressed pleasure as its chief aim.

- The early Christians expected Jesus to return at any time. For them, his second coming would complete the Day of the Lord, prophesied by the prophets, and begun with the first coming of Jesus.

- Gnosticism was a mixture of astrology, reincarnation, and Greek philosophy. Gnostics believed in a spiritual world, which was good, and the material world, which was evil. Gnostic beliefs affected the early church, and Paul spoke out against them in his letters to the Corinthian and Colossian churches.

- In idolatrous Athens, Paul found an altar with the inscription "To an unknown god" (Ac 17:23). Using this as a starting point, the apostle preached a stirring message about the one true God.

THE LAND OF THE BIBLE

IF WE TAKE A CLOSER LOOK at the lands of the Bible, we catch a fresh glimpse of the people who lived there. This has always been a difficult environment, filled with many challenges. It is home to lush farmland, but also barren deserts, sweltering heat, freezing rain, and the Dead Sea. Though it is masked today by modern cities and conveniences, the basic geography and temperament of this area has changed little since the days when Jesus walked the earth. When we get a feel for the hills and valleys, the rivers and lakes, the rainy seasons and the hot dry periods, we begin to understand how these natural elements affected the way people lived their lives.

The promised land of Canaan (Israel) was described as an earthly paradise that "flows with milk and honey" (Nu 13:27).

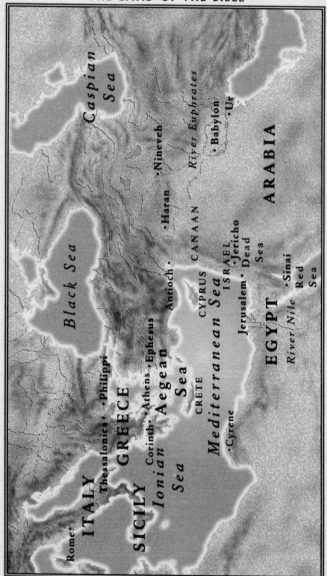

Geography of the Region

Surprisingly, the story of the Bible took place in a relatively small area. Palestine lies in the middle of a region called the *Fertile Crescent*, the name given to a belt of lush lands that includes Egypt (and the River Nile) to the south, and Mesopotamia (with its Tigris and Euphrates river systems) to the east. The Fertile Crescent is sandwiched between the vast arid world of the Arabian desert on one side, and the Mediterranean Sea on the other.

From early times, the people of God lived squarely in this corridor, which was well-traveled because of its strategic location. Back then, Egypt and Mesopotamia were major civilizations, and they developed important trade routes right through the heart of Israel. International routes such as the Transjordanian King's Highway intersected Palestine, making it a crucial point of cultural and trade interchange. Because of its position on the map, Palestine became not only an important crossroads, but a place that powerful nations vied for as they tried to dominate the Near East.

Fertile Crescent

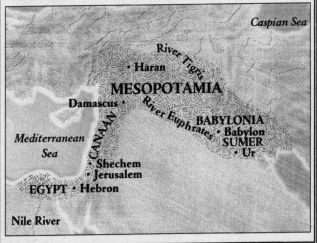

The Coastal Plain

When Israel captured the Promised Land, the coast lands were controlled by the Philistines. This area is made up of stretches of sand dunes in front of forests, lagoons, and swamps. This part of the Mediterranean coast was not particularly desirable during Old Testament times, and there was no major port in this area until King Herod the Great built an artificial harbor at Caesarea just before Jesus was born.

The Shephelah or Piedmont

Between the coastal plain and the central hill country is an area of low foothills (called the *Shephelah*) that used to be covered by sycamore trees. In Old Testament times, there were several skirmishes between the Philistines and the Israelites in this area. Today, much of the Shephelah is under cultivation.

The Central Hill Country

In Bible times, the capitals of the northern and southern kingdoms of Israel were both in this location. These highlands rise to just over 3,280 feet at the highest point, near Hebron. The western slope to the coast is gradual, while the east drops sharply into the Jordan Valley. Most of the region is composed of limestone, and the soil that exists is of poor quality. Cultivation is done on a small scale, and much of the area is used for raising livestock.

Even though this region contains Jerusalem, the only major highway is the one connecting the holy city with Hebron in the south and Nablus (Shechem) in the north. Most of the main roads through Palestine lie to the north of these hills, or run parallel with them along the coast.

The Jordan Valley

The Jordan River originates near Mt. Hermon and flows south into the Sea of Galilee. At the southern tip of the sea,

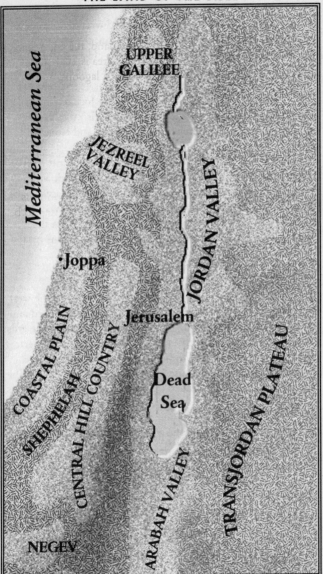

the river enters a deep gorge that is filled with dense vegetation. As the river then winds its way south, the water becomes increasingly salty as it meanders closer to the Dead Sea. This affects the type of crops that are planted along its banks. Wheat is planted in the north, and salt resistant barley is planted in the south. By the time the Jordan River reaches the Dead Sea, the water is so brackish that vegetation along its banks is limited to the poplar and tamarisk trees.

The Jordan Valley is part of a large geological rift or fissure that runs from just above the Sea of Galilee down to Africa. The valley is extremely deep and temperatures in the heart of this area (known as the *Ghor*) are oppressively hot. People are glad to travel as quickly as possible from the mountains on one side of the Ghor to the mountains on the other side.

The Transjordan

The uplands of this area are higher than those to the west and provide good pasture for the vast numbers of sheep and cattle raised on these lands. This is a well-watered fertile area that stands between the dry valley and the Arabian Desert. In Bible times, people living in this region were fairly protected from invaders because it was difficult to move into the Transjordan from the east or the west.

Ten Quick Geography Facts

- Most of the land surface in Palestine is made up of limestone and chalk.

- The water sinks through the limestone rocks to underground streams, where it can be recovered by digging wells.

- There are many limestone caves in this region.

- Wind and water erosion transform desert rocks into fantastic shapes!

- Flash floods can fill a dry valley several feet deep with water in a short span of time.

- The Galilee area of Palestine enjoys the highest annual rainfall and the richest soil in the region.

- Rainfall declines from west to east because the hill country blocks the storms that move in from the Mediterranean.

- An arid area known as the Judean wilderness is so barren that it has been associated with pain, trial, and death.

- The Judean wilderness and the southern Negeb desert have the most severe environments in Palestine.

- Jerusalem is 2,500 feet above sea level. Fifteen miles to the east, however, Jericho is 1,275 feet below sea level!

Rainfall and Climate

The climate of the Mediterranean lands is somewhere between temperate and tropical. Winters are wet and cool; summers are hot and dry. Because coastal areas lie in such close proximity to mountains and deserts, snow will blanket the tops of coastal mountains while fruit trees flourish in the plain.

The lowlands receive less rainfall than the mountain areas, and the latter tend to block rain-bearing winds from flowing inland. Going south, the annual rainfall lessens until arid desert conditions prevail. There can be great variations in annual rainfall from place to place, and the constantly moving desert margin overtakes certain areas from time to time, plunging them into drought and famine. The Bible speaks frequently about these extreme conditions. We read of dry years and famine, flooding rains, and years of plenty.

Famines—a Constant Threat

In Bible times, famines occurred for a number of reasons: lack of seasonal rainfall; destructive hailstorms; crops destroyed by locusts and caterpillars; war; the erosion of the land by the encroaching desert; and judgment by God because of sin.

The Bible records several famines and what people did when food was scarce.

- Famine in Palestine caused Abraham to go to Egypt to find food (Gen 12:10).
- Isaac went down to Gerar because of famine in Palestine (Gen 26:1–3).
- Famine in Palestine caused Jacob's sons to look for food in Egypt (Gen 41:54–57).
- Famine in Palestine caused Naomi to go into Moab (Ruth 1:1).
- God allowed a three-year famine in David's time because of Saul's sins (2Sa 21:1).
- Famine in Elijah's day was caused by the sins of Ahab and Israel (1Ki 17:1).
- There were three famines recorded in Elisha's time (2Ki 4; 6; 8).
- The famine in Jerusalem was caused by Nebuchadnezzar's siege (2Ki 25:2).
- During the famine in Nehemiah's day, the prophet preached a sermon and there was a revival among the people (Ne 5).
- Christians outside of Judea sent help to the believers there because they were suffering from a famine (Ac 11:28).

The Bible and the apocryphal books mention several times the importance of dew in the lives of Bible people. And as we look at the region, we discover that many areas with low rainfall rely on dew to water the land. Most of the areas with heavy dewfall are on the coast. Some areas may have dew as often as 200 nights each year.

There are great contrasts in the temperature range in the Near East. It may be a hot summer's day by the Dead Sea (100 degrees Fahrenheit), but a hundred miles away in Galilee, a cool rain may be falling. Winter can be miserably wet and cold in the highlands, but the lowlands experience some extreme weather as well. Summer weather on the coast and in the mountains average a mild 75 degrees. Temperate winds from the Mediterranean blow onshore to relieve some of the heat. However, there is a searing wind—known as the *hamsin*—that blows in from the south, and its effect can be felt all the way to the coast. Jesus even referred to the hamsin when he mentioned the scorching south wind (Lk 12:55).

Plants

The natural plant life of Bible lands was important to the everyday life of the people. Leaves, bark, stems, and gum from various plants were used to make medicines, oils, and cosmetics. A variety of reeds were useful for making paper and pens. Crops were grown for food and for making cloth. Dyes were extracted from some plants. And other plants were merely enjoyed for their beautiful blossoms! Here is a list of some interesting plants mentioned in the Bible.

PLANT	DESCRIPTION	REFERENCE
1. Aloe	a succulent plant used for cleansing bodies of the dead	Ps 45:8
2. Balm	an evergreen shrub used for medicinal purposes	Eze 27:17
3. Bulrush	a type of reed whose stems were used to make paper	Ex 2:3

PLANT	DESCRIPTION	REFERENCE
4. Cumin	used to flavor meat, and in eye medicine	Mt 23:23
5. Dill (anise)	used to flavor bread or cakes	Mt 23:23
6. Flaxstem	fibers used to make linen, string nets, and lamp wicks	Ex 9:31
7. Hyssop	this bushy plant was used for sprinkling blood and other purification rites in the Old Testament; on the cross, Jesus was given a sponge filled with vinegar on a branch of hyssop	Ex 12:22; Jn 19:29
8. Lilies of the field	may refer to a variety of wild flowers: anemone, crocus, poppy, narcissus, and yellow chrysanthemum	Mt 6:28
9. Mustard	a tiny seed that produces a great plant; Jesus likely referred to the black mustard used for oil as well as flavoring	Mt 13:31–32
10. Myrrh	light-yellow gum from a shrub grown in North Africa; used as a spice, medicine, holy oil, and embalming treatment	Mt 2:11
11. Pomegranate	a wild shrub with a red fruit, used for medicine and food	Ex 28:31–34

PLANT	DESCRIPTION	REFERENCE
12. Reed	a tall plant with purple flowers, used to make pens, paper, and measuring devices	Eze 40:3
13. Rose	the "rose" in the Bible is probably the narcissus or the mountain tulip	Isa 35:1; SS 2:1
14. Rush	used to make chair seats, baskets, and other items	Isa 35:7
15. Tares, thistles, thorns	these destructive weeds abound in the dry areas of Palestine, often choking the growth of young grain plants	Mt 13:24–30; Gen 3:18; Mt 7:16
16. Wormwood and gall	a bitter-tasting plant, wormwood and gall (possibly the juice of the opium poppy) are associated with sorrow and bitterness in the Bible	Dt 29:18; Mt 27:34

Trees

Trees were crucial to the Bible world. They affected climate and soil erosion, and on a practical level, their everyday value was immeasurable. People depended on trees for food, shelter, fuel, and building materials. There are more than 300 references to trees and wood in the Bible, and more than 25 different kinds of trees have been identified as having grown in Palestine. Today, most of the wooded parts of this area have been cut down.

In Bible times, trees that were identified with holy places were allowed to flourish. In some pagan cultures, people believed that their gods inhabited the trees, and sacrifices were often offered under trees. According to the Law, the Hebrews were forbidden to plant a tree near an altar (Dt 16:21). The following list identifies some of the major trees and shrubs of Palestine.

TREE OR SHRUB	DESCRIPTION	REFERENCE
1. Acacia (shittim)	one of the few trees to grow in the Sinai desert, the ark of the covenant was made from this wood	Ex 25:10
2. Almond	a favorite food, the nut also produced oil; Aaron's famous rod, which budded overnight and bore ripe fruit, was from this tree!	Nu 17:8
3. Cedar	the famous cedars of Lebanon are legend; today only a few of these trees remain, high in the mountains; the durable red wood was used to panel Solomon's temple and palace	1Ki 6–7
4. Cypress	this hard, durable red-toned wood is believed to have been used to construct Noah's ark	Gen 6:14

TREE OR SHRUB	DESCRIPTION	REFERENCE
5. Fig	these slow-growing trees bear fruit most of the year; the fig was a popular fruit in Bible times	Jdg 9:10–11
6. Fir and pine	the wood was used for building the temple, ship building, and making musical instruments	Eze 27:5
7. Frankincense	the gum collected from this tree (native to Arabia) was used as incense	Mt 2:11
8. Gourd	a large, fast-growing bush, this castor bean plant may have grown up overnight to shade Jonah from the sun	Jnh 4:6
9. Myrtle	a large, evergreen, sweet-smelling shrub used for wreaths and for making festival booths	Isa 41:19
10. Oak	there are many types of oak trees in Israel, some are evergreen; wood was used for oars and statues; black dye was obtained from the acorn cups of the Valonia oak	2Sa 18:9–10
11. Olive	an evergreen, one tree could supply an entire	Dt 24:20

TREE OR SHRUB	DESCRIPTION	REFERENCE
	family with fats; olive oil was used for cooking, as oil for lamps, and as a skin lotion; it was also used to anoint kings and priests; carvings and decorative work were made from the wood	
12. Palm (date)	a tall tree topped by a crown of huge leaves, the valuable fruit grew in clusters below the leaves; leaves were woven into mats, and the sap was fermented to make liquor or vinegar	Jn 12:13
13. Poplar	this fast-growing tree found in the hills of Palestine provides dense shade; the "willows" of Babylon, where the exiles mourned, were probably a type of poplar	Gen 30:37
14. Sycamore	a type of fig tree, the sycamore is known for its durability; Zacchaeus climbed this type of tree to get a better view of Jesus	Lk 19:4
15. Terebinth	this spreading tree is	Isa 6:13

TREE OR SHRUB	DESCRIPTION	REFERENCE
	common in the warm, dry, hilly places of Israel	
16. Vine	one of the earliest cultivated plants in biblical history, the vine produced one of the most important fruit crops in Israel; after the grapes were harvested, time was set aside for joyous festivities	Dt 8:8
17. Willow	These trees are found in thickets along the streams or rivers from Syria to Palestine	Job 40:22

Animals and Birds

A look at the animals and birds of the Bible lands gives us an idea of the kinds of creatures that thrived in this environment, their place in the natural habitat, and their importance to the lives of the people of the region. The Bible makes reference to a variety of animals, and birds are mentioned in 45 books of the Bible and 19 times in the apocryphal books. The animals and birds listed below are those most often mentioned in the Bible—and the most important ones.

WILD ANIMALS

- **Bear.** The Syrian brown bear lived in the hills and woods of Israel in Bible times. David had to protect his flocks against them, and two she-bears once attacked a group of boys who were ridiculing the prophet Elisha (1Sa 17:34–36).

- **Fox and jackal.** Both of these scavengers damaged crops. Jackals hunted in packs at night, and the fox went after grapes hanging on low vines (Jdg 15:4).

- **Leopard.** The prophets Isaiah and Jeremiah mention this wild animal that was clearly around in Bible times (Isa 11:6; Jer 13:23).

- **Lion.** Mentioned several times in the Bible, lions lived in the thickets of the Jordan Valley and were dangerous to flocks and people (Da 6:16–24).

- **Wolf.** These savage hunters would feed on smaller animals but would sometimes attack and kill deer, sheep, and even cattle (2Esd 5:18).

- **Deer and gazelle.** These wild animals were a major source of meat (Dt 12:15).

- **Badger.** This shy animal lived in colonies in rocky areas (Pr 30:26).

WORKING ANIMALS

- **Camel.** The Arabian camel was valuable to desert nomads, travelers, and merchants. It could live on poor food and go for several days without drinking. The camel could carry a load of about 400 pounds—as well as the rider. These beasts of burden are mentioned in the stories of Abraham, Jacob, and Job (Gen 12:16; 30:43; Job 1:3).

- **Donkey and mule.** These were the most common pack animals in Bible times. Surefooted and dependable, they also provided transportation for rich and poor alike. It was on a donkey that Jesus rode into Jerusalem on Palm Sunday (Mt 21:1–11).

- **Horse.** In Bible times, horses were owned by the rich, and first came to Israel during David's reign. They were primarily used in war (Jos 11:4).

FLOCKS AND HERDS

- **Cattle.** Herds of cattle were kept to provide milk, meat, and leather. Oxen were used to pull the plow, threshing-sledge, wagons, and carts. Cattle were also offered as temple sacrifices. Wealth was reckoned by the number of cattle and sheep a man owned. Bashan, east of Jordan, was known for its cattle (Gen 13:2).

- **Sheep and goat.** From ancient times, these animals were an important part of the lives of Bible people, many of whom depended on them for milk, cheese, meat, and clothing. Goatskins were used to make a variety of coverings—from water bottles to tents. Wool from sheep was used to make cloaks and tunics. Sheep and goats were also used in temple sacrifices. These animals were well suited to the craggy hill pasture areas of Palestine (Gen 27:9; Jn 10:1–12).

BIRDS OF PREY

- **Eagle and vulture.** These large birds were similar to one another. The eagle had a powerful beak, talons, and a wingspread of more than four feet. Mentioned often in the Bible, the eagle was a symbol of swiftness and strength. The vulture, wide ranging in its soaring, would feed on dead animals. Both the eagle and vulture were listed as unclean birds in Leviticus (Lev 11).

- **Owl.** Pictured in the Bible as inhabiting ruined and desolate places, many varieties of owls are known in Israel today (Isa 34:15).

- **Raven.** After the flood, Noah first sent out this black, flesh-eating bird to see if the land was dry (Gen 8:7).

BIRDS FOR FOOD AND SACRIFICE

- **Dove and pigeon.** Common in Israel, these birds were an important food source and were offered for sacrifice by the poor. After the Flood, it was a dove that brought back the first green leaf to Noah (Gen 8:8–12).

- **Partridge.** The eggs and flesh of this bird made a good meal (1Sa 26:20).

- **Quail.** These birds provided the Israelites with meat as they journeyed from Egypt during the time of the Exodus (Ex 16:13).

- **Sparrow.** Often used in reference to any small bird suitable for eating, it refers specifically to the hedge sparrow (Mt 10:29–31).

MIGRATORY BIRDS

- **Crane.** The prophet Jeremiah spoke of this large gray bird that is still a regular visitor to Israel. It feeds on seeds and leaves (Jer 8:7).

- **Peacock.** The peacock was imported to Israel by King Solomon, who used the graceful creatures to decorate his palace (1Ki 10:22).

- **Stork.** Black and white storks pass through Israel every year as they fly north from Arabia and Africa. They feed on small animal life—snakes, fish, mice, worms, and insects (Jer 8:7).

Rivers of Bible Lands

NAME OF RIVER	LOCATION	REFERENCE
Pishon	flows out of Eden around the land of Havilah	Gen 2:11
Gihon	flows out of Eden around the land of Cush	Gen 2:13
Tigris	flows out of Eden and east of Assyria	Gen 2:14
Euphrates	flows out of Eden and through the Taurus mountains	Gen 2:14

NAME OF RIVER	LOCATION	REFERENCE
Nile	Egypt	Gen 15:18
Jabbok	east of the Jordan, about halfway between the Dead Sea and the Sea of Galilee	Gen 32:22–30
Arnon	boundary river between Israel and Moab	Nu 21:13
Kishon	near the town of Megiddo	Jdg 5:21
Ahava	Babylonia	Ez 8:21
Chebar	Babylonia (the land of the Chaldeans)	Eze 1:1
Abana and Pharpar	rivers of Damascus	2Ki 5:12
Jordan	the principal river in Palestine	Jos 3:13–17
Yarmuk	six miles to the southeast of the Sea of Galilee, marked the southern boundary of ancient Bashan	an important river, though there is no biblical reference to the name "Yarmuk"

Water—a Scarce Resource

For us in the western world, fresh water is easily accessible at the turn of a tap. But for the average Israelite in Bible times, dealing with water was a daily struggle. It had to be found, saved, and carried from one place to another for personal use, for their animals, and for their crops. It is no wonder that abundant, clear water was a strong symbol of God's blessing in Bible times. Back then, people were grateful for a shower of rain, a clear brook, or a family well with a ready supply of water.

Constantly menaced by the desert at its door and limited winter rainfall, Israel has always had to conserve water. The Jordan is the only major river in this territory, and it empties into the Dead Sea, where water evaporates at the rate of 60 inches a year. Fortunately, the Jordan flows year round. Many smaller rivers and streams flow in the rainy season, but have dry beds during the rest of the year. How did people in Bible times deal with their water problems?

- **Wells.** Any family that owned a well was fortunate. Water was available right outside the home and it was likely to be cleaner than the water from a stream or storage cistern. From ancient times, ground water (rainfall that had seeped through the limestone rocks and collected underground) was drawn from deep wells—sometimes dug to a depth of 140 feet. However, once it was dug a well lasted for several generations. Besides family wells, there were community wells where villagers or city folk could draw water. There are several interesting Bible stories centered around these natural meeting places for people. Jacob met his future bride Rachel at one. The Samaritan woman had a life-changing conversation with Jesus at a well reportedly dug by the patriarch Jacob.

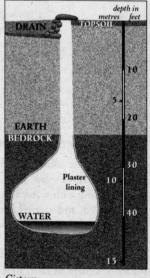

Cistern

- **Cisterns.** These were small reservoirs dug in the ground to collect and store rainwater. Dug to a depth of about 40 feet, they were bulb-shaped with a fairly narrow neck topped by a stone or wood cover. Water drained into the cistern from roofs, courtyards, streets, and—on occasion—open land. Water was drawn from the cistern using a bucket.

Cisterns were first built in the patriarchal period, and archaeologists have uncovered plaster-lined cisterns in Palestine with a capacity of 706 cubic feet. Many homes had their own cisterns, and they were especially popular in areas where there were no streams or rivers.

Famous Wells

LOCATION	DESCRIPTION	REFERENCE
1. Kadesh wilderness	where God spoke to Hagar	Gen 16:14
2. Beersheba	where Abraham made a covenant with Abimilech	Gen 21:30
3. Nahor	where Abraham's servant found Rebekah	Gen 24:11–20
4. Gerar	dug by Isaac	Gen 26:18
5. Haran	where Jacob met Rachel	Gen 29:1–12
6. Midian	where Moses met Zipporah	Ex 2:15–21
7. Bahurim	where two of David's spies hid from Absalom	2Sa 17:18–19
8. Ramah	where Saul looked for David	1Sa 19:18–24
9. Bethlehem	where David longed for a drink	2Sa 23:15
10. Samaria	where Jesus conversed with the Samaritan woman	Jn 4:6–26

- **Tunnels and Channels.** Walled cities in ancient times often had little or no water supply. People there had to bring in water from outside springs. To solve the problem, some remarkable underground channeling systems were developed. Tunnels and shafts were cut through the rocks beneath towns to bring in a good supply of water. During Hezekiah's reign, a tunnel was dug under the walls of Jerusalem to connect the city to a spring outside. The water was fed from the spring to a pool in the city. Over time, Jerusalem developed other systems, underground as well as above ground. Water brought in by tunnels or aqueducts emptied into open pools or large underground cisterns. Under the temple mount in Jerusalem, 37 cisterns have been found, and one huge cavern had a capacity of some two million gallons! The famous aqueduct at Caesarea and the cisterns of Masada are other excellent examples of the engineering ingenuity of people during Bible times. Even in dry or mountainous regions, the Israelites found creative ways to obtain and conserve water.

Minerals

Copper and iron have been found in Israel's rocks (Dt 8:9). Copper was mined from early on, and iron came later. During Bible times, the land's other major resources were building stones, pitch, sand, and clays. A variety of chemical salts were obtained from the Dead Sea area, and today the Dead Sea itself yields potash, bromine, and magnesium. From biblical days on, many materials had to be imported. Israel conducted a busy import/export trade with its neighbors.

Fisheries

Although the Jews never really controlled the Mediterranean coast lands (and were not known to be seafarers), fishing was an important part of their lives. Fish was a natural food resource in Palestine. Most fishing was done on the Sea of Galilee (also known as the Lake of Gennesaret or the Sea of Tiberias). An inland freshwater lake (13 miles long and 8 miles wide), the Sea of Galilee supported the livelihood of many fishermen. It was from among this group that Jesus chose his first disciples.

Fish from the Sea of Galilee was sold fresh or it was dried and kept for eating in the winter. Much of the fish sold in Jerusalem was brought in by non-Jewish merchants from Tyre and other places. Unfortunately, Israel's other large body of water, the Dead Sea, has always been too salty to support life. The prophet Ezekiel had a vision of fisherman spreading out their nets to dry along the shores of the Dead Sea because the catch there was so great (Eze 47:10). This, of course, has yet to happen.

Roads and Highways

Many journeys are recorded in the Bible. We read about Abraham moving from Ur to Canaan, the Israelites wandering through the desert, and the Queen of Sheba leaving Africa to visit King Solomon. Jesus traveled around quite a bit, and Paul's journeys took him over land and sea.

Road and trade routes crisscrossed Palestine and extended north and south. There were few paved roads until the Romans came along and built a fine system connecting the provinces they controlled to Rome itself. Here is a list of some significant roads mentioned in the Bible:

1. *The highway leading through Edom.* This was blocked by the Edomites, forcing the Israelites to find another route (Nu 20:19).
2. *The highway from Bethel to Shechem.* Travelers from Bethel or Shechem went along this road to get to Shiloh to celebrate the yearly festival of the Lord (Jdg 21:19).
3. *The Jerusalem to Jericho road.* The story of the good Samaritan took place along this road (Lk 10:30).
4. *The Bethpage to Jerusalem road.* Here Jesus mounted a young donkey and rode into Jerusalem on Palm Sunday (Mt 21:1–9).

5. *The Jerusalem to Emmaus road.* After his resurrection, Christ appeared to two of his followers as they were walking along this road (Lk 24:13).
6. *The Jerusalem to Damascus road.* Paul was converted to Christianity along this road (Ac 9:3).

A Look at the Land—
Then and Now

During the time of Jesus, Jews considered Jerusalem to be the most important place in Palestine. The pulse of the country lay in Judea and Galilee, west of the Jordan, and on either side of Samaria. Jews avoided going through Samaria as much as possible, and would cross the Jordan twice just to avoid the Samaritans.

Most of the Jewish towns were in the hill country where cultivation was done on terraces and in small fields, and where livestock was raised. The northern end of this region looked down on the Plain of Esdraelon, a strategic place in the ancient world. The north-south route known as the Via Maris (the way of the sea) cut through the plain on the way from Egypt to Damascus and Mesopotamia. Because of its important location, the plain has been the scene of many battles from Bible times right up to the 20th century.

Beyond the Plain of Esdraelon, the upland ranges begin again, gradually rising to the mountains of Lebanon. These hilly ranges form the region of Galilee, a busy area with many trade routes. People from other cultures and places were constantly coming and going through this area, and it was marked by great diversity. This was also an area where people lived well off the fertile farmlands and the Galilee fisheries. It was in this region that Jesus spent his boyhood years.

However, it must be noted that over the centuries some natural features have changed in the Mediterranean. When Israel entered the Promised Land, much of the higher elevations were wooded. Today, the forest landscape has almost gone. Trees were used for building and firewood, they were destroyed in times of war, and animals were allowed to destructively graze in forested areas. Consequently, woods were gradually replaced by a thorny scrub known as *maquis*, which is common throughout the Mediterranean lands.

During the last 50 years, some reforestation has taken place, and other landscape changes are in progress. Marshy areas have been drained and cultivated, groves of fruit trees have been planted in former woodlands, and some desert soils have been cultivated.

This is the land of the Bible—a small place on the earth's surface with some attractive features and many natural challenges. In spite of lush fertile areas, Palestine is primarily known as a barren, eroded, and hilly country with limited natural resources. It is a narrow band squeezed between the desert and the sea. Temperatures can be oppressively hot or freezing cold, rainfall is often unpredictable (and in some places almost nonexistent), and to top it all off, Palestine is part of one of the world's main earthquake zones!

Yet in spite of all this, the land of Israel has been one of the most desirable countries in the world. It is the vital land bridge to three continents: Europe, Asia, and Africa. This busy corridor (which narrows to as little as 40 miles) has been fought for time and again—from the days of the ancients until now.

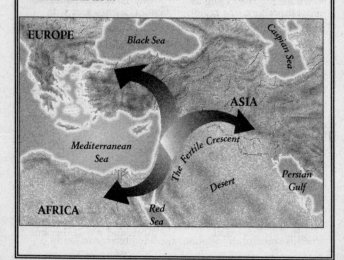

Bible Geography—15 Fascinating Facts

1. Salty and Deadly

The Dead Sea—the lowest point on the face of the earth—is the saltiest body of water in the world. The water is so dense you can't sink. This makes it the world's largest natural flotation device!

2. New Roads from Old

Until the Romans came along, roads and paths in biblical times were dirt tracks, which became impossibly muddy during rainy seasons. The pathways of these dirt roads would keep changing as caravans searched for smoother ground to cross.

3. Is It a Mirage?

Oases were wonderful places of relief set in the heart and heat of the desert regions. The Israelites stayed at the oasis of Kadesh-barnea in the northern Sinai desert. En-gedi, in the Judean wilderness near the Dead Sea, is famous for its spring and waterfall.

4. Down to Jericho

Did the Good Samaritan really go down from Jerusalem to Jericho? Actually, he went east and down. Jericho is 3,300 feet lower than Jerusalem—an amazing drop for a journey of only 15 miles!

5. Jerusalem: An Out-of-the-Way Place

Jerusalem was difficult to get to. It was not located on either of the great trade routes (The Way of the Sea or The King's Highway). So even though tiny Israel was squeezed between powerful empires—and armies frequently marched through it on their missions of conquest—Jerusalem remained fairly secure as Israel's capital.

6. Hell on Earth

The Hinnon Valley in Jerusalem was a place where residents burned their rubbish. As a result, it gained a reputation as a place of fiery abominations and it even became symbolic of hell. Its Hebrew name—ge'hin-nom—formed the basis for the New Testament word gehenna, which means "hell."

7. Egypt's Highway

The River Nile has always been the great highway of Egypt. It flows through the desert, with a fertile margin of cultivatable land on either bank.

8. Water From Below

The Jebusites who lived in Jerusalem before King David were responsible for an ingenious tunnel system that brought fresh water into their city from a hidden spring in the valley below. They tunneled straight down through the hill above the spring and tapped into an underground stream. They would lower buckets and fill them from this stream and not have to venture outside the walls of the city.

9. Where Did Jesus Die?

Jesus died at a place ominously called Golgotha, which is Aramaic for "skull." Its exact location is widely disputed. Many scholars believe that the present-day Church of the Holy Sepulcher marks the true site of Golgotha.

10. Where Was Jesus Buried?

The rock-cut Garden Tomb near Gordon's Calvary is thought by some to be the site of Jesus' burial, but it is possible the tomb is somewhere under the present-day Church of the Holy Sepulcher in Jerusalem.

11. Jericho—the World's Oldest City

A fine spring waters Jericho, which was first occupied in 9000 B.C. It was an oasis in the Jordan Valley and was called the "City of the Palms" in the Bible. The Israelites captured it under Joshua in the famous incident when its walls collapsed. It lay as a sparsely inhabited ruin for more than 1,000 years, until it was rebuilt by King Herod.

12. Where Was Tarshish?

The Book of Jonah tells us that Jonah took a ship going to Tarshish rather than to Nineveh, as God had commanded him. Tarshish was either part of the island of Sardinia (off the coast of Italy) or a region in far-off Spain. Jonah wanted to get as far away from Nineveh as possible!

13. Cavernous Caves

Caves are abundant in Palestine. Most caves were formed by the action of underground water. After the water table receded, the dry caves became useful as dwelling places (Gen 19:30), hiding places (1Sa 22:1), burial places (Gen 23), and storage.

14. How Fast Can a Camel Go?

People walking on foot could travel about 15 miles a day in Bible times. Donkey caravans could travel about 20 miles a day. Fully loaded camel caravans could cover 18 to 20 miles a day. But someone riding a fast camel could travel much farther—up to 70 miles a day!

15. Masada

One of the most spectacular sites in the Holy Land, the fortress of Masada sits on the flat top of a high rock bluff above the wilderness floor near the Dead Sea. The city began as a fortified Jewish community in the second century B.C. The Romans captured it in A.D. 6. Then, in A.D. 66, the Jews revolted and reclaimed it.

IDEAS AND BELIEFS OF THE BIBLE

THE BIBLE IS MUCH MORE than a colorful information book about people, places, and events of long ago. Beyond a collection of fascinating facts, interesting stories, and compelling literature, the Bible is a record of God's word to humanity. It is God's written instruction to those he has called to follow him. What does the Bible really tell us about heaven and hell? What is the true meaning of redemption or salvation? In this section, we will look at some of the key teachings and themes in both the Old and New Testaments.

The Bible teaches that Jesus died on the cross to bring the world salvation from sin.

Angels

These influential messengers of God are supernatural beings who surround God's throne in heaven. Their work in heaven is to worship God. On earth they are God's couriers, bringing his word and assistance to people. Gabriel and Michael are two important angels named in the Bible, and it was Gabriel who announced the birth of Jesus. The Old Testament term "the angel of the Lord" was used as a way of describing how God sometimes came to people in human form (Ps 103:20–21; Mt 1:20; Lk 1:26–38).

Angels—20 Quick Facts

1. They are created by God (Eph 3:9).
2. They report directly to God (Job 1:6).
3. They are named 273 times in 34 of the books of the Bible.
4. They were present at the Creation (Job 38).
5. They announced the birth of Jesus to the shepherds (Lk 2:9–14).
6. They were created to live forever (Rev 4:8).
7. Their heavenly work is to worship and glorify God (Rev 4:8).
8. Their earthly work is to help God's people (Heb 1:14).
9. They are spirit beings, not human beings (Heb 1:14).
10. They are numberless (Dt 33:2).
11. They possess free will (Jude 6).
12. They express joy (Job 38:7).
13. They express longing (1Pe 1:12).
14. They are mighty (Ps 103:20).
15. They are wise (Da 9:21).
16. They move swiftly (Rev 14:6).
17. Some are cherubim—an order of angels (Eze 10:20).
18. Some are seraphim—six-winged angels (Isa 6:1–8).
19. They do not know everything (Mt 24:36).
20. They will join all Christians in the heavenly Jerusalem (Heb 12:22–23).

Apostles

Jesus chose 12 apostles to be his special followers—to preach, to heal, and to carry on his work after he left earth. These "sent ones" were a select group who had been with Jesus from the beginning. They had also seen Jesus after he rose from the dead, and they watched him ascend into heaven. Before he left, Jesus told the apostles to take his message to all nations, and he promised to be with them always.

Before the death of Jesus, Judas Iscariot fell away from this group. Before Pentecost, Matthias became an apostle. After the death of Stephen, the evangelist Paul became known as an emissary of Jesus. Paul's dramatic conversion on the Damascus road transformed him into a great missionary witness for Jesus Christ (Lk 6:12–16; Ac 9).

Ascension

After Jesus rose from the dead, he spent a number of days with his disciples. Gathering at Mt. Olivet with his faithful followers, Jesus gave them his final message, and

then he was carried up into heaven. After Jesus left, heavenly messengers assured the disciples that Jesus would come back one day in the same way that he had left.

Even though the ascension marked the end of Jesus' ministry on earth, it was certainly not the end of his work. He left to be with God his father, and to share the glory of heaven. From there, he now reigns over the entire universe, represents his followers before God, and sends the Holy Spirit to be their helper (Ac 1:6–11; Heb 1:1–4; 4:14–16).

Baptism

In New Testament times, baptism meant more than ceremonial cleansing. It marked a real change of heart, it was a public declaration of faith, and it was a symbolic picture of a complete break with sin and the start of a new life in Jesus Christ (Ro 6:3–11).

Significant Signs

Just as baptism is a sign of repentance, the Bible mentions other important events or symbols that have special significance.

SIGN	MEANING
1. Rainbow	God will never send another flood to destroy everyone (Gen 9:13–17)
2. Ten plagues in Egypt	a demonstration of the power of God for both the Egyptians and the Israelites to see (Ex 10:2)
3. Unleavened bread	a sign of the deliverance of Israel from the bondage of Egypt (Ex 13:7–9)
4. Sabbath	a holy day set apart to honor the Lord and to rest (Ex 31:13)
5. Twelve stones	a reminder of God's power in parting the Jordan so that Israel and the ark of the covenant could cross over (Jos 4:1–7)
6. Manna in the ark of the covenant	a reminder of God's provision of food to his followers in the desert (Ex 16:32)
7. Purim	a feast to remember the salvation of the Jews from the wicked Haman (Est 9:28)
8. Virgin birth	a sign of the incarnation (Isa 7:14)
9. Lord's Supper	a remembrance of the broken body and shed blood of Christ (Lk 22:19)
10. Speaking in tongues	a sign of God's power to unbelievers (1Co 14:22)

Body

The apostle Paul uses the idea of the human body as a rather unique picture of the church. He depicts Christians as different parts of the body with specific functions and roles, all working together and relying on one another in order to operate well as the church.

In the New Testament, the Christian is told to take care of his or her physical body. Scripture teaches that the body is the dwelling place of the Holy Spirit, and it is to be used for God's glory (Ro 12:1–2; 1Co 12:12–30).

Church

In the New Testament, the word "church" always refers to a community of believers—never to a building. In fact, for several generations the first Christians did not have specific buildings for worship. They met in homes and other places. Paul taught that Christ was the head of the church, and that the gatherings of Christians everywhere were part of his body. In these early church communities, there were few official leaders. Some gatherings were guided by elders or bishops, but it was normal for everyone to share his or her gift and to take part in service and worship (Mt 16:18; Eph 4:11–16; 1Co 12:12–28).

Early Christians in Rome listen to a reading of the epistle of Paul.

A Secret Password

The drawing of a fish was an important sign to the first Christians. It was written as graffiti and used as a secret password when Christians were being persecuted by the Romans. The fish symbol stood for five words of special importance to the early believers:

I	X	Θ	Y	Σ
Jesus	Christ	God's	Son	Savior

The first letter in each of these words formed an acrostic of the Greek word for fish, *ichthus*. Thus, whenever a Christian saw the sign of a fish, it was an instant reminder of who Jesus was, and of the need to tell others about him.

Besides a quickly etched mark, drawings and paintings by Christians back then might include beautiful renderings of the fish symbol. Often the markings on a grave included a fish to suggest that the dead person was a Christian. Today, some Christians wear a pin of a fish on their clothing, or some place a plaque in a church or home with a fish on it. There are even bumper stickers on cars that bear the fish symbol.

Covenant

Although there are several covenants, treaties, and agreements mentioned in the Bible, there are two major biblical covenants that the Bible itself is arranged around: the Old and the New. In the Old Testament, God made a covenant with Moses when the Ten Commandments were given to God's people to live by. In the New Testament, the "new" covenant is based on the death of Jesus—the final sacrifice for sin. The letter to the Hebrews compares both these covenants and points out that the new covenant offers many things unavailable under the covenant of Moses, including freedom from sin (Ex 19:3–6; 20:1–17; Heb 10).

Creation

The Bible says that God created everything. He made a perfect, good world that included plants, animals, sunshine, water, and people. In this delightful environment the first humans enjoyed a close relationship with each other and with God. However, this perfection was spoiled by sin when Adam and Eve chose to disobey God. From that point on, the perfection of creation vanished. The Bible teaches, however, that one day in the future all things will be made new, and the believer (who is called a "new creation") will share in the fullness of that new order (Gen 1–3; Ro 8:18–23; Rev 21–22).

Cross

Jesus was executed on a criminal's cross because of false charges brought against him. However, he was called to this sinless death by God himself to pay for the sins of the world. In Jesus' death on the cross, we see the profound nature of God's love for humanity. As a result of Jesus' perfect and complete sacrifice, people can be reconciled both to God and to each other. In the cross, we see all the powers of evil defeated by God. Thus the cross has become the universal symbol of the Christian faith (Mt 27; Ro 5:6–11).

Faith

The key to living the Christian life is to have faith in God. This means to put thoughtful trust and confidence in a God who can be counted on. The Christian faith is not a religion of self-effort, good deeds, and keeping the Law. Rather, it is a life of reliance on Jesus Christ and the Holy Spirit to give the help needed to live in a way that pleases God (1Jn 5:1–5; Gal 2–6).

The Fall

The Bible traces sin back to the dawn of history. When Adam and Eve disobeyed God, the "Fall" began. Instead of open fellowship with God, the pair were banished from the beauty and ease of the garden to a life of backbreaking hardship. Since the fall of Adam and Eve, all of creation has joined in their rebellion against God. Sin and death has spread throughout humanity, so that every part of the world is tainted by the Fall (Gen 1–3; Ro 1:18–32).

Forgiveness

God loves human beings and delights in forgiving them. The Bible clearly teaches that when people repent and turn away from wrongdoing, God quickly blots away their sin. In turn, Christians should excuse others because they themselves have been pardoned by God. And although there may be times when believers fall into sin, they can turn to God for forgiveness and restoration (Eph 4:32; 1Jn 1:9).

Gospel

The word "gospel" means "good news." The Bible teaches that people do not need to be cut off from God because of their sin. Jesus Christ can bring forgiveness and new life—that is the Bible's good news (Mk 1:1; Jn 3:16).

Grace

God is good to us because he loves us, and for no other reason. This, in essence, is the "grace" of God. In the Old Testament, God demonstrated his goodness to Israel countless times. In the New Testament, the grace of God is evident in the coming of Jesus.

Through the work of Jesus, God freely gives salvation to undeserving humans, and extends his grace into the believer's life from beginning to end. The apostle Paul often started or finished his letters to Christians with a prayer for God's grace (Dt 7:6–9; Eph 2:8–9).

Jesus gives sight to a blind man.

Healing

Many miraculous healings are recorded throughout the Scriptures, but they take on particular theological significance in the New Testament. When Jesus came, he announced a whole new order in which sin, sickness, and death would be overpowered. Although not completed yet, the new order began with Jesus' resurrection and looks forward to being completed in the future.

While on earth, Jesus demonstrated not only the power to forgive sins but to heal sickness, disease, and disability. Since then, the healing work of Jesus has been carried on by some of his disciples. However, the final removal of all illness will not happen until the kingdom of God is fully established—only then will all tears, pain, and death cease (Nu 21:4–9; Mt 8:5–13; Jas 5:14–16; Rev 21:1–5).

The Healing Miracles of Jesus

	MATTHEW	MARK	LUKE	JOHN
Leper	8:2–3	1:40–42	5:12–13	
Centurion's servant	8:5–13		7:1–10	
Peter's mother-in-law	8:14–15	1:30–31	4:38–39	
Two demoniacs	8:28–34	5:1–15	8:27–35	
Woman with hemorrhages	9:20–22	5:25–29	8:43–48	
Two blind men	9:27–31			
Demoniac who was mute	9:32–33			
Man with a withered hand	12:10–13	3:1–5	6:6–10	
Demoniac who was blind and mute	12:22			
Canaanite woman's daughter	15:21–28	7:24–30		
Boy with epilepsy	17:14–18	9:17–29	9:38–43	

	MATTHEW	MARK	LUKE	JOHN
Two blind men	20:29–34	10:46–52	18:35–43	
Deaf man with a speech impediment		7:31–37		
Man with an unclean spirit		1:23–26	4:33–35	
Blind man at Bethsaida		8:22–26		
Woman bent double			13:11–13	
Man with dropsy			14:1–4	
Ten lepers			17:11–19	
Slave's ear			22:50–51	
Official's son			4:46–54	
Sick man at Beth-zatha				5:1–9
Man born blind				9:1–7

Heaven

Where is heaven? Although the Hebrews used this word to refer to the sky, and the biblical phrase "heaven and earth" implies the whole universe, we do not really know where heaven is located. The Bible, however, clearly teaches that heaven is the home of God, Jesus Christ, and the angels. It is also the future home of all believers—the place where they will worship God forever.

What is heaven like? Not only will it be "home" for all God's people, but it will be a place to rest and share in God's work. In heaven, all Christians across the centuries will be safe, happy, and perfect in God's presence. There will be unending joy and life in this new land of perpetual day (Ne 9:6; 1Pe 1:3–5; Rev 4; 21–22).

The Celestial Home

The Bible gives us some broad clues about what to expect when we get to heaven. Here are 10 facts that help fill in the picture of the celestial home:

1. Heaven is joyful. The Bible tells us to expect joy and pleasure in God's presence (Ps 16:11).

2. Heaven is healthy. In the new order, there will be no place for pain, sorrow, or death (Rev 21:4).

3. Heaven is musical. What type of music will be in heaven? The Bible mentions harps and choirs of angels (Rev 5:8–9).

4. Heaven is busy. The Bible does not say that we will recline on clouds and play heavenly harps all eternal day long. Our work in heaven will be to serve Jesus Christ (Rev 22:3).

5. Heaven is diverse. The worldwide community of Christians, from all periods of history and all cultures will join together in heaven to worship God in perfect unity (Php 2:10–11; 1Th 4:17).

6. Heaven has other names. It is called the holy city and the new Jerusalem (Rev 21:2).

7. Heaven is beautiful. It is described as having the glory of God, the radiance of a rare jewel, and appearing clear as glass (Rev 21:12, 18).

8. Heaven is being made ready. Jesus told his followers that he was going away to prepare a place for them, but that he would return for them one day and take them to be with him (Jn 14:3).

9. Heaven is for believers. Jesus told Nicodemus that no one can be part of the kingdom of God without being born again by the Spirit of God (Jn 3).

10. Heaven is a city. In several instances the Bible refers to heaven as a glorious city being prepared for the "bride" of Christ, the church (Rev 21).

Hell

The Bible teaches that hell is the place of eternal punishment for those who live in disobedience to God. It is described in the Scriptures in horrifying terms: the hell of fire (Mt. 18:8–9); unquenchable fire (Mt 3:12); the lake of fire and sulfur—and a place of perpetual torment (Rev 20:10–15). Clearly, this vivid imagery implies that hell is a place of constant misery. It is reserved for Satan, his angels, and all those who reject God.

In some instances, the word "hell" has been used with another meaning to describe the Hebrew word *Sheol* ("Hades" in Greek). In this instance, "hell" means the place of the dead, not the place of eternal punishment. There is some mention of Hades in the Bible, and several more references in the apocryphal books (Ac 2:27; Tob 4:19; Sir 51:6).

Judgment

God is the supreme ruler and judge of the universe. At the last judgment, everyone will be judged according to the knowledge they have about God. Those who do not know the Law, or the good news about Jesus, will be judged by what they know of God from creation, and how they have followed their own conscience. Believers will be judged on the basis of their relationship to Jesus. At this final sorting out of good from evil, the Judge of all the earth will act fairly and mercifully. The actual task of judging will be given to Jesus Christ himself (Ps 96:10; Ac 10:42; Heb 12:22–27; Rev 20:12–15).

Justification

Because sin cuts us off from a holy God, there is nothing we can do to measure up to his standards. Only God's action on our behalf can "justify" us in his eyes. God accepts us into his family because of the work of Christ on the cross. Christ took our punishment for sin on himself so that we could be acquitted and made righteous before God. The believer is therefore justified by God's grace, and accepts this position in Jesus Christ through faith (2Co 5:21; Ro 3).

Kingdom of God

In his preaching and teaching, Jesus declared that the kingdom of God had arrived. He used parable stories to explain the meaning of this concept. The Jews thought that deliverance from the Romans would usher in the kingdom. However, Jesus taught that the life of the kingdom started from small beginnings that would then grow and spread throughout the world.

The kingdom of God is an action where God rules: It was demonstrated in the life and work of Jesus; It is alive in the hearts of repentant sinners; It shows up in the life and actions of the obedient believer. The kingdom will be completed in the future, at the time of the new heaven and the new earth (Mt 5:1–20).

The Law

The Law (Torah) was given by God to help his people know how to live. This body of law presented in the first five books of the Bible included the Ten Commandments and religious, social, and dietary rules. These guidelines were basic to right living back then, and they are still a type of moral imperative for all humanity.

However, the coming of Jesus marked the fulfillment of the Law. Since it was impossible to keep the Law perfectly and atone for sin, a perfect one-time sacrifice was necessary to bring freedom from bondage to the old system. Jesus came to be that sacrifice. He fulfilled the deepest meaning of the Law. The New Testament teaches that salvation does not come by obedience to the Law; it comes through Christ and the pardon he offers for sin (Ex 20–34; Ro 8:3–4; Heb 7:18–19).

Rules and Commandments—Ten Quick Facts

- The Ten Commandments are listed twice—first in Exodus 20, and then in Deuteronomy 5. They are also referred to as "the ten words" (Ex 34:28; Dt 4:13; 10:4).

- The Jewish rabbis counted 613 separate commandments in the Law of Moses.

- Jesus summarized the entire Law of Moses by saying that "You shall love the Lord your God with all your heart, and with all your soul, and with all your mind...And ...You shall love your neighbor as yourself" (Mt 22:37–40).

- The Book of Leviticus contains instructions for the Levites—the order of priests for whom the book is named.

- In the Law of Moses, 365 commandments are stated negatively.

- In the Book of Numbers, the Israelites are counted and given instructions before entering the promised land of Canaan.

- In the Law of Moses, 248 commands are stated positively.

- Deuteronomy means "second law," and this book repeats and adds to many of the laws found in Exodus, Leviticus, and Numbers.

- It was said that 611 of the 613 commandments were given through Moses. Interestingly enough, the number 611 is the numerical value of the word *Torah*, which means "law," "commandment," or "instruction."

- The great Jewish rabbi Hillel was asked by a skeptic to teach him the entire Torah while standing on one leg. Hillel's response was, "What is hateful to yourself do not do to another. This is the whole Torah; go and study it; the rest is commentary."

Life

From the time that God created the world and infused the first person with the breath of life, the whole of creation has been dependent on God for life itself. Not only life, but death for every living thing is in the hands of the creator and sustainer of the universe. The Bible also speaks about "eternal life" as a free and lasting gift to anyone who becomes a Christian (Gen 2:7; Jn 1:1–18; 10:10, 28).

Love

The character of God is love. Several Old Testament writers emphasize God's tender love and care for the people of Israel. The New Testament stresses the self-giving love of Jesus as the kind of love that joins God the Father with his son, Jesus Christ. It is this same love that God has for humanity, and it can only become part of the believer's life through the gift of God. This God-given love is the mark of God's presence in the life of every Christian. Believers who unselfishly love each other show the world that they are true disciples of Christ (Hos 11:1–4; Jn 3:16; 1Co 13).

Mercy

Even though the Israelites often broke their side of the covenant-agreement with God, he showed great mercy to his people. Instead of abandoning them, he offered them his patient love and ready forgiveness—his mercy in action. It is because of God's mercy that he offers salvation through Jesus Christ to those who are lost and without hope (Ps 23:6; Ro 9:15; Eph 2:4).

Miracles

Many people witnessed the extraordinary miracles that Jesus performed. Among his many feats, he healed the sick, turned water into wine, calmed a storm, and brought the dead back to life. These mighty works were done by the power of God. Jesus did miracles to show his compassion,

The miracle of loaves and fishes.

and to demonstrate that the age of the kingdom of God had dawned. These "wonders"—as they were called—were signs that Jesus was the Messiah.

The disciples were also empowered by Jesus to do miraculous works, and these remained part of the experience of the early church. These signs and wonders were always done in the name and authority of God (Mt 8:2–3; 8:23–27; 9:18–19; Ac 3:6–10).

Old Testament "Wonders"

There are many unusual events and dramatic signs recorded in the Old Testament that make the New Testament miracles seem almost tame by comparison. We read of Lot's wife turning into a pillar of salt (Gen 19:24–28), Balaam's speaking donkey (Nu 22:20–35), and Elijah dashing off to heaven in a fiery chariot (2Ki 2:9–11). Here is a list of some of the more startling marvels:

1. Moses at the blazing bush that did not burn (Ex 3:1–14)
2. Moses' leprous hand (Ex 4:6–12)
3. The ten plagues (Ex 4; 8–12)
4. The Red Sea parting (Ex 14:21–31)
5. Aaron's budding rod (Nu 17)
6. The collapse of Jericho's walls (Jos 6)
7. Samson's destruction of Dagon's temple (Jdg 16:23–31)
8. The unfailing jar of meal and jug of oil (1Ki 17:13–16)
9. Elijah's triumph over the priests of Baal (1Ki 18)
10. Healing of the poisonous stew (2Ki 4:38–41)
11. The floating ax head (2Ki 6:1–7)
12. A dead man revived through Elisha's bones (2Ki 13:21)
13. Shadrach, Meshach, Abednego, and the fiery furnace (Da 3)
14. The mysterious handwriting on the wall (Da 5:5, 25)
15. Daniel in the lion's den (Da 6)

Parables

Jesus often taught in parables: These were stories about everyday life that were tied to spiritual truths (Mt 5:14–15; Mk 2:22; Lk 13:18–19).

Peace

The Hebrew word for "peace" has several shades of meaning. It implies safety, harmony, personal good health and long life, and unity in the community. The Bible is clear that God is the author of the precious gift of peace. And perfect peace will characterize the new age when God will finally establish the fullness of his kingdom.

The Messiah is described as the "Prince of Peace" who came and preached the good news to everyone. His gift to every believer is peace with God and unity in the community of Christians. On the eve of his departure from earth, Jesus left the gift of his peace with the disciples—a deep inner assurance unaffected by circumstances (Isa 9:6; Jn 14:27; Ro 5:1; Eph 2:14–18).

Prayer

People communicate with God through prayer. The Israelites in the Old Testament prayed three times every day. In the New Testament (at the request of the disciples), Jesus taught his followers how to pray. The apostle Paul believed that prayer should have a central place in the life of the believer and the church as a whole. The Scriptures teach that it is the work of the Holy Spirit to assist Christians in prayer, turning their minds toward God, and bringing their requests to the heavenly father. Prayer involves confession of sin, petition, thanksgiving, and worship. God desires our fellowship with him through prayer, and is moved to act through the prayers of his people (1Sa 12:23; Ps 62:8; Mt 6:9–13; Php 4:6; Col 4:2; Ro 8:26).

The Way of Prayer

In the Lord's pattern for prayer, he includes a number of important elements that should be part of our own prayers. Among these components are petition, confession, and praise and thanksgiving (Mt 6:9–13). Prayer was very much a part of the lives of many Bible personalities. Here is a partial list of significant Bible prayers which include some of the elements of the Lord's Prayer.

PETITION

1. Abraham asked the Lord for an heir. (Gen 15:2–3)
2. Moses prayed for a glimpse of God's glory. (Ex 33:18)
3. David prayed for deliverance from his enemies. (Ps 31)
4. Stephen prayed for his murderers. (Ac 7:59–60)
5. Paul prayed three times for the removal of a personal difficulty. (2Co 12:7–10)

CONFESSION AND FORGIVENESS

1. David asked for forgiveness for numbering the people. (2Sa 24:10)
2. David implored God to forgive him for his many sins, including his affair with Bathsheba. (Ps 51)
3. Manasseh prayed for forgiveness and asked the Lord to restore to him his kingdom. (2Ch 33:11–13)
4. Job confessed his pride and repented in dust and ashes. (Job 42:1–6)
5. The prodigal son confessed his sin against God and his father. (Lk 15:11–24)

PRAISE AND THANKSGIVING

1. Moses and Israel praised God for deliverance at the Red Sea. (Ex 15)
2. Hannah praised God for the birth of her son Samuel. (1Sa 2:1–10)
3. Mary praised God for being chosen to be the mother of the Lord. (Lk 1:46–55)
4. The angels praised God for the birth of Jesus. (Lk 2:13–14)
5. Paul and Silas praised God while they were in prison. (Ac 16:25)

Prophecy

Prophets were an important part of the Bible panorama. Called to their line of work by God, they spoke with his authority, delivering messages of judgment, repentance, hope, and forgiveness. Prophecies were clear messages to the people about what God would do now and in the future to correct a particular problem or situation. Most prophetic messages referred directly to a specific situation in the prophet's own day. There were times in biblical history when false prophets emerged, working right alongside the true prophets. When their predictions did not come true, however, they were put to

Ezekiel prophesying

death because they tried to lead the people away from God, and they were a threat to Israel's faith and security.

In the Bible, there are certain prophecies that are different from the traditional God-inspired prophetic voice. These prophecies belong to a particular type of literature known as *apocalyptic*. The prophecies of the Book of Revelation and the Book of Daniel fall into this category. This kind of writing contains imagery and symbolism that depict the coming of the end of the world and God's judgment.

With the coming of the Holy Spirit in the early church, all Christians were given the right to proclaim God's message of salvation. And the New Testament declares that the gift of prophecy is bestowed upon some believers in order to strengthen the church as a whole (Am 7:14–15; Dt 13:1–5; 1Co 12:10, 29).

Visions of the End

A major topic in apocalyptic literature is the end of time. In the Bible, the significant apocalyptic portions are Ezekiel 40–48, Daniel 7–12, Zechariah 9–14, and the Book of Revelation.

The Book of Revelation is the longest example of apocalyptic literature in the Bible. It presents the apostle John's visions and prophecies of the last days and the new spiritual order. The book is rich with symbols. It speaks of strange creatures—a great red dragon with seven heads and ten horns and seven crowns on its head, a beast that looked like a leopard with feet like a bear's and a mouth like a lion's! It also mentions hosts of angels, and it describes armies and battles, a lake of fire, and a bottomless pit.

Throughout the book, however, the consistent message woven into the prophetic imagery is the ultimate triumph of Christ over all forces of evil.

Redemption

By his life, death, and resurrection, Jesus paid the price that would set people free from sin. This work of his is known as redemption. By his blood sacrifice, he recovered those enslaved to wrongdoing. Christians are therefore redeemed, and the apostle Paul encourages them to live in freedom and to not fall back into old patterns of sin and entrapment. The apostle also points out that full freedom will have to wait until the end of the age when Christ returns, and all things will be made new (Mk 10:45; 1Co 6:20; Ro 6:12–14; 8:19–23).

Repentance

Repentance involves turning away from sin and leaving it behind. In the Old Testament, people showed sorrow for sin by wearing sackcloth and ashes, offering sacrifices, and fasting. In the New Testament, Jesus called for a radical approach to repentance—an inward change of heart, not outward rituals. He commanded people everywhere to turn from their evil ways and repent in order to become a part of the kingdom of God (Joel 2:12–13; Lk 18:9–14; Lk 19:1–10; Ac 17:30).

Resurrection

One of the key facts of the Christian faith is that Jesus rose from the dead. The apostles saw him on a number of occasions after his resurrection, and in his first letter to the Corinthian church, Paul lists a number of people who encountered Jesus alive. Because of the empty grave and the absence of the

Jesus appearing to his disciples

body, the authorities could not disprove the claim that Jesus had risen from the dead.

The power of the resurrection is vital to believers. The New Testament teaches that they will share in the resurrection at the end of the age. Naturally, Christians face physical death like everyone else, but they can count on a future life with Christ. In this new spiritual existence, there will be the resurrection of the complete person in a new and perfect body (Mt 28; Mk 16; Lk 24; Jn 20; 1Co 15).

Revelation

People know about God because he chooses to reveal himself. Since he is unapproachable in his purity, majesty, and holiness, we must rely on his revelation if we are to know anything about him. God has revealed something about himself through the world he has created. All during the history of Israel, God showed glimpses of himself through his actions and through the words spoken by his prophets and leaders.

In the New Testament, he fully revealed himself in his son, Jesus Christ. He became a person, and lived in community with others. Yet, many people did not recognize who he really was.

Another important revelation is the Bible itself. It is the revealed word of God, the inspired record of God's doings from the dawn of creation to the time of the New Testament apostles and the growth of the early church (Ex 3; Am 3:7; Jn 1:14; Heb 1:1–2).

Salvation

The Bible tells us that God sent his son into the world to save people from their sins. Jesus dealt with the sin problem in his death and resurrection. Those who put their faith in Christ and accept his work on their behalf are now "saved." This gift of salvation is offered to anyone who calls on the Lord in repentance. However, the full significance of salvation will not be experienced until the end of the age and the return of Christ, the Savior.

Besides spiritual deliverance, the Old and New Testaments speak of salvation in broader terms. When God rescued the Israelites from Egyptian bondage, it was a major act of salvation. References to salvation in the New Testament include freedom from imprisonment, disease, and demonic possession (Isa 60:16; Mt 1:21; Eph 2:8–9; Ro 10:13).

Second Coming of Christ

When Jesus came to earth as a baby, his arrival was hardly noticed. His impact on the world was definite, but small and quiet at first. During his time of ministry here, Jesus promised that he would return at the end of the world. His second coming would be unlike his first, because this time he would come with power and glory for everyone to see, and his second coming would mark the time of judgment.

The world still awaits the second coming of Christ. The Bible teaches that when he returns, it will be the moment of final salvation for all Christians, both living and dead. At his second coming, Jesus will take all believers with him forever in the place that he has prepared for them. The Bible does not tell us when that day will be, but encourages Christians to live in readiness for Christ's unexpected return (Mt 26:64; Php 3:20; 1Th 4:13–5:11; Rev 19–22).

Sin

Although the Bible does not deal with the issue of where sin came from, it describes this condition and its effects clearly. Sin is basically rebellion against God, and it permeates all of society. People are instinctively at enmity with God. The Bible is full of stories that show this natural human bent in action.

From the biblical record we learn that although sin started with Satan, people are responsible (and guilty) for their own wrongdoing. Because sin is an offense to God, he defeated its power in the work of Jesus Christ on the cross. In this "fallen" world of ours, however, wrongdoing still abounds, and the full significance of Christ's work on the cross will not be experienced until Jesus returns to redeem his church. On that day, sin and evil will no longer exist (Gen 3; Ps 51; Isa 1:18–20; Ro 1:18–2:11).

Soul

In the Bible the word "soul" means a person's entire being. Greeks had the idea that the immortal soul was caged in a decaying body, but this was not the Christian view. In biblical thought, the soul included mind, will, and personality—besides flesh and bone (Ps 103:1; Mt 10:28).

Suffering

Part of the consequence of sin is the misfortune of suffering. Pain and hardship strike at believer and unbeliever alike. Sometimes it would seem that the innocent suffer while the guilty enjoy relatively pain-free lives. The Book of Job deals with the problem of suffering, innocent people, and the hand of God in it all.

The suffering of Job

In the life of Jesus, we see suffering as a way of life (Isa 53). Totally innocent, Jesus took on the rejection, hatred, and sin of others in order to bring salvation to the lost. God took responsibility for the problem of suffering in the death of his son. However, suffering will not finally go away until all things are made new in the future (Gen 3:15–19; 2Co 12:6–9; Heb 12:3–11).

Temptation

There are two classic accounts of temptation in the Bible. In the story of Adam and Eve, the serpent leads the woman into doubt and confusion about God's will, and she gives in to temptation by eating the fruit from the forbidden tree. In

the second instance, Satan tempts Jesus in the wilderness, but Jesus rebukes the evil one by quoting the word of God to him.

Clearly, the Scripture shows that God allows his people to be tested, but it also points out that they should be on guard against temptation, assured that God will not allow his people to be tempted beyond what they can bear (Gen 3; Mt 4; Eph 6:10–18).

Worship

God commands his people to worship him, and to give him the honor due to him for who he is, for the world he has created, for his work of redemption through Jesus Christ, and for his blessings and gifts. God is not interested in outward forms of worship; he is only interested in praise that comes from the heart. True God-centered worship is reflected in a life lived to honor him. The Psalms are filled with eloquent words of worship and praise to the Lord.

In the New Testament, Christians joined together to worship God. Empowered by the Holy Spirit, they sang hymns and psalms of praise to the Lord. Paul and Silas even praised him when they were imprisoned.

However, the Bible also teaches that worship is not simply restricted to life on earth. In heaven, the great hosts of angels worship the Lord, and when the entire church is finally redeemed, God's whole creation will praise and worship him forever (Ps 29; 136; Ac 2:43–47; Col 3:16; Rev 15).

A Dozen Ways to Worship God

1. Meet regularly with other Christians to honor God (Ac 2:46–47).
2. Proclaim the word of God (1Ti 4:13).
3. Respond in gratitude to the word of God (Ex 24:3).
4. Celebrate communion (Ac 2:46).
5. Observe Christian creeds (1Co 11:2).
6. Sing psalms, hymns, and spiritual songs (Eph 5:19).
7. Pray in the Spirit (Eph 6:18).
8. Present your whole person to God (Ro 12:1).
9. Offer a sacrifice of praise (Heb 13:15).
10. Confess the name of God (Heb 13:15).
11. Do good (Heb 13:16).
12. Share with others (Heb 13:16).

THE PEOPLE OF THE BIBLE

MANY BIBLE PERSONALITIES are familiar to most of us. We are well acquainted with Adam and Eve and their misadventures in Eden. The saga of Moses—from the hiding place in the bulrushes to the view of the Promised Land—is well known. But how many of us are as familiar with Elymas, Onesiphorus, or Epaphroditus? And what about Jesus? The Bible portrays him as a sinless human being, the Son of God, and a great teacher. But did you know he also broke many Sabbath rules, chased people out of the temple, and overturned tables? This section should reveal more about some of the Bible characters you thought you knew—as well as introduce some of the ones you didn't!

Samson and Delilah are two memorable characters from the Book of Judges.

Personalities You Should Know

These quick sketches of some major Bible characters indicate the main highlights of their lives, and also include little-known facts that bring them to life before our view.

Aaron *(15th century B.C.)*

Aaron (oldest son of Amran and Jochebed) was Moses' brother, a Levite, and the high priest of Israel. He helped Moses free the Israelites and lead them out of Egypt. Aaron was Moses' public speaker, and he used his rod to perform many miracles, even to strike the waters of Egypt and turn them to blood. In the wilderness, he helped Moses defeat the Amalekites. When his authority was questioned, Aaron's rod budded, blossomed, and bore ripe almonds —a sign that showed he was God's choice as high priest.

At times, Aaron disobeyed God. He allowed the Israelites to build an idol in Moses' absence, and another time he sided with Miriam against Moses. On both these occasions, Moses begged God to show Aaron mercy, and God did so. Aaron died when he was 123, just before the Israelites entered the Promised Land. (For further study, see Ex 4; 6–7; 17; 28–29; 32; Nu 4; 12; 14–15; 18; 20.)

Abraham *(22nd century B.C.)*

Abraham (Abram) and his family were called by God to leave Haran and go to a new land. Abraham obeyed. He moved his family and flocks from place to place, even going to Egypt for food, until God directed him to the new land, Canaan. God promised to make Abraham the founder of the Hebrew nation, and Hagar, his wife's slave-girl, bore him a son. This, however, was not the promised child.

When Abraham and his wife Sarah (Sarai) were old, she gave birth to Isaac—the firstborn of the Hebrew nation. Some years later, God tested Abraham's faith when he told him to offer Isaac as a sacrifice. Again, Abraham obeyed.

Just as he was about to lay the knife on his child, God's angel stopped him. Isaac's life was spared and God renewed his promises to Abraham—the Bible's most outstanding example of faith. (For further study, see Gen 11:27–25:11; Ac 13:26; Ro 4; Heb 7:5; 11:8; 19.)

Daniel *(6th century B.C.)*

The fine son of a wealthy Jewish family, Daniel was taken captive to pagan Babylon when he was young. While Daniel and three Jewish friends were in training as King Nebuchadnezzar's courtiers, they honored God.

Filled with godly wisdom, Daniel was able to interpret Nebuchadnezzar's strange dreams. Years later, when Belshazzar was king, the elderly Daniel deciphered an ominous message that appeared on the palace walls. That same night the king was killed and the Persians captured Babylon.

Daniel's fame grew and he became an important official. Others were jealous of his position and plotted to do him in. Daniel was thrown in among lions, but God preserved his life. Daniel went on to record a number of dreams, visions, and prophecies concerning the future. (For further study, see the Book of Daniel; Jer 25:11–12; 29:10; 1Mac 1–6; Rev 1:12–16.)

Israel's Kings and Rulers

THE UNITED KINGDOM

1. Saul	Israel's first king (1Sa 9–10)
2. David	Israel's second and best-loved king (2Sa 1–24)

3. Solomon — David's son, known for his wisdom and riches (1Ki 1–11)

THE NORTHERN KINGDOM (ISRAEL)

1. Jeroboam I — left Israel with a legacy of idolatry (1Ki 11:26–14:20)

2. Nadab — son of Jeroboam, continued idol worship (1Ki 15:25–28)

3. Baasha — ruled for 24 years, and was cursed for his sin by the prophet Jehu (1Ki 15:27–16:7)

4. Elah — son of Baasha, killed while drunk (1Ki 16:6–14)

5. Zimri — committed suicide after ruling for a week (1Ki 16:9–20)

6. Omri — capable ruler who, unfortunately, continued Jeroboam's legacy of paganism (1Ki 16:15–28)

7. Ahab — corrupt husband of Jezebel, condemned by Elijah, and killed in battle (1Ki 16:28–22:40)

8. Ahaziah — Ahab's son and evil successor (1Ki 22:40–2Ki 1:18)

9. Jehoram — Ahaziah's younger brother and successor, he ended Baal worship but did not fully reform (2Ki 3:1–9:25)

10. Jehu — famous for his chariot riding and ending Ahab's pagan dynasty (2Ki 9:1–10:36)

11. Jehoahaz — Jehu's son, his army was almost destroyed by the king of Aram (2Ki 13:1–19)

12. Jehoash — son of Jehoahaz, he was king of Israel for 16 years (2Ki 13:10–14:6)

13. Jeroboam II — reigned during the time of Jonah the prophet (2Ki 14:23–29)

14. Zechariah — Jeroboam's son; reigned for six months

	and then was assassinated by Shallum (2Ki 14:19–15:2)
15. Shallum	reigned for a month and then was killed by Menahem (2Ki 15:14–22)
16. Menahem	an exacting, cruel king, he reigned for 10 years (2Ki 15:14–22)
17. Pekahiah	Menahem's son, he ruled for two years, then was killed by his army captain, Pekah (2Ki 15:22–26)
18. Pekah	ruled for 21 years and maintained idol worship in Israel (2Ki 15:27–31)
19. Hoshea	last king of Israel after the monarchy split; he was defeated by King Shalmaneser V of Assyria; Samaria, the capital of Israel, was captured and the people taken captive to Assyria (2Ki 17)

THE SOUTHERN KINGDOM (JUDAH)

1. Rehoboam	Solomon's son, who sparked a civil war with the northern tribe of Israel (1Ki 11:43–12:24)
2. Abijam	defeated Jeroboam in battle (1Ki 14:31–15:8)
3. Asa	son of Abijam, Judah's first godly king (1Ki 15:8–14)
4. Jehoshaphat	Asa's son, another godly king (1Ki 22:41–50)
5. Jehoram	married Athaliah, the evil daughter of Ahab and Jezebel (2Ki 8:16–24)
6. Ahaziah	son of Jehoram and Athaliah (2Ki 8:24–9:29)
7. Athaliah	seized the throne after Ahaziah's death and had all the royal offspring murdered except Joash, who was hidden from his brutal grandmother (2Ki 11:1–20)

8. Joash	Ahaziah's son and ruler after Athaliah was executed (2Ki 11:1–12:21)
9. Amaziah	son of Joash (2Ki 14:1–20)
10. Azariah (Uzziah)	son of Amaziah; strong, powerful king who fortified Jerusalem; he allowed his subjects to worship idols and was struck with leprosy (2Ki 15:1–7)
11. Jotham	Azariah's son who fortified Jerusalem (2Ki 15:32–38)
12. Ahaz	Jotham's pagan son who reigned for 16 years (2Ki 16:1–20)
13. Hezekiah	king of Judah after his father, Ahaz; Hezekiah put an end to idol worship; God saved Judah from Assyria, and added 15 years to Hezekiah's life (2Ki 18–20)
14. Manasseh	son of Hezekiah (2Ki 21:1–18)
15. Amon	Manasseh's son, killed by his own servants (2Ki 21:19–26)
16. Josiah	leader of national reform (2Ki 22:1–23:30)
17. Jehoahaz	Josiah's son, deposed after 90 days (2Ki 23:31–33)
18. Jehoiakim	Josiah's son who persecuted Jeremiah (2Ki 23:34–24:5; Jer 36)
19. Jehoiachin	Jehoiakim's son who provoked God's anger (2Ki 24:6–16)
20. Zedekiah	uncle of Jehoiachin, blinded and taken into exile in Babylon (2Ki 24:17–25:30)

David (11th century B.C.)

David, youngest son of Jesse of Bethlehem, was a shepherd boy when Samuel the prophet came and secretly anointed him as Israel's next king. Time passed and David was sent to take food to his brothers in the army. While there, he took up the challenge to fight big Goliath, the champion soldier of the Philistines. After he killed the giant, King Saul became jealous of the young shepherd, whose music often soothed the temperamental king.

After Saul's death, David became king in Judah. His popular reign was marked by many achievements. He made Jerusalem his capital, brought the ark of the covenant there, and made preparations to build the temple.

David's great life was not without tragic personal failings: He committed adultery, plotted murder, experienced the death of a child, and had trouble with his sons. Yet David always turned to the Lord for forgiveness and renewal. He was a great king, a fearless soldier, and a creative writer and musician. Many psalms are attributed to David, the man whom the Bible describes as close to the heart of God! (For further study, see 1Sa 16–31; the Second Book of Samuel; 1Ki 1–2.)

Deborah *(12th century B.C.)*

One of Israel's greatest judges, Deborah was the only woman on record to hold this position of leadership. She was highly regarded for her moral authority and wisdom. When the Israelites were being oppressed by the Canaanites (led by Jabin), Deborah was given instructions from God. She told Barek of Naphtali to gather an army on Mount Tabor to face the enemy. Barek would only agree to go if Deborah went with the army. She complied, providing essential leadership and inspiration. As the Canaanites advanced, a violent rainstorm flooded the area, bogging down their horses and chariots in mud. The Israelites were able to overpower them. Sisera, the Canaanite general, fled and was later killed. (For further study, see Jdg 4–5.)

Elijah *(9th century B.C.)*

Elijah the prophet lived and worked in Israel during King Ahab's reign. He was sent by God to judge the king and his pagan wife Jezebel for worshiping Baal and killing God's prophets. God sent a drought, and Elijah had to go into hiding for his own safety. God provided him with food from the mouth of ravens, and later from the hands of a widow— whose dead son was brought back to life by Elijah's prayer of faith.

In the third year of the drought, Elijah confronted Ahab and they agreed to a showdown at Mt. Carmel between the prophets of Baal and Elijah's God. Baal and his cohorts failed miserably, Elijah and the God of Israel won the contest, the priests of Baal were killed, and the drought ended that day. God protected Elijah in further dealings with the rebellious Jezebel and Ahab, and the prophet continued to warn and confront them about their wanton sins.

Before his work was finished, Elijah prepared Elisha to continue his work, and the prophet witnessed the death of the dreadful Ahab. After this, God took Elijah to heaven in a chariot of fire, and the prophet's mantle fell on Elisha's shoulders. (For further study, see 1Ki 17–19; 21; 2Ki 1–2; Mal 4:5; Mt 11:14; 17:1–13; 27:47–49; Jas 5:16–18.)

Esther *(5th century B.C.)*

After King Ahasuerus (Xerxes) divorced his wife Vashti, he chose the lovely young Jewish woman Hadassah (Esther) to be his wife. When she moved into the palace, her cousin Mordecai, who had been her guardian, advised her to keep her Jewish identity hidden from the Persian royal court.

When Haman, the imperious and cruel chief minister, schemed to wipe out all the Jews in the area because of his hatred toward Mordecai, Esther stepped in. She approached the king, gained his pleasure and interest, then courageously revealed Haman's plan to exterminate her people. Outraged by Haman's conspiracy, the king ordered his death and appointed Mordecai chief minister in Haman's place. On the day Haman had appointed for the annihilation of the Jews, Esther's people turned on their enemies and wiped them out. This amazing turn of events is remembered at the Feast of Purim, an important festival in the Jewish calendar. (For further study, see the Book of Esther and Additions to Esther.)

Eve

Described as the "mother of all living," Eve was created by God to provide companionship to Adam in the garden of Eden. She was tempted by the clever serpent into tasting the fruit from the tree of knowledge of good and evil—the one thing that God had instructed them to avoid. She persuaded Adam to join her in disobeying God, bringing sin into the world. Her curse was to experience suffering in childbirth and to have her mutual partnership with Adam give way to a relationship of conflict and inequity. God sent them out of the garden forever. Eve later bore Adam many children, including Cain, Abel, and Seth. (For further study, see Gen 1:26–31; 2:18–25; 3; 4:1–2, 25; 2Co 11:3; 1Ti 2:13.)

God

The biblical narrative is the story of God and his dealings with humanity. From Genesis to Revelation, God is pictured as the beginning and end of history—its Creator, Sustainer, and Redeemer. The Bible does not contain a formal definition of God, nor do any of its writers argue for his existence, which is presumed throughout Scripture. Yet even though we cannot fully capture the essence and character of God, we can be certain of many things about him from the Bible. Here are a number of important facts about God's perfections, the Godhead, and his moral character traits:

• God is omniscient—he knows everything (Isa 40:13–14).

• God is infinite spirit—he is without the limitations of his creatures (Jn 4:24).

• God is eternal—he is everywhere (Ps 139).

- God is sovereign and all-powerful (Isa 46:9–11).

- There is only one God, and he reveals himself in three forms—Father, Son, and Holy Spirit (Gen 1:26; Mt 28:19; 2Co 13:14).

- God is holy and pure—he cannot tolerate sin (1Pe 1:15).

- God is true, righteous, and just (Heb 6:18; Ps 119:137).

- God is faithful and loving (Ps 89:1–2).

- God is kind, good, and compassionate (Ps 107:8).

- God is the Creator and Judge of the universe (Isa 40).

From beginning to end, God's story is one of profound love for humanity. We see him as a compassionate creator concerned about Adam's loneliness and as a shaper of history who called Abraham to faith. God revealed himself as a loving father when he led and disciplined his wayward people. He was a moral authority, thundering from Mt. Sinai, and a delighted father enjoying the baptism of his son, Jesus.

God's pure love and holy righteousness motivated him to send his son to deal with the problem of sin. The coming of the long-expected Messiah gave humanity the chance to come home to God. It was in the humanity of Jesus that God revealed himself most clearly. The Bible declares that God was the power behind the death, resurrection, and ascension of Jesus; and it was God who orchestrated the phenomenal spread of Christianity. However, God's leading and directing history did not end there.

He promises his people a hope and a future beyond the grave. It is he who will usher in the end of the age, and establish a new heaven and earth (Rev 21). By putting together what is yet to be with what has already been, the Bible makes it clear that all of history lies within the purpose and power of God.

Holy Spirit

Christian tradition has often relegated the Holy Spirit to a shadowy behind-the-scenes role in religious life. But this is by far an inaccurate picture. The Holy Spirit—who has always been present—is an equal partner in the Godhead. He was involved in the birth of Creation, active throughout the making of the Bible story, and he will be involved at the end of history, doing the work of God in particular ways.

The Bible best describes the Spirit as "wind, breath" (Hebrew, *ruah;* Greek, *pneuma*). This portrays his invisible power and ability to move freely everywhere. The Spirit of the Lord rushed on Samson, then left just as quickly (Jdg 14:19; 16:20). At the baptism of Jesus, the Holy Spirit descended on him like a dove, assuring him of God's love and delight in him (Mt 3:16–17). In the Pentecost narrative, the Spirit came in the form of rushing wind and divided tongues of fire, spreading power and unity over a crowd of waiting pilgrims (Ac 2).

The Old Testament records a number of intermittent interactions between the Holy Spirit and a variety of people—from childless women to babes in the womb, from soldiers in battle to fugitives in hiding, from kings to peasants, and from priests to beggars.

In the New Testament, the image of the Spirit's work is specifically tied to the life of Jesus, to his coming at Pentecost, and to the life of the believer and the work of the church. God's Spirit not only lives in the believer and helps in the daily living of spiritual life (Ro 8), but he also gives spiritual gifts for the good of the church (1Co 12:7), and equips the church for ministry to others (Eph 4:12).

The Holy Spirit—a Panoramic View

TRAITS	NAMES	MINISTRIES
1. Omnipresent (Ps 139:7)	Spirit of God (1Co 3:16)	Active in creation (Gen 1:2)
2. Omniscient (1Co 2:10–11)	Spirit of Christ (Ro 8:9)	Inspired the writing of the Scriptures (2Ti 3:16)
3. Omnipotent (Gen 1:2)	Eternal Spirit (Heb 9:14)	Helped Israel in the wilderness (Neh 9:20)
4. Eternal (Heb 9:14)	Spirit of truth (Jn 16:13)	Restrains Satan's power (Eph 6:10–18)
5. Equal with the father and with the Son (Mt 28:19–20)	Spirit of life (Ro 8:2)	Anointed Jesus (Mt 3:16)
6. He has a will (1Co 12:11)	Advocate (Jn 14:26)	Empowered Jesus (Mt 12:28)
7. He speaks (Ac 8:29)	Spirit of the Lord (Jdg 3:10)	Empowered the church (Ac 2)
8. He loves (Ro 15:30)	Spirit of the living God (2Co 3:3)	Indwells the believer (Ro 8:9)
9. He grieves (Eph 4:30)	Holy Spirit of promise (Eph 1:13)	Assures and guides the believer (Ro 8:14–15)
10. He prays (Ro 8:26)		Raises Christians from the dead (Ro 8:11)

Isaiah *(8th century B.C.)*

An outstanding poet, writer, and statesman who lived in Jerusalem, Isaiah is considered the greatest Old Testament prophet. He lived during the reigns of Uzziah, Jotham, Ahaz, and Hezekiah. When he was about 25, he had a profound vision of God, and from that day on devoted himself to the vocation of prophecy.

Isaiah had a wife and two sons, both of whom were given symbolic names as a sign of what God was going to do among his people: Shear-jashub ("the remnant will return") and Maher-shalal-hash-baz ("the spoil speeds and the prey hastens")—a reference to the impending downfall of Samaria.

The two small kingdoms of Israel and Judah, often at odds with each other, were under the threat of advancing Assyria (the dominant power in Mesopotamia) and Egyptian military assaults from the south. Throughout this time of political and military threat, Isaiah's basic message warned against looking for safety in armies and ever-shifting alliances with various nations. His faith and vision led him to proclaim that God, and only God, had established and would protect the Hebrew nation.

More than a prophetic advisor to Judah's kings, Isaiah spoke out against idolatry, religious hypocrisy, and the rich and famous who ignored the plight of the poor. The prophet cared passionately about righteous living, and he did not hesitate to drive home the truth about social justice.

Even though Judah could not escape the consequences of their disobedience, Isaiah's message of warning included an element of hope. In time, God would destroy the enemies of the Jews and bring them back from exile. Isaiah also looked forward to the day when God's suffering servant—the Messiah—would come. (For further study, see 2Ki 19:1–7; the Book of Isaiah.)

Jacob *(20th century B.C.)*

When he was born, Jacob was clutching his first-born twin brother's heel. From that moment on, there was rivalry and conflict between Jacob and Esau that would last for years to come. Matters were exacerbated years later when Jacob persuaded Esau to give up his rights as the first-born son in exchange for a bowl of stew. Thus Jacob—pretending to be Esau—gained Isaac's special blessing. When the plot was uncovered, Esau was enraged and planned to kill his cunning twin brother.

Jacob escaped to relatives in Haran. On the way there, God vowed to keep his promise to Abraham through Jacob and his descendants. Jacob worked for Laban, his uncle, for 20 years. He first married Laban's daughter Leah through the trickery of his uncle, then her younger sister Rachel, whom he loved.

While in Haran, Jacob became the father of many sons and a daughter by Leah and two maids in his household. He waited years for the birth of Joseph, then later Benjamin, by his beloved Rachel (who died giving birth to their second son). Jacob favored these two boys over his other children, and long-established family patterns of favoritism and jealousy continued.

Although Laban continued his practice of cheating and deceiving his nephew, Jacob built up his own flocks of sheep and goats, and left with his household for home. He never returned to Haran again. On his way home, Jacob had an unusual and significant encounter with an angel in human form. At this point his name was changed from Jacob to "Israel" which means "one who strives with God."

After this, Jacob and Esau were warmly reunited, but afterwards they went their separate ways. Jacob lived in the land of Canaan until his son Joseph invited him to settle in Egypt. Before he died, Jacob blessed his 12 sons, who became the 12 tribes of Israel—the fulfillment of God's promise to Abraham. (For further study, see Gen 26–35; 37:18–28; 38–47; Ro 9:13.)

Jesus *(1st century A.D.)*

The name Jesus (meaning "salvation") was common among Jews during the Greco-Roman occupation, but Jesus of Nazareth was no common man. He is the historical figure whom Christians believe to be the Son of God incarnate—that is, God-in-the-flesh.

Close to the end of the short three-year ministry of Jesus, it became clear that the Jewish leaders were afraid of his claims and power, and they wanted to kill him. Judas betrayed his leader, helping the enemies of Jesus find and capture him at night. Jesus was arrested in the Garden of Gethsemane, close to Jerusalem, and he was tried and condemned by a Jewish court before dawn. Pilate, the Roman governor, ratified his death sentence for the sake of the crowd, even though he knew that Jesus was innocent of any charges.

Jesus was crucified and buried in the tomb of Joseph of Arimathaea. Three days later, a group of women found the tomb empty and an angel told them that Jesus was alive. During the next 40 days, his followers and many others saw him, and were convinced by his resurrection that he was truly the Son of God. Then Jesus ascended to the glory of heaven, and his followers were left with the assurance that he would return one day. (For further study, see the Books of Matthew, Mark, Luke, and John; other New Testament books offer reflections on his significance to humanity.)

Jesus Christ—Both Man and God

THE HUMANITY OF JESUS	THE DEITY OF JESUS
He had a human mother (Lk 1:31)	He healed disease (Mt 8:1–4)
He had a human body (Mt 26:12)	He cast out demons (Mt 8:16–17)
He grew (Lk 2:40)	He had authority over all people (Jn 17:2)
He increased in wisdom (Lk 2:52)	He had power over nature (Mt 8:26)
He prayed (Mk 1:35)	He had power over sin (Mt 9:1–8)
He was tempted (Mt 4:1)	He had power over death (Lk 7:14–15)
He learned obedience (Heb 5:8)	He knew all about Nathanael (Jn 1)
He was hungry (Mt 4:2)	He knew all about Judas (Jn 6:70)
He was thirsty (Jn 4:7)	He knew all about the Samaritan woman (Jn 4:24)
He was tired (Jn 4:6)	He is omnipresent today (Mt 18:20)
He slept (Mt 8:24)	He was worshiped as God by a leper (Mt 8:2)
He loved others (Mk 10:21)	He was worshiped as God by Thomas (Jn 20:28)

He was angry (Mk 3:5)

He was worshiped as God by his disciples (Mt 14:33)

He wept (Jn 11:35)

He judges (Jn 5:22)

He was troubled (Mk 14:33–34)

He forgave wrongdoing (Mk 2:5)

He sweated profusely (Lk 22:44)

He gives eternal life (Jn 10:28)

He suffered (1Pe 4:1)

Paul called him God (Gal 2:20)

He bled (Jn 19:34)

Peter identified him with God (1Pe 3:22)

He died (Mt 27:50)

Jude called him God (Jude 25)

He was buried (Mt 27:59–60)

He rose from the dead (Mt 28:5–6)

Mary *(1st century B.C.)*

The young Jewish virgin was engaged to Joseph the carpenter, a descendant of Abraham and David, when the angel Gabriel visited her with some startling news. Mary was

amazed to learn that she would soon become the mother of Jesus, the Messiah and Son of God. When the angel told her that she would become pregnant by the power of the Holy Spirit, Mary accepted this assignment for her life in spite of the social pressure and shame associated with a pregnancy before marriage.

Before Jesus was born, Mary visited her cousin Elizabeth, who was also expecting a baby. When the women greeted each other, the baby in Elizabeth's womb (John the Baptist) moved in delight at hearing the voice of the mother of Jesus. Overcome with joy, Mary broke out in a song of praise (historically known as the Magnificat). She praised God for his mercy to the humble and poor and for his justice upon the rich and the proud.

Mary and Joseph left Nazareth to register in Bethlehem for a Roman census, and it was there that Jesus was born. His humble birth in an animal holding was acknowledged by angels and shepherds. When Jesus was presented at the temple eight days after his birth, Simeon and Anna honored him as the long-awaited Messiah. Some time later, after a visit from wise men from the East, the family had to escape to Egypt because King Herod, perceiving the baby Jesus as a rival, wanted to kill him.

An involved parent, Mary was present at all the major milestones in her son's life. She was searching for her missing 12-year-old when he was at the temple confounding the teachers. Mary was there at Cana when Jesus—prompted by her—performed his first miracle. She stood at the foot of the cross and watched her son suffer an excruciating death. And Mary was with the disciples when they met together to pray after Jesus' ascension. Mary led a life of quiet dignity and strength, strong faith, and enormous purpose.(For further study, see Mt 1:16–25; 13:54–57; Lk 1–2; Jn 2:1–5; 19:25–27; Ac 1:14; Gal 4:4.)

Miriam *(15th century B.C.)*

The sister of Moses and Aaron, Miriam played an instrumental role in saving the nation of Israel. When she was just a girl of 12, the King of Egypt ordered all Jewish baby boys slaughtered as a means of population control—including her newborn brother Moses. Her mother put the young boy in a makeshift lifeboat and floated him down the Nile. He was discovered by Pharaoh's daughter, who decided to keep the Jewish child. Miriam, who had watched from a distance, struck up a conversation and offered to fetch a Hebrew woman to nurse the baby. She then brought her own mother. Miriam had saved Moses' life and returned him to his mother's arms!

During the Exodus of the Israelites from Egypt, Miriam shared leadership with her two brothers. Her strength and guidance were evident. After the parting of the Red Sea, she led thousands of the women in joyful singing and dancing in triumphant worship. But Miriam did not always support her brother and sing praises. She spoke out against Moses when he married a Cushite (Ethiopian) woman, and later joined Aaron in public rebellion against Moses' leadership. For this, she was struck with leprosy by God. Moses cried out to the Lord to forgive her sins and Miriam was healed, but only after she was quarantined outside the camp for seven days. (For further study, see Ex 15:20–21; Nu 12:1–15; 20:1; 26:59; Dt 24:9; 1Ch 6:3; Mic 6:4.)

Moses *(15th century B.C.)*

Born and brought up in Egypt, Moses became a great leader who freed the Israelites from slavery, led them through the wilderness, and brought them to the borders of Canaan. Although a Hebrew, he was brought up by the daughter of the Pharaoh and educated at the palace as an Egyptian.

Angered one day by the cruel treatment of the Israelites, Moses killed an Egyptian overseer. For his own safety, Moses fled into the desert and lived there for years as a shepherd. He married the daughter of Jethro, the man who took him in when he escaped.

Forty years after leaving Egypt, God spoke to Moses from a burning desert bush. He told Moses to go back to Egypt to rescue the Israelites from the Pharaoh's grasp. Along with his brother Aaron, Moses spoke to the Pharaoh, who refused to let the people go. God plagued the Egyptians with trouble, until finally the Pharaoh released the Israelites. The Egyptian army pursued their former slaves as far as the Red Sea, but the Israelites escaped into the desert and the Egyptian army was drowned.

At Mt. Sinai, God gave Moses the Law and instructions for building the tent of worship (tabernacle). During their time in the wilderness, the people often turned against Moses, complaining about food, water, and other desert conditions. They even forgot about God's power and turned to idol worship. Because of their faithlessness, the people were condemned to wander in the desert until all those who rebelled had died.

Before Moses handed the leadership of the people to Joshua, he gave God's Law to the new generation of Israelites. When he gave the people his final blessing, Moses climbed Mt. Nebo so he could glimpse Canaan, the Promised Land that he could not enter because of his own earlier sin. Moses—a great man of God—then died in the desert of Moab. (For further study, see Ex 2–40; the Book of Numbers; the Book of Deuteronomy.)

Paul *(1st century A.D.)*

A dominant personality in the early church movement, Paul was an outstanding champion of Jesus Christ—an apostle and missionary whose letters make up a large part of the New Testament. Born a Jew, Paul was a Roman citizen educated in Jerusalem by Rabbi Gamaliel. At first, a Pharisee who strongly opposed the Christian movement, Paul supported the persecuting of Christians and was present at the stoning of Stephen.

In a dramatic incident on the Damascus road, Paul became converted to Christianity. After his baptism in Damascus, Paul immediately started preaching. When the Jews plotted to kill him, Paul moved on to Jerusalem. The Christians there were skeptical of Paul, but Barnabas, a kind, encouraging Christian leader, introduced him to the apostles, and the Christian community embraced the new convert. Again, Paul's life was threatened, so he returned to Tarsus. Paul and Barnabas helped establish the church at Antioch in Syria.

Later, the two men embarked on a trip to take the Christian message to many people in Cyprus and Asia Minor. The missionaries then reported back to the church in Antioch. Paul went on to help the Jewish Christians in Jerusalem understand and accept that Jesus Christ came to be the Savior of all ethnic groups.

Silas was Paul's helper on his second missionary journey. They visited the church in Galatia, then Timothy joined them in Lystra. From Troas they sailed to Greece, where they were joined by Luke, the author of the Gospel and Acts. At Philippi, Paul and Silas were beaten and imprisoned. After their release, they traveled through Greece and Paul ended up in Corinth, where he stayed for more than a year.

On his third missionary trek, Paul did intensive ministry in Ephesus. Days were long as he worked to support himself and did preaching and teaching. After three winters there, working among Jews and Greeks, Paul moved on to Corinth to prepare for his visit to Rome. Then once more he traveled on to Jerusalem to tell the believers there of the spread of the Christian faith. He was arrested in Jerusalem, then sent to Caesarea to be tried. Imprisoned for two years, Paul was eventually sent to Rome for trial.

The sea journey to Rome included a shipwreck, lack of food, and a venomous snake bite on the island of Malta. Yet

God preserved Paul and his company through it all. When Paul got to Rome, he was kept under house arrest for more than two years. During this time he boldly preached the good news.

The Bible does not record Paul's death, but in his last message to Timothy just before the traditional date of his death, Paul indicates that his end is near. The fourth-century church historian Eusebius states that Paul was executed in Rome by Nero in 67 A.D. (For further study, see the Book of Acts; and the following books of the New Testament: Romans; 1 and 2 Corinthians; Galatians; Ephesians; Philippians; Colossians; 1 and 2 Thessalonians; 1 and 2 Timothy; Titus; Philemon)

Peter *(1st century A.D.)*

A fisherman by trade, Peter was called by Jesus to be a disciple. Along with the call came a change of name: Known by everyone as Simon, his name was changed to Peter (which means "rock") by Jesus. It was this disciple who would later identify Jesus as the Christ, the Son of the living God. And in response to Peter's confession, Jesus would promise to establish the church on him, and give him the keys to the kingdom of heaven.

Peter was one of Jesus' closest followers. He was with Jesus at the transfiguration and in the Garden of Gethsemane just before his arrest. Although fiercely loyal to his leader, he was quick to deny ever knowing Jesus, and he deeply regretted this betrayal. However, Jesus loved and understood this impetuous disciple of his, and at Lake Galilee instructed him to be a shepherd to the Christian "flock." Jesus was certain of Peter's strength of character, his ability to lead, and his commitment to the kingdom of God.

At Pentecost, Peter preached boldly about Jesus to the crowd of pilgrims in Jerusalem, and about 3,000 became believers. At first Peter only shared the gospel with the Jews,

but God sent him a special vision to show him that he must take the message of the kingdom of God to non-Jews also.

Later, King Herod saw to it that Peter was arrested and imprisoned, but the apostle escaped because of the fervent prayer of believers at the house of Mary, and an angel of the Lord was sent to release him. Herod was furious at the news, and Peter went elsewhere to avoid further harm. Not much is known of Peter's activities after this point, but he is credited with the authorship of two New Testament letters. Church tradition holds that he suffered martyrdom at the hands of the Roman Emperor Nero in the middle of the first century A.D. (For further study, see Mt 16–17; Mk 8–9, 14; Lk 9, 22; Jn 13:31–38; 18:15–27; 21:15–23; Ac 1–5; 9–12; 15; the First Letter of Peter; the Second Letter of Peter.)

Ruth *(12th century B.C.)*

The story of Ruth is an inspiring tale of a non-Jewish woman whose romance with an Israelite resulted in her becoming an ancestor of the Messiah. During a great famine, Naomi, along with her husband and two sons, were forced to leave Bethlehem in search of food. While in Moab, her husband died and her sons, Mahlon and Chilion, married the Moabite women Ruth and Orpah. The sons also died, leaving the women widowed. Naomi planned to return to Bethlehem and told the two women to go back to their mothers, but Ruth refused to leave Naomi. (Ancient customs held that a widow was a servant of the dead husband's family.) Once in Bethlehem, the hand of God guided Ruth to work in a wheat field, where the owner, Boaz, was drawn to her. Under Jewish law, a dead man's nearest relative had the right to marry or "redeem" the widow. If he refused, that right would pass on to the nearest kin. Boaz was a distant relative of Mahlon, so he waited at the city gate for a closer relative to claim redemption rights to Ruth. One was willing to buy the dead husband's land, but not marry Ruth, thus giving the rights to Boaz. Ruth and Boaz were married and had a son named Obed, who became the grandfather of David. (For further study, see the Book of Ruth.)

Samuel *(11th century B.C.)*

The long-awaited son of Elkanah and Hannah, Samuel grew up to be the last great judge in Israel and one of its fine prophets. When Samuel was a toddler, Hannah kept her promise to God and brought the child to the shrine at Shiloh to be raised by Eli the priest.

One night while Samuel was under Eli's care, God spoke to him about the downfall of the house of Eli because of the corruption of Eli's two sons. When Israel was defeated by the Philistines at the battle of Aphek, Eli's two sons were killed and the sacred ark of the covenant was captured. When Eli heard the news, he was devastated and fell over backward, breaking his neck.

Samuel was now faced with a difficult situation. The Israelites felt that God no longer cared about them. At Mizpah, Samuel told the people to turn away from pagan gods, to repent, and to serve the God of Israel only. Once again the Philistine army approached to attack God's people, and Samuel cried to the Lord for help. The Philistines were thrown into confusion and retreated. Samuel marked this victory by setting up a stone to the Lord and naming the place Ebenezer, meaning "stone of help." After this, Samuel ruled Israel all his life.

When Samuel was old, he appointed his sons Joel and Abijah as judges and handed his work over to them. But the Israelites were displeased with their lack of justice and asked for a monarch instead. Samuel was against this idea at first, but God guided him to anoint Saul as Israel's first king. After Saul proved to be a disobedient and willful king, Samuel secretly anointed David as the next in line for the monarchy.

All of Israel mourned when the distinguished prophet and judge died. Samuel was an uncompromising man of God, diligent in a variety of roles in the religious and political life of Israel. The New Testament upholds Samuel as one of the great heroes of faith. (For further study, see 1Sa 1–16; 19; 28; Ps 99:6; Heb 11:32.)

Satan

Appropriately, his name means "adversary," and Satan is portrayed in the Bible as the foremost enemy of God and humanity. Known by a host of names that serve to identify him as the source of all aspects of evil, Satan began his earthly career with the temptation of Adam and Eve. The prophet Ezekiel portrays Satan as a created being who once resided in heaven in a perfect, blameless state. However, he grew proud and desired to be like God and rule over him. Because of his flawed ambition and self-deification, Satan was thrown out of heaven and given the limited position of "ruler of the power of the air" (Eph 2:2). Thus began the adversarial relationship between God and Satan, good and evil, holiness and sin, life and death.

Satan's Names

Most commonly known by the name Satan (adversary), this designation appears some 52 times in the Bible. Another frequent name—devil (slanderer)—appears 35 times. He is also called by many other descriptive names that help to identify the nature and work of Satan.

1. The ruler of the power of the air (Eph 2:2)
2. The god of this world (2Co 4:4)
3. The ruler of this world (Jn 12:31)
4. Day Star, son of Dawn (Isa 14:12)
5. The dragon (Rev 12:7)
6. The angel of the bottomless pit (Rev 9:11)
7. Abaddon or Apollyon (destruction, ruin) (Rev 9:11)
8. Beelzebul (Mt 12:24)
9. Beliar (2Co 6:15)
10. The evil one (Mt 13:38)
11. The tempter (1Th 3:5)
12. The accuser of our comrades (Rev 12:10)
13. An angel of light (2Co 11:14–15)
14. A murderer (Jn 8:44)
15. The father of lies (Jn 8:44)
16. The enemy (Mt 13:39)

Even though Satan is without the powers of God, he still has the ability to seduce the human race. Thus the struggle between Satan and people is a constant theme throughout the Bible.

However, the Bible teaches that Satan's ultimate power was broken through the work of Jesus on the cross (Heb 2:14). The victory over sin and death was won by God then, but the final defeat of Satan, his angels, and his followers will not be realized until after the final judgment (Rev 20). Until then, Satan continues his attempts to destroy God's plan and usurp his position.

Women of Power

In biblical times, the status of women was restricted and perceived as much less important than the place of men. A woman was defined by her relationship to men: She was a father's daughter, a husband's wife or widow, a king's queen, or—for that matter—his concubine. Caught in a cultural bind, a woman had few rights or opportunities and seldom a career. Most women were mothers and homemakers. Yet throughout biblical history, there were exceptional women who defied their restrictive societal mold. These were women of extraordinary individuality and courage who were compelled to act and speak out. Some of these women were known for their godly ways and good deeds; others were notoriously evil; but all were women of power.

1. **Jael.** Pretending to offer Israel's enemy, Sisera, protection, Jael drove a peg into the army captain's head, killing him while he slept in her tent (Jdg 4:17–22; 5:24–27).

2. **Bathsheba.** In spite of her ignoble entry into David's life, Bathsheba maneuvered herself into a position of political power in the royal court during David's latter years. She convinced David to make Solomon the next king of Israel, and after David's death she exerted power and influence over her son, King Solomon (2Sa 11–12; 1Ki 1–2).

3. **A wise woman of Tekoa.** She played a strategic role in helping King David reconcile with his son Absalom (2Sa 14:1–23).

4. **Jezebel.** A strong-willed and evil queen, Jezebel succeeded in forcing Baal worship on her husband Ahab, the royal household, and on Israel. She massacred God's prophets, cut down Naboth, and sent the prophet Elijah into hiding (1Ki 16:31; 18:4, 13, 19; 19:1–2; 21).

5. **Huldah.** A wise prophet who gave advice to Hilkiah the priest (and a deputation sent by King Josiah) on the ancient scroll of God's Law discovered in the temple (2Ki 22:14–20).

6. **Judith.** The apocryphal tale of Judith is one of resourcefulness and courage. When Israel was under siege by the Assyrians and the situation seemed hopeless, Judith encouraged the townspeople to trust God for a victory. Disarming the unsuspecting Assyrian general by her kind friendship, Judith overpowered Holofernes, cutting off his head. His troops fled, and Israel won an easy victory (Book of Judith).

7. **Herodias.** When John the Baptist spoke out against the adulterous marriage of Herodias to King Herod (Antipas), she had John arrested and put in prison. Not satisfied with that, she asked for his head and had John the Baptist executed (Mk 6:17–29).

8. **Priscilla.** When Priscilla chose to marry Aquila, the Jewish former slave, she undoubtedly shocked her wealthy Roman family, and certainly those in her social setting. Priscilla and Aquila were clearly leaders in the early church, they were partners with Paul in tent-making, and they both had a part in the discipleship of the eloquent Apollos (Ac 18:24–26).

9. **Phoebe.** Probably an officer in her own church at Cenchrea, Phoebe was known for assisting the apostle Paul during his visits to Corinth and Cenchrea, for helping many other people, and for her community service. She was a valued member of the early church (Ro 16:1–2).

Who's Who from Abel to Zerubbabel

The Bible identifies at least 4,000 individuals, as well as nations and groups of people. This abbreviated list highlights a cross-section of Bible personalities. Almost every entry includes a definition or description of the person's name. (However, readers should know that the meanings given are merely educated guesses by scholars.) A brief description of each character is also provided, as well as the first Biblical reference for that person.

Abel (breath or vapor or son; possibly meadow): The second son of Adam and Eve, he was murdered by his brother Cain (Gen 4:2).

Abishag (possibly my father was a wanderer): A capable and attractive woman chosen to nurse the elderly David. She may also be the central female figure of the Song of Solomon (1Ki 1:3).

Absalom (father of peace): David's son; he tried to usurp the throne from his father (2Sa 3:3).

Adam (human being or humanity): The first man, and husband of Eve. Their sin caused a curse on all humanity (Gen 1:26–27).

Adonijah (The Lord is my Lord): One of David's sons; he was executed by Solomon for attempting to usurp the throne (2Sa 3:4).

Amalek (warlike): A son of Eliphaz and the forefather of the Amalekites (Gen 36:12).

Amram (the kinsman is exalted): A descendant of Levi and an ancestor of Aaron, Moses, and Miriam (Ex 6:18).

Ananias (The Lord is gracious): A follower of Christ who was struck dead for trying to deceive the apostles (Ac 5:1).

Anna (grace): A prophet and woman of prayer in Christ's time; she was of the tribe of Asher (Lk 2:36–38).

Apollos (possibly a destroyer): A Jewish Christian and enthusiastic student of the Scriptures (Ac 18:24).

Aquila (eagle): Husband of Priscilla and friend of Paul (Ac 18:2).

Augustus (consecrated or holy) **Caesar**: The imperial name of Octavian, Julius Caesar's nephew who became emperor of Rome. Jesus was born during his reign, which lasted until A.D. 14 (Lk 2:1).

Balaam (possibly devourer): A prophet that the king of Moab persuaded to curse Israel. However, God put words of blessing in Balaam's mouth instead (Nu 22:5).

Barabbas (father's son or son of Abba): A murderer who was released to the people instead of Jesus (Mt 27:16).

Barnabas (son of encouragement): A Jewish Christian who traveled with Paul; he was known for his ability to encourage others (Ac 4:36).

Bernice (victorious): She and her brother Agrippa (with whom she had an incestuous relationship) sat in judgment on Paul (Ac 25:13).

Caesar: The name of a branch of the family of the Julii that eventually gained control of the Roman government. Later it came to be known as the formal title of the Roman emperors.

Caiaphas (meaning unknown): The high priest who played a major role in the trial of Jesus (Mt 26:3).

Cain (to acquire): The eldest son of Adam and Eve; he murdered his brother Abel (Gen 4:1).

Caleb (dog or rabid): One of the spies sent out by Moses to evaluate the Promised Land (Nu 13:6).

Candace (pure): A dynastic title of the queens of Ethiopia (Ac 8:27).

Claudius Caesar (meaning unknown): The Roman emperor who banished the Jews from Rome (Ac 11:28).

Cyrus the Great (son): Founder of the Persian Empire; he freed the captive Jews and allowed them to return to their land (2Ch 36:22).

Delilah (small or dainty): The Philistines paid Delilah to find out the secret of Samson's strength—and then betray him (Jdg 16:4).

Dinah (justice): The daughter of Jacob and Leah who was violated by Hamor. This act resulted in tribal war (Gen 30:21).

Elizabeth (God is my oath): Married to Zechariah the priest, and mother of John the Baptist (Lk 1:5).

Elymas: This false prophet opposed Saul and Barnabas at Paphos. He was also called Bar-Jesus, son of Jesus (Ac 13:6).

Epaphroditus (handsome or charming): A Philippian Christian who worked so strenuously that he lost his health (Php 2:25).

Esau (hairy or shaggy): Jacob's twin brother and ancestor of the tribe of Edom. He sold his birthright to Jacob (Gen 25:25).

Ezekiel (God strengthens): A prophet who was taken captive to Babylon. He prophesied to the exiles in Mesopotamia (Eze 1:3).

Felix (happy): The Roman governor of Judea who presided over Paul's trial at Caesarea (Ac 23:24).

Festus (joyful): The successor of Felix; he continued the trial of Paul started under Felix (Ac 24:47).

Gideon (cutter or hewer): The outstanding judge of Israel who delivered his people from Midian (Jdg 6:11).

Habakkuk (embracer or wrestler): A prophet during the reigns of Jehoiakim and Josiah (Hab 1:1).

Hosea (The Lord has saved): A prophet of Israel; he spoke out against the idolatries of Israel and Samaria (Hos 1:1).

Hur (meaning unknown): One of the men who held up the arms of Moses during the battle with Amalek (Ex 17:10).

Isaac (laughing or he laughed): The son born to Abraham and Sarah in their old age. The father of Esau and Jacob and an ancestor of Jesus (Gen 17:19).

Ishmael (God heard): The son of Abraham and Hagar; he established a clan of desert dwellers considered to be the ancestors of today's Arab nations (Gen 16:11).

Jairus (The Lord enlightens): A ruler of the synagogue near Capernaum; Jesus raised his daughter from the dead (Mk 5:22).

James (supplanter): One of Jesus' 12 disciples; he was the son of Zebedee and brother of John. James was put to death by Herod Agrippa I (Mt 4:21).

James: The brother of Jesus, James became a believer after Christ's resurrection. He became a leader of the church at Jerusalem, and wrote the Letter of James (Mt 13:55).

Jemimah (little dove): The first daughter of Job to be born after he was restored from his troubles (Job 42:14).

Jeremiah (The Lord establishes or the Lord is exalted): A prophet whose work covered the reigns of the last five kings of Judah (2Ch 35:25).

Jesse (meaning unknown): David's father and an ancestor of Jesus (Ru 4:17).

Job (meaning unknown): A godly man; he endured fierce trial that resulted in tremendous blessing (Job 1:1).

Jochebed (The Lord is glory): A descendant of Levi and the mother of Moses (Ex 6:20).

John (the Lord has been gracious) **the Baptist:** He came to prepare the way for the Messiah (Mt 3:1).

John the Apostle: One of the 12 apostles. The fourth Gospel, three epistles, and the Book of Revelation are all ascribed to his authorship (Mt 4:21).

Jonah (dove): A Hebrew prophet sent to preach to the people of Nineveh (2Ki 14:25).

Jonathan (The Lord has given): Saul's son and David's close friend (1Sa 13:2).

Joseph (may God add): The son of Jacob and Rachel; he was sold into slavery in Egypt but then rose to the position of prime minister there (Gen 37).

Joshua (The Lord is salvation): Moses' successor; he led the conquest of the Promised Land (Ex 17:9).

Lazarus (God has helped): The brother of Mary and Martha. Jesus raised him from the dead (Lk 16:20).

Lot (concealed or covering): Abraham's nephew; he escaped from corrupt Sodom (Gen 11:27).

Mark (large hammer): A Christian convert and Paul's helper; he wrote the second Gospel (Ac 12:12).

Martha (lady): The sister of Mary and Lazarus who lived in Bethany (Lk 10:38).

Mordecai (consecrated to Marduk [a pagan god]): A Jewish exile who helped Esther save the Jews (Est 2:5).

Naaman (pleasantness): A Syrian general healed of leprosy by bathing in the Jordan River (2Ki 5:1).

Nehemiah (The Lord comforts): The governor of Jerusalem who helped rebuild that city (Ne 1:1).

Nicodemus (victor over the people): A pharisee who visited Jesus at night, and assisted in Christ's burial (Jn 3:1).

Noah (rest or comfort): The patriarch chosen to build the ark. He and his family survived the Flood (Gen 5:29).

Onesimus (profitable or useful): A Christian slave whom Paul defends as a brother in Christ in a letter to Philemon (Col 4:9).

Orpah (possibly neck): Naomi's daughter-in-law (Ru 1:4).

Philip (lover of horses): One of the 12 apostles of Christ (Mt 10:3).

Potiphar (who Re [the sun god] has given): The Egyptian captain of the guard who became Joseph's master (Gen 37:36).

Publius (common or popular): The governor of Malta who graciously received Paul and his group when they were shipwrecked (Ac 28:7).

Rachel (ewe): The daughter of Laban, beloved wife of Jacob, and mother of Joseph and Benjamin (Gen 29:6).

Rahab (broad): The prostitute of Jericho who helped the Hebrew spies; she became an ancestor of Jesus (Jos 2:1).

Rebekah (meaning unknown): Isaac's wife and the mother of Jacob and Esau (Gen 22:23).

Samson (sun's man or distinguished): A judge of Israel for 20 years; his great physical strength and moral weakness made him notorious (Jdg 13:24).

Sapphira (beautiful or sapphire): The wife of Ananias; she was struck dead by God for deceiving the Holy Spirit (Ac 5:1).

Sargon (he [the god] has established the kingship): An important Assyrian king who completed the siege of Samaria and carried the Israelites into exile (Isa 20:1).

Silas (of the woods): Companion of Paul on his second missionary journey; he was imprisoned with Paul at Philippi (Ac 15:22).

Simon (he hears): One of Jesus' 12 apostles; he was called "the Zealot" (Mt 10:4).

Stephen (crown or crown-bearer): One of the seven deacons in the early church; he became the first martyr of the church (Ac 6:5).

Syntyche (fortunate): A woman of the church at Philippi (Php 4:2).

Tabitha (gazelle): The Christian woman of Joppa whom the apostle Peter raised from the dead (Ac 9:36).

Thomas (the twin): One of the 12 apostles; at first he doubted Christ's resurrection (Mt 10:3).

Tiglath-pileser (my trust is in the heir of [the temple] E-sharra): A king of Assyria who conquered northern Palestine and deported many from Naphtali (2Ki 15:19).

Timothy (man who honors God): The son of a Jewish mother and Greek father; the young convert traveled extensively with Paul (Ac 16:1).

Vashti (beautiful woman): The queen of Persia who was divorced by her husband because she refused to attend his great feast (Est 1:9).

Zacchaeus (pure): A tax collector whom Jesus visited when he was in Jericho (Lk 19:2).

Zerubbabel (seed of Babylon): The leader of the remnant who returned from the Exile; he began the rebuilding of the temple (Ezr 3:19).

Clans, People Groups, and Nations

The 12 Tribes of Israel

Each Hebrew tribe was made up of all the descendants from one of the sons of the patriarch Jacob. The leader of each clan was known as a ruler, head, or chief. The 12 tribes of Israel were grouped according to their fathers' houses while they were in Egypt. After they left the Pharaoh's land, the whole group began to operate as the 12 clans of Israel (Ex 24:4). And while they traveled through the wilderness, each group was assigned its place in which to march and to camp. When the Israelites were numbered, the tribe of Levi was not counted because God had set them apart to take care of Israel's religious life. They had to keep and transport the tabernacle and its furniture, and they were responsible for worship and sacrifices.

The 12 sons of Jacob were Reuben, Simeon, Levi, Judah, Zebulun, Issachar, Dan, Gad, Asher, Naphtali, Joseph (later divided into Ephraim and Manasseh), and Benjamin. Although they were all fathered by Jacob, they had four mothers: Leah and Rachel (Jacob's wives), and Bilhah and Zilpah (household maids and concubines).

Before the Hebrew people entered the Promised Land, two tribes, Reuben and Gad (and part of Manasseh), decided to settle on the east side of the Jordan. When Canaan was conquered, it was divided between the remaining tribes.

During the time of the Judges, each clan determined its own laws and lifestyle. When David became king, he ruled over the whole land and Israel was unified. Jerusalem became the capital of the country—the political as well as the religious hub of the nation (2Ch 12:13).

After the death of Solomon, the tribes divided into two groups. Judah and Benjamin became one nation, the kingdom of Judah. And to the north of them, the remaining tribes formed the kingdom of Israel. This division continued until

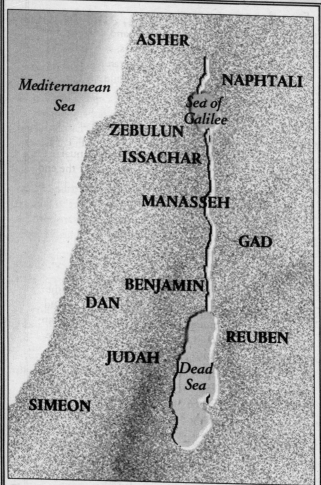

The tribal divisions of Israel

both kingdoms went into captivity, Israel in 721 B.C. to Assyria, and Judah in 586 B.C. to Babylon. These captivities marked the end of the tribal distinctions among the Hebrews.

The Egyptians

The might of ancient Egyptian culture and religion is well attested to by its many buildings, structures, and artifacts that still exist today. Besides the famous pyramids, the images of Pharaohs dominate many large building works, and huge pillars of the great hall in the Temple of Amun at Karnak still stand.

The life and culture of ancient Egypt centered around the great Nile river. Peasant farmers (most of Egypt's population during the time of Moses) depended on its annual flooding to irrigate crops and provide rich mud. At the end of the harvest, grain was always carefully recorded and stored. The Nile was also an important "highway" for travel. Egyptians quickly learned to make boats and use the waterway to their advantage. Besides the Nile, other parts of the region were also important. The deserts contained valuable metals, including copper and gold, and there was stone available for making the pyramids and temples.

At the top of Egypt's social order was the Pharaoh, the king and chief negotiator between Egypt's pagan gods and the people. Second in command were two viziers who managed the vast political and social order of the culture. The people of this highly organized culture enjoyed many periods of greatness, but eventually became part of the Persian Empire, then later the Greek Ptolemies ruled Egypt until the coming of the Roman Empire.

The Canaanites

Renowned for their trading and crafts—and the first nation to develop an alphabet—the Canaanites were a people who settled at the eastern end of the Mediterranean Sea by about 2000 B.C. By Joshua's day, the land had been divided up into small, strongly fortified cities, each with its own king. The Canaanites traded up and down the Mediterranean Sea in their merchant ships. Their main ports were Tyre, Sidon, Berytus (Beirut), and Byblos.

The Philistines

The land of the Philistines consisted of five coastal cities: Ekron, Ashdod, Ashkelon, Gath, and Gaza. The settlers were originally warlike sea people who came from Crete in the 13th and 12th centuries B.C. They gave their name—Palestine—to the entire country. They brought iron to the area, using it to make tools and weapons, which gave them a great advantage in war.

The Assyrians

For much of the Old Testament period the Assyrians occupied the area that is now Iraq. From about 900 B.C. the Assyrian Empire was established. The Assyrians were known to be shamelessly cruel in war. They paraded their captors about before they blinded them and burnt them to death.

The ruler, Ashurbanipal, made Nineveh the center for literature and the arts. There were thousands of clay tablets with the history and traditions of Mesopotamia written down on them.

The Babylonians

One of the oldest cultures in the Middle East, Babylon first rose to prominence about 1850 B.C. Their first noteworthy king was Hammurabi, who was known for his diplomacy and his work in revising the laws of Babylon and having them engraved on stone. Another well-known king (who came along 1,200 years later) was Nebuchadnezzar. He was responsible for Babylon's hanging gardens (one of the ancient wonders of the world) and the construction of superb buildings that made Babylon famous. During Nebuchadnezzar's reign, Jerusalem was struck down and many Jews were taken captive to Babylon.

The great Babylonian empire was known for its system of writing (which spread throughout the Near East) and its developments in astronomy and mathematics. The divisions

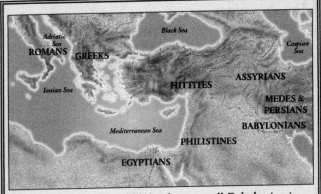

of the circle, the hour, and the day were all Babylonian in origin, and were later borrowed and developed by the Greeks.

The Persians

The setting of the Bible books of Ezra, Nehemiah, Esther, and part of Daniel belonged to the time of the Persian Empire under Cyrus the Great and the kings after him. Their borders stretched east to India, northwest to Macedonia, and south to Egypt. Cyrus divided the far-reaching empire into provinces that were controlled by rulers or satraps (who were Persian or Median nobles).

Aramaic became the diplomatic language of the empire. The different cultures of the empire, however, were encouraged to keep their own customs and religion. When Babylon was captured, the exiled Jews were given assistance to go back home to Judah. It was during the reign of Darius I that Haggai and Zechariah began to prophesy and the work on rebuilding the temple resumed (Ezr 5–6).

The Greeks

In the fifth century B.C., the most famous city in Greece was Athens. It was rich, powerful, had beautiful buildings—including the acclaimed Parthenon still standing today—and was known to be a model of democracy. This remarkable city became the home of many creative thinkers—Socrates, Plato, and Euripedes among them.

The brilliant soldier Alexander the Great defeated the Persians in 334 B.C., conquered Syria and Egypt (founding Alexandria), and went east to India. Wherever his armies went they spread the language, culture, and ideas of Greece (Hellenism). Greek became the international language of the Mediterranean lands, and even the Jews were influenced by it. In the second century B.C., the Old Testament was translated into Greek. This translation—known as the Septuagint—was most familiar to the first Christians.

The Romans

Following the Greeks with their philosophies, ideals, and culture came the practical Romans with their excellent roads, sturdy aqueducts, public baths, and spectator sports. From the time that Carthage (modern Tunisia) was destroyed in 146 B.C., the Romans became a world power, extending their control all around the Mediterranean Sea.

However, there were many years of war as various generals and dictators vied for power throughout the sprawling empire. Eventually, in 27 B.C. Octavian (Augustus) brought peace to the region. It was during his reign that Jesus was born. Palestine, under Roman jurisdiction, was ruled by a king of the Herod dynasty at the time. When this family failed to rule, Rome sent a procurator to govern Judea.

At first, Rome protected and took care of the Jews, but they eventually grew tired of Jewish nationalism and religion. In turn, Jews were angered by Roman misrule, foreign oppression, and heavy taxation; and Jewish Zealot guerrillas constantly badgered the Roman troops.

By the time of the spread of Christianity, believers paid dearly for their faith. Rome's paganism led to the cult of emperor worship, Christianity was not tolerated, and many believers were thrown into public arenas, made to fight wild animals, and then burnt to death.

Bible People—Fascinating Facts

- Methuselah, the oldest person in the Bible, lived to the ripe old age of 969 years. He fathered his first son, Lamech, when he was 187 years old!

- Jacob buried his beloved wife Rachel near Bethlehem, and built a pillar on her grave. Today nomadic Arabs bury their children near her tomb.

- Naomi lost her husband and two sons. Her name means "pleasant" but she told people to call her Mara, which means "bitter," because of her misfortune.

- Ahilud, who lived during the time of the judges, must have been rather short. Supporting pillars for roof beams in his house were only five feet three inches tall!

- The Phrygians were a warlike people who traded in copper and slaves. Several of their rulers were named Midas and were buried in richly furnished tombs.

- Several good Bible characters had troubled sons: Aaron's two sons offered unsanctioned sacrifices (Lev 10); Eli's two sons were scoundrels (1Sa 2); and Samuel's two sons took bribes and perverted justice (1Sa 8).

- The Edomites, descended from Esau, often clashed with the Israelites. They were delighted when Israel fell, and the prophet Obadiah condemned them for this (Ps 137:7).

- Onesiphorus was a real friend to Paul. When Paul was imprisoned in Rome, Onesiphorus went to Rome and eagerly searched until he found the apostle. There Onesiphorus encouraged him greatly. Paul could not help but contrast his friend's example with that of Phylegus and Hermogenes, who abandoned him and the Gospel he preached (2Ti 1:15–18; 2:17–18).

INDEX